Exploring Oregon's Historic House Museums

By the same author

Exploring Oregon's Historic Courthouses

Exploring Oregon's Historic House Museums

Kathleen M. Wiederhold

Oregon State University Press
Corvallis

Publication of this book was made possible in part
by a contribution from
The Delmer Goode Fund
The Oregon State University Press is grateful for this support

Cover photographs of the Drain House (Drain) and Pittock Mansion (Portland) by Kathleen M. Wiederhold.

The paper in this book meets the guidelines for permanence and durability of the Committee on Production Guidelines for Book Longevity of the Council on Library Resources and the minimum requirements of the American National Standard for Permanence of Paper for Printed Library Materials Z39.48-1984.

Library of Congress Cataloging-in-Publication Data
Wiederhold, Kathleen M.
  Exploring Oregon's historic house museums / Kathleen M. Wiederhold.—
1st ed.
      p. cm.
Includes bibliographical references and index.
  ISBN 0-87071-483-X (alk. paper)
  1. Historical museums—Oregon—Guidebooks.
2. Dwellings—Oregon—Guidebooks. 3. Oregon—Guidebooks.
4. Oregon—Biography. I. Title.
  F773 .W54 2000
  917.9504'44—dc21

                              00-009285

**OREGON STATE
UNIVERSITY**

Oregon State University Press
101 Waldo Hall
Corvallis OR 97331-6407
541-737-3166 • fax 541-737-3170
http://osu.orst.edu/dept/press

Table of Contents

Acknowledgements

Writing a book takes a great amount of effort, more than most people can imagine. The completion of such a project, however, lends itself to introspection and gratitude for those who have helped me in the past and during this particular work.

My grandmother Nellie Wiederhold, with her quiet yet steely determination, showed me the importance of being strong; her unconditional love nurtured me in periods of drought. Jeanette Baker, who took a risk with me, still takes chances because of her lightheartedness and sense of play. She sets an example today.

James T. Walker, Brigitte Patrick, and Jeff Gray were all instructors who singled me out and taught me important lessons.

Lisa Kristen-Scott is a good friend who helped me during the times I needed her.

Theresa Wiederhold, Patrick Wiederhold, and Mary Catherine Wiederhold form a support network for me. I am proud that despite obstacles, they preserve towards their goals. Katherine and Christopher, both treasures, are a special source of joy to me.

Arlene and Dave Rand give me loving support. They continually teach me that love is expressed not in the grand gestures but in little actions like yellow vegetables and comfort food.

During this project, the Multnomah County Library provided obscure reference books. While I revel in the luxury of my own private library, writing this book made me a fan of the public library system.

Historic house museums require countless hours of maintenance done by volunteers—unsung heroes in my mind—who care about history and preserving the past. Without organizations such as historical societies and other historical organizations, Oregon simply would not have these museums.

People at the State Historic Preservation Office work to preserve significant buildings. A special thanks to Susan Haylock for her prompt and efficient help.

Ruth Powers, Professor Philip Dole, and Elizabeth Potter all had an early vision about recording and saving Oregon's historic houses.

The Oregon Society of the Daughters of the American Revolution operates four museums in the state (three of which are house museums), and were one of the early preservers of significant houses in the state. The outstanding women I spoke with included Virginia Burgh, Dorothy Schriever, and Charlotte White.

I would especially like to thank the people who showed me the house and/or gave me their time:

Adler House: Colleen Brooks and Chary Mires
Aurora Colony Museum: Daniel McElhinny
Beekman House: Jan Wright
Brunk House: Georgia and Howard Wildfang
Bush House: Jennifer Hagloch
Butterfield Cottage: Helen Gaston
Bybee Howell House: Jennifer Black
Caples House: Shari Ouillette
Deepwood Estate: Ross Sutherland
Dibble House: Isobel Williams
Drain House: Kristin Martin
Ermatinger House: Marge Harding and Rocky Smith Jr.
Flavel House: Liisa Penner, Michelle Schmitter, Julie Staton, and Lisa Studts
Flippin House: Margaret Doyle, Norma Hendrickson, and Marge Tuomi
Floed-Lane House: Audrey Hakanson
Fort Dalles Museum: Paula Kuttner
Fort Rock Valley Homestead Village Museum: Jean Flegel and Vivian
    Stratton
Foster House: Joanne Broadhurst
Frazier Farmhouse: Diane Biggs
Harlow House: Sharon Nesbit
Hoover-Minthorn House: Eileen Jette
Hughes House: Laura Rhodes
Kam Wah Chung Museum: Carolyn Micnhimer
Lindgren Cabin: Gene Knapp and Helena Perttu
McLoughlin House: Nancy Wilson
Mission Mill Museum: Jennifer Stark
Monteith House: Doug Killin
Morse House: Nora Hagerty and Jan Mueller
Moyer House: Anna Schroeder
Naucke: Sandy Hare
Newell House: Trisha McManus
Pittock Mansion: Lucy Smith McLean
Rose Farm: Bob Higgins
Schminck Memorial Museum: Sherrain Glen
Schmidt House: Mollie Means
Settlemier House: Cindy Thomas
Shelton-McMurphey-Johnson House: Mary Ellen West
Stevens-Crawford House: Patrick Harris and David Leckband
Tigard House: Kathy Palmer
Yaquina Lighthouse: Loretta Harrison

Amy Houchen gave me the seed of the idea and provided me with the preliminary list of house museums.

Without the hardworking people at Oregon State University Press, many books about Oregon would not be published. I salute Jeffrey Grass, Jo Alexander, Tom Booth, Pennie Coe, Lea Ann McGill, and Warren Slesinger. Jo Alexander and Tom Booth are the finest people with whom to work, and I admire both professionally and, more importantly, personally.

Alan Viewig, a photography maven, was unfailing in his generosity with his expertise and equipment.

Sieglinde Smith, who read my manuscript, saved me countless hours during a time when I was under deadline pressure. Her help, both in Portland and as a traveling companion, reflects her great kindness and her dedication to preserving history. I am proud and lucky that she is my friend.

Bruce Ostly, in addition to reading my manuscript and being a resource about building construction, was a source of deep wisdom. His love and support sustained me while I wrote this book. He has added to my life in countless ways.

Introduction

Oregon's historic house museums are time capsules that preserve our past domestic life and provide a place to experience the architecture and artifacts of the most intimate part of our lives, the home. They help us to understand the evolution of common items that we have around us today, such as sofas and sinks, and showcase both ordinary and unusual objects that Oregonians used in everyday life.

This book also explores the lives lived in these houses. Buildings and objects become meaningful if we understand the human connection. By visiting the home where wealthy Sally Bush fed tramps, or seeing the cedar plank cabin that sixty-seven-year-old Erik Lindgren built with his own hands, we broaden our understanding of how Oregonians have lived.

Houses Included in this Book

Each of the houses profiled in the book has regular operating hours. However, some museums, such as the Adler house and Bybee-Howell house, are open only during the summer. Others, such as Rose Farm and the Settlemier house, are open only one day a month, usually on a Sunday. All the houses have scheduled hours. Since volunteers run many of these museums and the operating hours can change, call ahead to ensure that the house will be open. While visits to the house museums may take a little planning, they are definitely worth the effort.

Historical societies sometimes purchase historic houses and use them as museums to display local artifacts. Even though the structure is a house, the primary emphasis is to display historical items rather than to recreate a home atmosphere. I toured many of these museums and made judgments as to whether they were actually house museums. The decision to omit a museum sometimes was not easy, as many have a small budget and any additional publicity would be helpful.

Variety of Oregon's House Museums

Each house museum in the state is unique. This book features houses built from 1841 to 1936, and owned by those spanning the economic spectrum from poor to wealthy, including some noteworthy in Oregon's history, from John McLoughlin to Wayne Morse.

Oregon's house museums range from small cabins like the Webster dwelling in Fort Rock to opulent homes like the Pittock mansion in

Portland. Some museums were farms, like the Brunk house near Dallas, while others are located in town, such as the Moyer house in Brownsville. The book includes three "castles," so designated by local residents because they are relatively grand.

Interiors of Oregon's House Museums

Tours can be guided or self-guided, and some museums offer both types. A few tours are unique, such as the living history tour at the Beekman house, where the "family members" are in character.

Some of the state's house museums, such as the Kam Wah Chung Museum and the Bush house, are preserved with the household furnishings and items that were owned by the original occupants. Many display household items donated by members of the local community; these collections, while sometimes portraying aspects of a house interior that are historically inaccurate, do present opportunities for whimsy.

Some of the houses, such as the Dibble House, also display items of local history. Other houses have special collections of domestic items, such as the one hundred sixty pressed-glass goblets at the Schminck house.

Oregon's house museums afford glimpses of how Oregonians lived and the things they had around them in their homes. The complete picture is often illusive, despite our best efforts. For those who want a better understanding of our domestic past, I recommend first perusing the books in the General Sources section.

Background on Oregon's House Museums

Prior to the 1970s, some significant dwellings such as the McLoughlin house and Flavel house were used as museums displaying local history. Their preservation, however, sometimes generated protest. Citizens filed court injunctions against moving the McLoughlin house, now a National Historic Site, to its current location on the bluff in Oregon City.

Ruth Powers stands out as a dedicated preservationist of Oregon's pioneer houses. Called by one of her admirers after her death in 1995 the "empress of historic preservation" in Oregon, she spent her own money to save many of today's house museums, such as the Rose Farm in Oregon City and Foster Farm in Eagle Creek.

Today, historical societies are some of the most common owners of Oregon's house museums. Ruth Powers transferred many of her houses to historical societies; others were simply bequeathed to these organizations, sometimes along with the furnishing, because the owner had an affinity for history. Other museums have been saved because they were the home of someone or some event significant in Oregon's history. A few house museums, such as Deepwood in Salem or Pittock in Portland, were purchased by the city because they are opulent structures. Frequently in these cases, while the municipality maintains the exterior, an organization such as the Friends of Deepwood is responsible for running the house and maintaining the furnishings.

How the Book Is Organized

The house museums are grouped by geographical area. Each chapter profiles one house, except when a museum has multiple houses, such as the Fort Dalles Museum or the Fort Rock Valley Homestead Village Museum.

Each chapter begins with an address, directions, and neighborhood map. For many of the houses, the directions are given from the freeway. If a visitor could be could be coming from either direction, the directions state, for example, "turn east" instead of "turn right." This section also notes whether the house is listed on the National Register of Historic Places, meaning that it has been deemed to be significant architecturally and/or historically. Additional Attractions suggests other places such as nearby house museums or parks to visit while in the area.

The History section provides an overview of the people who built the house or who were significantly involved with it at a later time period. This section provides a context for understanding the house, why it was constructed, and for whom.

The Setting section includes important features about the museum's site or the area in close proximity.

The Exterior section examines significant aspects of the appearance of the house, including characteristics that define its architectural style and features that distinguish the building.

The Interior section, the largest section of each chapter, provides a step-by-step tour of the inside of the house and is more detailed than the usual overview given by the docent. It provides insight into aspects of the floor plan, interior design, technology of the time, and the artifacts on display. For perspective, I have included quotes from people of the times. When available, I also have included rich stories connected with the house.

Important Tips About Your Visit

Because historic house museums usually are run on a shoestring budget and are staffed by volunteers, their operating hours and admission charge can change frequently. To ensure the most up-to-date information, call ahead before visiting.

Many house museums are decorated for Christmas and are open special hours during that season. Some houses are also open during local festivals. I have not listed these additional opening times because they tend to vary from year to year, but again, I recommend calling the house for further information.

Handicap accessibility varies from house to house. If this is a concern, please call the house for information before visiting.

Location of Oregon's Historic House Museums

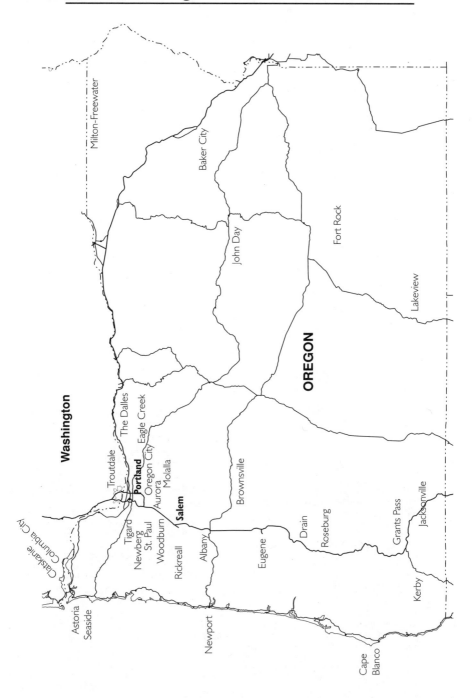

Portland Area

Bybee-Howell House

National Register of Historic Places
Built: 1856

13901 N.W. Howell Park Rd
Sauvie Island
503-621-3344 (museum)
503-222-1741 (Oregon Historical Society)

The Bybee-Howell house has exceptionally fine architectural detailing for its early date. While little remains in the house from either the Bybee or Howell families, the Oregon Historical Society has installed historically accurate furnishings, some of which reference people who were connected with Sauvie Island.

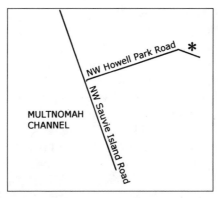

Directions: From Highway 30, follow the sign to Sauvie Island. After crossing the bridge, follow the road as it curves to the left. Drive approximately one mile north to N.W. Howell Park Road, and turn right. A grassy parking area is on your left; the house is just beyond it.
Open: Mid-June to Labor Day; Saturday–Sunday
Hours: 12:00–5:00
Admission: Donation
Tour: Guided
Entry: At the rear of the house

Additional Attractions: A small agricultural museum is located in the barn in the back of the house. Howell Park includes picnicking facilities.

History

James Bybee, born in Kentucky in 1818, crossed the Plains in 1847. He went to the California gold mines, and unlike most, he succeeded in coming back to Oregon with considerable wealth. In 1854, he was sufficiently involved in the local political scene to be appointed one of the three first commissioners in Multnomah County. Sometime in 1855, James Bybee and his wife Julia Ann Miller Bybee began building the house on a 640-acre claim on the southern end of Sauvie Island.

The couple eventually had eleven children, five of whom died in childhood. In 1873, for some unknown reason, the Bybees sold their property to Joseph and John Howell, whose parents, Dr. Benjamin and Elizabeth Howell, owned land to the north and west of the Bybee claim. After John Howell married in 1875, he and his bride, Amelia Rulifson, moved into the house, eventually acquiring more than one thousand acres for their cattle feeding operation. Joseph Howell was a skilled amateur botanist, as was his other brother, Thomas, author of the acclaimed *Flora of Northwest America.*

In the mid 1950s, the Howell family still owned the house, but it stood vacant and ramshackle. Thomas Vaughn, then executive director of the Oregon Historical Society, recalled when he first saw the house, it was "surrounded by blackberries, vines and interesting shrubs. ... I noted the fine roofline and the double chimneys poking from the vines. ... Buried in its own dreams, it sent messages of a forgotten past and another century." The structure was so dilapidated, Vaughn later noted, that "a sharp wind would have toppled the tired old frame house."

Multnomah County purchased the house in 1961 along with seventy-five acres for use as a park and game refuge. Volunteers spent thousands of hours to restore the house. Workers cleared the land, restored and leveled the foundation, and drove out the swarm of wild bees occupying the southwest corner of the building. The Oregon Historical Society currently operates the museum.

Setting

The Bybee-Howell house rests on a rise, perhaps to avoid spring flooding. Behind the house today is a pioneer orchard developed from cuttings of the oldest apple, pear, and plum trees in the Pacific Northwest.

Exterior

The Bybee-Howell house represents the building tradition in Oregon making a transition from crude cabins to more refined housing. This dwelling's fine detailing in the Classical Revival style was more sophisticated than the average settler's home at the time.

The house has a cornice, which runs along the front and wraps around its sides, forming a full pediment on the gable when most structures in Oregon merely had a suggestion of one. The porch, rebuilt in the 1960s, has squared columns, as does the balustrade above, which encloses the second floor balcony. While corner boards were left plain for many houses, these are designed as slender pilasters, mimicking the shape of the porch columns.

Interior

The tour begins in the kitchen, now located at the rear of the Bybee-Howell house. The kitchen was originally in a separate building, which protected the house in case of fire and kept heat away from the dwelling during the summer, but by 1868, it was attached to the back of the house. Visitor John Nevin King thought the room was worth noting, as he wrote in a letter that the house was "well built and is substantial, having eight larger sized rooms & kitchen."

The Bybee-Howell house has unusually fine detailing for an early Oregon home.

In the adjoining dining room, one gets a sense of the Bybees' wealth. Historians believe that the house was the first in Oregon to have plaster walls and ceilings. The Bybees also installed central plaster medallions on the ceilings of the central hall, parlor, and dining room. Both the dining room and the study feature built-in cupboards, and the house has six closets, an unusual amount of storage space for an early Oregon home.

The house was constructed with a traditional floor plan with four rooms per floor and a central hall. However, a puzzling anomaly is a second floor bedroom which has no access to the upstairs hall; the only entrance is via a stairway from the ground floor textile room. Perhaps it was intended to be a servant's quarters or rented to a boarder. Laborers did reside at the house while the Bybees lived there; in fact, one of the daughters married one.

One part of a pioneer woman's responsibilities was the time-consuming job of spinning, illustrated by the tools in the textile room. The carders on the fireplace illustrate the first step, the removal of dirt and tangles in the wool. Once the clean wool had been spun in the spinning wheel, a clock reel like the one by the window both measured the yarn and formed it into skeins. By the chair facing the fire, the historical society has placed two handspun and hand-dyed balls of yarn, the work of Lucinda Brown, who settled in Silverton in 1846.

The men's study features hunting items. The print over the fireplace sets the tone: a man, woman, and their children stand in front of their camp, inspecting the kill. On one wall hangs the head of a deer killed at Crater Lake in 1916. There are also three duck decoys, the most detailed of which is an early twentieth-century wooden mallard hen that was found on the property in the 1960s. The museum's only item owned by James Bybee is the leather hunting pouch for his bullets, which rests on the desk.

The horse picture (circa 1890s) hanging on the wall commemorates James Bybee's horse racing endeavors. His obituary referred to him as the "King of the Oregon Turf," a title also given to his racehorse, Rye Straw, which won a much-heralded contest in 1880. Bybee was one of the earliest and most successful breeders of racehorses in Oregon. Although he did not smoke or drink, according to a granddaughter, he did indulge in wagers. Some family stories suggest that James and Julia Bybee separated because of disagreements over the education of their children, but another source gave James Bybee's gambling as the reason the couple sold the house and then became estranged.

Other items in the study reference the Howells. Dr. Howell was the island's first physician, and on the table by the cherry-red wing chair lies a homeopathic kit in a folding leather box with twenty-four glass vials

The house includes features such as a dining room fireplace and built-in cupboard.

topped with corks, though this did not belong to Dr. Howell. Nearby is the scarificator of Dr. Forbes Barclay, who once practiced at the Hudson's Bay Company at Fort Vancouver. The scarificator, brought from Scotland in 1841, was a bloodletting tool. When the lever was pushed, twelve razor blades flicked out.

The one item in the study that did belong to Benjamin Howell is the collection of minerals, dating back to his years in New Jersey, which is stored in the chest of drawers. The collection also contains minerals and shells from Sauvie Island and other parts of the world, and the dates of the samples indicate that the Howell family added to the collection over the years. Other items from Sauvie Island are also displayed in the room: stuffed birds believed to have been caught on the island, a hoe found on the property, and mortar, pestle, and sinkers believed to have been used by the Indians on the island.

The parlor, the most formal room in the house, appropriately has the most architectural features. It has one of the house's three ceiling medallions, as well as crown molding and a fireplace mantel designed with fluted pilasters. The furnishings suggest the good taste appropriate for a room used as the center of social events. One prominent piece is the 1835 Empire-styled couch covered with black horsehair upholstery, a shiny fabric favored for much of the nineteenth century. Horsehair fabric also covers the piano stool, which was shipped around Cape Horn in 1857.

One furniture piece obsolete today is the firescreen. The screen, displaying a needlepoint floral design, is attached to a wood stand, which can be raised and lowered as desired. Many women of the time wore makeup made of lard, and the firescreen was used to divert the heat from melting the makeup.

On the second floor, a cutaway in the wall now allows the viewing of the bedroom that was initially accessible only by the stairway from the textile room. This is one of the two bedrooms with a fireplace, undoubtedly a necessity since the room would have been cut off from any warm air in the rest of the house. The historical society has decorated this room as a little girl's bedroom. Generally, bedroom furniture was purchased either in separate pieces or as a set; the pieces in this room do not match, although they are painted to appear similar.

Toys are frequently instruments to instruct, which also was true in the nineteenth century. On the spool-turned side table rest twenty spelling blocks with letters, pictures, and numerals. The lid of the box in which they were kept proclaims on one side, "Children learn best when the hands assist the head." Other toys in the room are miniatures of grownup furnishings, preparing the little girl for her coming life, and include a crib, tea set, butter churn, and firescreen.

The toys are different in the boy's room across the hall. One of the toys on the bookshelf is a wooden Noah's ark (circa 1850s). Mass-produced arks were first made in the mid-eighteenth century, although the finest were made between 1860 and 1870 and sometimes contained upwards of four hundred animals. Novelty mechanical banks, like the one on the bookshelf, first appeared about 1870. When a lever is pressed on this bank (which really depicts a bank), a teller advances and receives the coin that he then deposits in the back.

Visitors are often surprised to see the vibrant red and green carpet in the master bedroom, but it came from a contemporaneous house. Modern interior decorators designed the historically inspired wallpaper, called Fleuretts. The decorators also designed the fabric for the coverlet and drapes, which is called Camas Landing for its print suggesting thistles, ferns, and camas leaves.

The pine board chest at the end of the bed displays faded Norwegian rosemaling, a type of floral painting. The chest standing at the end of the bed in the bedroom across the hall originated from the Hudson's Bay Company. This chest is lined with camphor wood and was intended for trade; the flat-top design made it easy to stack. It represents the connection between the Hudson's Bay Company and Sauvie Island; during Dr. John McLoughlin's tenure, the company drove cows across the river and used the island as a farm.

Pittock Mansion

National Register of Historic Places
Built: 1914

3229 N.W. Pittock Drive
Portland
503-823-3624 (museum)

The Pittock Mansion is the grandest dwelling of all of Oregon's historic house museums, and the only one rightfully called a "mansion." Located on a hill about one thousand feet above Portland, the site has a premier view of the city and mountains.

Directions: In downtown Portland, proceed west on W. Burnside Street past N.W. 23rd Avenue. Go about one mile and watch for the blinking yellow light at the intersection of Barnes Road. Turn right and follow the signs to the mansion.

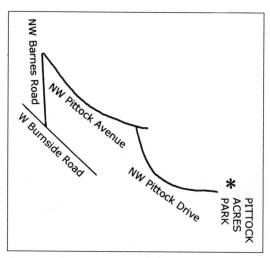

Open: Year-around, except major holidays and in January
Hours: Daily 12:00–4:00 (house); 7:00 a.m.–9:00 p.m. (grounds)
Admission: $5.00 adults; $4.50 over sixty-five; $2.50 children six to eighteen (house). Access to the grounds is free.
Tour: Guided or self-tour
Entry: At the door under the porte cochere

Additional Attractions: On the grounds are the Gate Lodge, formerly a groundskeeper's residence and now a restaurant, and a three-bay garage, now a gift shop.

The mansion stands in Pittock Acres Park, which has hiking trails.

History

Henry Pittock was born in London, England, in 1834. Five years later, he immigrated with his family to Pittsburgh. After traveling over the Oregon Trail with his brother Robert, Henry Pittock arrived in Portland in 1853 and eventually got a job as a "printer's devil" (apprentice) with Thomas Jefferson Dryer, the founder, publisher, and editor of the *Oregonian*. Dryer was an accomplished politician, speaker, and writer, but he was, according to Pittock, "entirely indifferent to income and outgo. He simply could not bring himself to pay attention to details." Pittock himself excelled in these skills; he advanced to foreman and for a time was a partner in the newspaper.

Henry Pittock married Georgiana Burton in June 1860 when he was twenty-six and she was sixteen. Later that year, Dryer, having accepted an appointment as commissioner to the Sandwich Islands (now Hawaii), transferred the ownership of the *Oregonian* to Pittock, who was owed a considerable amount of back wages. Over the next decades, Henry Pittock would build the *Oregonian* into the principal newspaper in the region despite numerous competitors.

The Pittocks had four girls and two boys, and lived most of their married life in houses on land now considered part of downtown Portland. Georgiana Pittock, who became a local leader in social welfare activities, organized a city rose show on the lawn at her home at SW Ninth and Washington streets in 1888. The event eventually would grow to become the Portland Rose Festival.

The family fortune increased after the Pittocks invested in pulp and paper mills. Henry Pittock, along with two other partners, established a paper mill at the Park Place area in Oregon City. With another partner, he later formed a company, bought acreage around LaCamas Lake in Washington State, built a pulp mill, and established the mill town of Camas. Other investments in mills followed, as well as real estate ventures such as the Sellwood and Fulton Park neighborhoods of Portland. Along with son-in-law Frederick Leadbetter, Henry Pittock purchased acreage at the confluence of the Willamette and Columbia rivers, which was acquired years later by the Port of Portland and developed into the Rivergate Industrial District.

In 1909, after years of living in relatively modest houses, the Pittocks commissioned thirty-five-year-old Edward Foulkes to design a new home. At the time, Henry was seventy-five, and Georgiana was sixty-five. Speculations about their move to a luxurious mansion at that stage in their lives ranged from an editorial taunt in a rival newspaper to a charge of displaying wealth. Why they selected the relatively unknown Foulkes, who had previously designed churches and commercial projects, is now lost. One possibility is that his brother worked for the *Oregonian.*

Construction started in late 1912, and the Pittocks were able to move into the $350,000 house in the summer of 1914. Their daughter Kate, her husband Lockwood Hebard, daughter Lucy, her husband John Gantenbein, and their three children also lived in the house. One of these children, Peter Gantenbein, was born at the mansion. Two orphaned nieces, Louise Gallien and Helen Van Houten, also lived with the Pittocks.

Georgiana Pittock lived in the house for only four years before she died in 1918; Henry followed her in 1919. The Pittock family continued to live there until 1958, when Peter Gantenbein put the house up for sale, distributed some of the furniture to family members, and sold the rest at auction. The mansion suffered during the 1962 Columbus Day Storm, when winds up to one hundred miles an hour blew over trees, which broke windows and damaged the roof. Leaking water spoiled the finish in many rooms and warped the oak strip flooring in the second floor hall. The City of Portland purchased the building in April 1964, and began repairs and restoration to the house. The Pittock Mansion Society, formed in 1968, manages the museum collection.

Setting

The site of the Pittock mansion encompasses about forty-six acres, although only about four acres are cultivated. The Willamette and Columbia rivers are visible from the grounds, and on clear days, five mountains can be seen: Mount Rainer, Mount St. Helens, Mount Adams, Mount Hood, and Mount Jefferson.

Exterior

The side of the house now visible from the walkway is really the rear. For the best view of the house, walk under the porte cochere and around to the front. Here, you can see that the center section of the structure is flanked by backswept wings. In the most prominent position of the house is the first-floor drawing room, which is skirted by a terrace that extends around to the wings. The drawing room is positioned to have a dramatic view to the east, while rooms in the wings have a view of Portland to the northeast and southeast.

Georgiana Pittock reportedly wanted a Colonial Revival house, a popular style that was being designed for both large and small houses. Henry Pittock apparently wanted a grander style. Foulkes designed the house in the French Renaissance Chateau style, which was based on the French chateaux and castles of the sixteenth century. Masonry walls are one of the elements of the style, and the Pittock mansion has a sandstone exterior with a reinforced concrete structure. At a time when residences were typically built with wood or masonry, the sturdiness of the Pittock is unusual. Alfred Staehli, an architect specializing in historic preservation, has noted that this and other elements show that the mansion was built more as a commercial structure than as a typical residence.

The mansion is designed so that the rooms have a sweeping view from the northeast to the southeast.

The Pittock mansion displays other characteristics of the style: rounded towers with conical roofs, and the main steep hipped roof. On the front above the main roofline are two rows of dormers, one row with a hipped roof and the other with bull's eye windows. At the turn of the twentieth century, part of the attic was the servants' quarters, and hired help at the Pittock mansion had good views.

Perhaps because of the grandeur of the architecture, Foulkes believed that the front door did not have to impress a visitor. Today, only by looking carefully does it become obvious that the front door is the located in the northern tower. Under a pediment with classical detailing, the front entrance consists of a single door embellished with bronze grillwork that displays in the center a rosette encircled by leaves.

Interior

The front door was not used very frequently at the mansion, as most of the family used the porte cochere door, the entrance that visitors use today. The porte cochere protected the Pittocks from the weather while getting in and out of their automobiles, one of which was a right-handed drive 1914 Pierce Arrow touring car. Although Georgiana Pittock was restricted in movement due to a stroke, she had the chauffeur drive her around Portland almost every afternoon.

The grand marble stairway dominates the hall. The white marble stairs match the marble floors and the cream-colored imitation Caen stone walls. The bronze railing with the eucalyptus banister appears serpentine as it curves up to the second floor and flows down to the basement. Besides the impressive scale, the mansion also has fine detailing, such as the wave and poppy scroll that follows the turns of the staircase.

Louise Gallien, one of the nieces, remembered that the Pittocks placed their Christmas tree on the landing between the first and second floor, and it was tall enough to touch the top of the second-floor ceiling. The children would sometimes roller skate in the hall, as there were few other level, smooth surfaces around the house. At one point after Henry and Georgiana Pittock died, the Pittock offspring were unable to afford help, and the daughters would wash the marble floor once a week as part of the house's routine cleaning. Peter Gantenbein, who also washed the floor from the second floor down to the basement in later years, reported the chore was a "mankiller."

The hall is designed like the center of a wheel, with the main rooms radiating out from it. The first room near the porte cochere entrance is the library, where the Pittocks retired every night. The mansion is called a "period house" because the rooms are architecturally embellished to

A marble staircase dominates the Pittock hall.

represent different periods. The library is designed in the style of the Jacobean period. One of the main features of that style is the quatrefoil design in the ceiling, which is emphasized by indirect lighting. Although the library has oak paneled walls, the patterned frieze above is of plaster, styled to look like carved oak, because of fire concerns due to the proximity of the indirect lighting.

The door molding displays a Tudor-style arch with a dragon figure in the oak leaves, a design repeated in the fireplace mantel. Above the mantel is a carved coat of arms. Eric Ladd, the caretaker during the 1950s and early 1960s, remembered that daughter Caroline "put him [Henry] up to [having that] carving." The coat of arms, which displays a head of armor and a rampant lion, was not appreciated by all. Eric Ladd noted that "people thought it was a little pretentious ... In fact that coat of arms [was] ... always covered with the pictures."

The best view of the coat of arms is from the doorway off the curved corridor that leads to the front door vestibule. The house had the latest innovations in heating, even in this vestibule. A thermostat on the wall indicates that the heat in each room could be individually adjusted. A small lever on the oak front door allowed the glass window to be opened for ventilation.

Not all were welcome at the front door. One day Georgiana Pittock was conferring with Henry, the chauffeur, in the library about her plans for her daily trip, when they heard a noise at the front door. Henry went to open the door, and was astonished to see a bear standing up on his back paws. He shut the door in a hurry. They called and found out that the bear had escaped from the zoo, then located in Washington Park. The ursine visitor was later recaptured.

Welcomed guests might have been escorted into the drawing room, although family members recall that it was called the music room and was only outfitted with a few chairs and the 1887 Steinway grand piano, which is still there. This room features a 7- by 11-foot plate-glass window with a view of the city and the mountains in the distance. If the room was infrequently used, then many missed this panorama.

Befitting its formal status, the French Renaissance-styled oval drawing room is the most embellished in the house. The heavy cast plaster cornice includes dentils and a frieze with winged cherubs, each holding a heraldic shield amid vines and clusters of leaves. The two crystal chandeliers and the wall sconces, although electric, are designed to appear as though they were holding candles.

The inclusion of a Turkish smoking room in the Pittock mansion was a holdover from the exotic rooms of the late Victorian movement. Louise Gallien reported that few people actually smoked in this room, and the red, green, silver, and gold paint is original. To make the flooring, craftsman Bruno Dombrowski had to steam and bend the strips of oak around the perimeter to fit the circular space.

The dining room is designed in the Arts and Crafts style. The ceiling beams are of Honduran mahogany instead of the more usual oak. Paneling on each side of the built-in buffet opens to reveal a place to store glassware. Other storage in the dining room was in the seventeenth-century Italian chest, which once held tennis rackets. The Pittocks had hired an interior designer for their new house, who had started purchasing a few pieces such as the Italian chest. Both Peter Gantenbein and Eric Ladd recalled a story that representatives from Meier & Frank, a local department store, went to Henry Pittock and told him that they would stop advertising in the newspaper if he didn't furnish his home with their merchandise. While the Pittocks had a few good pieces, Eric Ladd suggested that, as a result, much of the mansion was furnished with mass-produced pieces.

Although the family used the dining room for Sunday dinners of roast chicken, and other special occasions, they generally dined in the less ornate breakfast room located off the hall. All eleven members of the family ate breakfast there, starting with grapefruit at 8:00 a.m. If Henry Pittock had not finished reading the *Oregonian* before the meal, he would continue at the table.

The fruits and vegetables grown on the grounds made their way to the Pittock table. Raspberries, huckleberries, and apples grew on the estate. The groundskeeper, besides tending the flowers, also planted vegetables such as corn, beans, peas, and carrots. The Pittocks had a greenhouse, which was heated with steam from the house furnace. Commenting on how much it cost to keep a greenhouse and raise the vegetables, one morning Henry Pittock noted that "this tomato cost fifty dollars."

The large plate glass window in the music
room has a panoramic view of the city and
surrounding mountains.

The door on the other side of the china closet in the breakfast room
leads to a hall and then to the kitchen, pantries, and service stairway. Also
in this area is an insulated room designed to keep food cool, a luxury
before the time of refrigerators. The kitchen has been remodeled, but the
Pittock Mansion Society hopes to restore it to its original appearance and
open it to the public.

In 1982, one of the mansion visitors was a former servant who shared
her memories of working for the Pittocks as an upstairs maid and cook.
She recalled that, during her employment, there were very few servants.
At the time of the mansion's construction, factory jobs were offering
both better pay and more autonomy than servant positions, and the
number of available women and men for these jobs was shrinking.
However, the mansion was constructed with several labor-saving devices,
which not only made the duties easier but also allowed the Pittocks to
function with less help.

Central heating was one of these labor-saving devices, replacing
fireplaces, which required a good deal of work. Another invention was
the central vacuum system. After the turn of the twentieth century,
concerns over sanitation and a healthy environment increased, and a central
vacuum system was seen as promoting health. Unlike portable vacuums

that allowed the "germ-laden" air back into the room, the Pittock system exhausted the dust and germs outdoors via a chimney flue located in the basement furnace room.

Another convenience was the elevator, which helped Georgiana Pittock after her stroke. The architect even designed the interior of the elevator, including fine wood and a leaded amber glass ceiling panel. Despite the sturdiness of the elevator, the children were not allowed to play in it. Louise Gallien recalled, "I guess we all started out having a gay old time, going up and down. But they soon put a stop to that!"

The Pittocks believed in employing other young artisans besides the architect when they constructed the mansion. Frederick Baker was in his twenties when he created most of the light fixtures, including the 250- to 300-pound hall chandelier that was originally covered with gold leaf. Baker recalled later that he got the commission because he "used to hang around the old *Morning Oregonian* and shoot the breeze with the artists. I heard that Mr. Pittock was going to build a swell big home up on the hill. The boys told me to go ahead and make some sketches, and they would try to get Mr. Pittock to look at them." The mansion was Baker's first commission, and he went on to design the lighting in such prominent Portland places as Temple Beth Israel, Multnomah County Central Library, and the U. S. National Bank at SW Stark between Sixth and Broadway.

Hiring young artisans proved an unexpected benefit later, since many were still alive when the city attempted restoration. Baker helped to reconstruct the lighting fixtures, and Bruno Dombrowski repaired the water-damaged oak floor in the second-floor hall. Alexander Bolton Pierce, an architect involved with restoring the house, recalled that "the water had caused the floor to swell almost to eight inches out of line." Heavy weights helped to flatten out the wood.

In the second-floor hall hang portraits of Henry and Georgiana Pittock painted by Albert Salzbrenner in 1912 and 1913, respectively. They originally hung in the library, but not everyone was pleased with them. When Henry Pittock's brother came, Louise Gallien later recalled "how critical he was of the pictures, which made a little hard feeling there. The first thing he said was they didn't belong there! And Uncle Henry was quite disturbed, but ... I can remember him saying to his wife, 'We aren't going to change them; I want you right there where I can look at you.' "

The second floor is divided into three suites. In the writing room to the right, Henry and Georgiana Pittock's daughter Kate Hebard worked on the household accounts. Two phones are located in this room, one on the wall and one on the desk. At the time the mansion was constructed, Portland had two competing phone companies, Pacific Bell and Home Telephone, and the two systems were entirely separate. Many houses and businesses had telephone service from both companies; the *Oregonian* had two switchboards side by side.

Kate Hebard shared the adjoining bedroom with Lockwood Hebard, her second husband. She must have been skilled at handling accounting figures, but he apparently was skilled at handling human figures. Peter Gantenbein recalled that "Kate's friends were always subjected to his pinching." Granddaughter Elizabeth Cronin Meier related that "he had an automobile parts business, but it was always a failure. Finally Aunt Kate said … that it was cheaper to pay his debts and keep him out of business than to keep him in business."

Louise Gallien and Helen (the other niece) slept in the adjoining bedroom accessed though the dressing room and bathroom. Henry and Georgiana Pittock occupied separate bedrooms in the next suite. Henry Pittock likely enjoyed his view of the mountains from his bedroom. He was an avid hiker and climber, and Peter Gantenbein recollected that he was in the first group to climb Mount Hood. He applied his work ethic to his sport. Peter Gantenbein noted that "someone would say, 'Let's sit down and rest,' and he said, 'The man who sits down never reaches the top.' "

Henry Pittock's adjoining exclusive bathroom has a bathtub and a sitz bath in which he reportedly soaked his feet. The grandchildren thought the most fascinating feature in the entire house was the shower, which still intrigues visitors today. Besides the shower head above, the bather can use the four-level needle spray or turn the handle once labeled "liver" for a waist high wash. In addition, a bidet spray rises from below, and a "test" handle allows checking the temperature with a toe before stepping into the shower.

This bathroom occupied the southern tower; Georgiana Pittock's sewing room was in the northern tower. In her adjoining bedroom is an intercom, another labor-saving device. Nineteen stations are still listed on the phone ranging from "Mr. Pittock" to "3ᵈ Service" (likely the servant quarters on the third floor).

Georgiana Pittock shared her bathroom with Lucy, her husband John, and their three children. Historians believe that Lucy and John's two daughters occupied the sleeping porch, an arrangement that was in fashion after the turn of the twentieth century, as the health conscious believed that clean air was the antidote to germs. Like the sleeping porch in Kate Hebard's suite, it was designed with the maximum number of windows and waterproof decking on the floor. A drain in the middle of the floor removed any rainwater that came in through opened windows.

Peter Gantenbein was born in Lucy and John's bedroom shortly after the family moved into the mansion. Growing up in the Pittock house some distance from the nearest neighbors limited the number of possible playmates. Louise Gallien recalled a time when she and others were sitting on the lawn, and Peter Gantenbein was off playing by himself. She heard him talking to someone, and "casually walked up in back of him to see what he was talking about. When I got close he said, 'Now God: you catch it. It's your turn!' And he was throwing his ball up in the air. I guess he was lonesome—there weren't any other children up there to play with and he was telling God he wanted him to play ball with him!"

The plans labeled the rooms in the basement for adult amusement. The elliptical room was to be a social hall and billiard room, and the two flanking circular rooms were to be card nooks. Today, the rooms are used for interpretive exhibits on the Pittocks and the house. For those who like to look at plans, the society has put up a copy of each of the mansion's four floor plans on the walls.

Unfortunately, significant changes have occurred in the basement service areas, and a visitor today can only get a sense of the original layout. The men's restroom was once a kitchen storeroom and wine room, while the women's restroom now occupies what was the cook's quarters, which had a bedroom, bathroom, and closet. A male cook once resided here, but his tenure in the house did not last long. Peter Gantenbein believed he was fired because he was enamoured with the upstairs maid, and "he'd get up to the maids' rooms through the backstairs and he did [that] all the time."

A glass door in the hall gives a glimpse of a spacious and well-lit laundry room, another feature of the mansion. Although not available to viewing, behind another door in the basement is the original electrical service that operated on a marble slab. Even the service areas at the Pittock were luxurious.

Ermatinger House

National Register of Historic Places
Built: 1845
619 Sixth Street
Oregon City
503-650-1851 (museum)
503-557-9199 (Oregon City Parks & Recreation: Carnegie Center)

The Ermatinger house can easily be overlooked because it appears like an average dwelling. It is, however, the third oldest house in Oregon.

Directions: From McLoughlin Boulevard, turn south on Tenth Street, cross the railroad track, and head up to Singer Hill. At the top of the hill, follow the street as it veers left and turns into Seventh Street. After about two blocks, at the signalized intersection of Seventh and Washington streets, turn right. Go one block, and turn left on Sixth Street. The house is on the left at the end of the block.

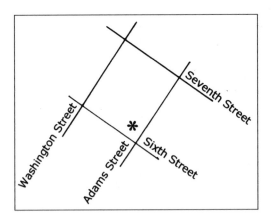

Open: Year around except in the last half of December and the month of January
Hours: Wednesday–Sunday, 12:00–4:00
Admission: $3.00 adults; $2.00 seniors and students
Tour: Guided. The house also has a living history tour and tea; call the house for details.

Entry: At the front door. If no one is there, inquire at the Carnegie Center on the next block west.

Additional Attractions: The Stevens-Crawford House, another house museum, is located on the same block at 603 Sixth Street (see page 36). The Dr. John McLoughlin house is located three blocks northwest at 713 Center Street (see page 23).

Also located in Oregon City is Rose Farm, another house museum (see page 30).

History

Francis Ermatinger was born in Portugal in 1798 and educated in England. In 1818 he joined the Hudson's Bay Company and in 1825 came to Fort Vancouver to work for John McLoughlin, eventually rising to the position of chief trader with the Northwest Indians. In 1841, he married Catherine Sinclair, Marguerite McLoughlin's granddaughter, and was placed in charge of the Hudson's Bay Company store in Oregon City. John McLoughlin deeded him land for the house, which was completed in 1845. However, he only lived here about a year before he was transferred to England, leaving his wife and daughter Frances behind. Two years later, he was sent to Canada with his family. During the 1860s, the house became a boarding house.

In 1909, the Hawley Pulp and Paper mill expansion threatened the McLoughlin and Ermatinger houses. The McLoughlin Memorial Association moved the McLoughlin house up the hill to its present location, and the Ermatinger house was moved to Eleventh and Center streets. Various occupants inhabited the house, and its significance was largely forgotten.

Ruth Powers, who preserved many historic houses in Oregon, purchased the house in 1986. The structure's second location was unsuitable for showing the house to the public, and Powers offered to pay for the move if the city would donate a lot. On moving day they inched the house down on ramps onto Eleventh Street, then pulled it by winches up the hill and towed it to its present-day site.

From 1987 to 1996, the house operated as a private museum, and it gained local notoriety in 1996. Between tours for visiting schoolchildren, a caretaker supplemented her income by selling drugs. A spokesman for the sheriff's office reported that "she just seemed like a nice old grandma, just a real sweet little old lady." To her credit, the caretaker did make the undercover officers buying her drugs wait until she had completed the tours for students visiting the house on a field trip.

The City of Oregon City then acquired the house, and currently operates the museum.

Exterior

Frontier conditions demanded that early building practices in Oregon be simple. The Ermatinger house appears plain today, especially when compared to the 1908 Stevens-Crawford house on the same block directly west, but it was constructed while many families were still living in log cabins. Most houses were without the luxury of the Ermatinger house's many windows and the long porch across the front.

The design of the house displays elements of the Federal style with an entablature surrounding the roofline and the rebuilt porch also with an entablature and square columns. On the front facade, the upper windows have six-over-six panes, although the first-floor windows have six-over-nine panes and extend to the floor. The five-light front door transom helped illuminate the hall.

An extension, discernible by the gable roof, was added to the rear about 1910. On the second floor of the addition facing north is a small door, although where it led is now unknown.

Although his house was grand for its time, Francis Ermatinger was only able to live in it for about a year before he was transferred to England.

Interior

Today many houses, such as the Flavel house in Astoria or the Moyer house in Brownsville, have been turned into museums because they were the grandest houses in the area. The Ermatinger house, however, is celebrated because of its age, now over one hundred fifty years. The interior lacks fine craftsmanship, so the house affords a glimpse of more common workmanship. Rough boards constitute the floor and ceiling. Wallpaper now covers the walls in the sitting room to the right of the front door, but it cannot hide the unevenness of the boards.

The house is the site of several ghost stories, including one based in the kitchen. Before the structure was moved up to the bluff, it had a cellar. Today, the house has only a crawl space, and in the kitchen, behind what was once the cellar door, a stairway now ends abruptly at a dirt floor. One story about the house is that a caretaker went down the stairway to the cellar and the door was locked behind her. She was alone there, without a means of communication, for hours, until the door was mysteriously unlocked. On the door frame is a rust-colored figure of a cross, one of four found in the house. Who put them there—or why—remains a mystery.

Another ghost story is about an old sea captain, but why he supposedly haunts the house, or who he was, is not known. The ghost is said to sit at the end of the table near the entrance to the kitchen and makes his presence known by pulling out that chair. A docent reported that one afternoon, after saying good-bye to a colleague and locking up the back door, he crossed the dining room to go out to the street to retrieve the museum sign on the sidewalk. When he returned, the chair was pulled out about two feet from the table.

In the front room off the dining room, which possibly

The dining room is the location of one of the Ermatinger House's reported ghost visitations.

Asa Lovejoy and Francis Pettygrove flipped the coin to determine Portland's name in this house.

served as the parlor at that time, Francis Pettygrove and Asa Lovejoy flipped a penny to determine whether their land should be called Boston, after Lovejoy's hometown, or Portland, after Pettygrove's. The reputed penny is now part of the Oregon Historical Society's collection in Portland, but a penny from the time sits on the table underneath glass. The coin is larger than the size of today's quarter, perhaps implying the greater purchasing power of the penny in the nineteenth century. While the profiles of former presidents grace our current coins, this 1837 penny shows the Goddess of Liberty. At that time, Abraham Lincoln, now depicted on contemporary pennies, was only twenty-eight years old.

Upstairs, four bedrooms are located off the main hall in the original section of the house. Another ghost story concerns the northeastern bedroom. The ghost, called the Little Girl, is believed to like ribbons. One day a docent, vacuuming the rug after a day of visitors, went downstairs but returned to turn off a light. She then found part of a ribbon lying across the rug where she had just vacuumed.

A piece of ribbon from the little girl's room was mysteriously found in a foot warmer, which rested on the bed on the southwest corner of the house. Like the cellar door closet, this room also bears a cross on the closet doorframe. The other two crosses are located in the adjoining bedroom: one on the windowsill and another on the doorframe in the hall. Why this room has two of these religious symbols is unknown, and much of the Ermatinger house remains a mystery.

McLoughlin House

National Historic Site
Built: 1845

713 Center Street
Oregon City
503-656-5146 (museum)

John McLoughlin's position in the community can be likened today to the president of a major corporation. With his position, he had power, influence, and wealth, and the house he built with his assets was really a mansion at the time. The memorabilia and furnishing inside the house also reflect his prestige.

Directions: From McLoughlin Boulevard, turn south on Tenth Street (away from the river). After crossing the railroad tracks, Tenth turns into a road climbing Singer Hill. At the top of the hill, follow the curve in the street as it veers left, and go one block. Turn left on Center Street; the house is one-half block on the left.

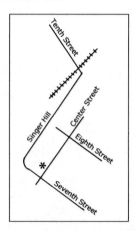

Open: Year around except for holidays and January, Tuesday–Sunday
Hours: Tuesday–Saturday, 10:00–4:00; Sunday, 1:00–4:00
Admission: $4.00 adults; $3.00 seniors; $2.00 students
Tour: Guided (last complete tour 3:15)
Entry: Pay admission at the adjoining Dr. Forbes Barclay house (719 Center Street).

Additional Attractions: Dr. Forbes Barclay was an associate of McLoughlin's at Fort Vancouver, and his 1849 house is currently used as a gift shop and meeting room of the McLoughlin Memorial Association.

Francis Ermatinger, who worked for McLoughlin, owned the house, now a museum, at 619 Sixth Street (see page 18). The Stevens-Crawford House, another house museum, is located on the same block at 603 Sixth Street (see page 36).

Also located in Oregon City is Rose Farm (see page 30).

History

John McLoughlin was born in 1794 to a Quebec farming family. At the age of nineteen, he joined the North West Company, a fur-trading concern, as a physician, and he worked his way up to management. After the North West Company merged with the Hudson's Bay Company in 1821, he was sent to the Oregon Country to organize Fort Vancouver, which became the hub of the Northwest fur trade. At that time, England and the United States had joint ownership in the Oregon Country, and the British-based Hudson's Bay Company was attempting to establish a toehold.

John McLoughlin and Governor George Simpson, the top Hudson's Bay Company official in North America, claimed in 1829 the land around the Willamette Falls, a promising source of hydro power. McLoughlin's relationship with Simpson had always been uneasy, as the governor had been disturbed about his hospitality to American settlers. In 1845, McLoughlin resigned from the Hudson's Bay Company, paid $20,000 for the claim at the falls, and moved to Oregon City and to this house. He became a U.S. citizen in 1851 and became mayor of the town that same year.

Despite his many years of kindness to the pioneers, they disputed his land claim. When the donation land claim law was put into effect in 1850, every prior claim was reaffirmed except his. It was a bitter blow, and the claim was still under dispute when he died in 1857, three years after his wife, Marguerite.

The surrounding area gradually became industrial, and in 1867, Eloisa Harvey, the McLoughlins' daughter, and her husband sold the house. The new owners named the building the Phoenix Hotel, and rented the rooms to Chinese mill woolen workers. When a fire burned the nearby mill in 1872, the building was threatened but unharmed.

The Phoenix Hotel gradually fell into disrepute, a condition that was memorialized in a ditty of the day, "It was [sic] at the Phoenix Hotel that the bugs and roaches do dwell." The building at one point became a "house of negotiable affection" and was abandoned to squatters. Eventually, the Hawley Pulp and Paper Mill Company bought the property for expansion of their operations. In 1909, the mill offered the building free to anyone who would move it, and the McLoughlin Memorial Association was organized. However, not everyone wanted to save the house. A pamphlet circulated opposing the idea stated that the house was a "haunt of shame and disgrace … It has been used for vile and disreputable purposes so long that no decent, purity loving citizen can associate it with any good purpose."

Nevertheless, with donations such as $48 raised at the "Bachelor Girls" dance, the association raised over $1,000 to move the house up the bluff to a lot that John McLoughlin had designated as a public park. However, the house, winched by horse, was moved only a few blocks before an injunction was served on the officers of the association to prevent moving of the house through town, and the move was stalled for three days.

The road up the side of the hill was narrow in one section, so narrow that more than half of the building would hang over the edge. The movers thought they needed to build a trestle, but there were no funds for this.

The stately McLoughlin house was considered a mansion when it was constructed.

Instead, they ingeniously devised a way to tip the house by loading the cliff side of it with sand, gravel, and cement. A second injunction was served while the house was on the cliff, but the its placement was so precarious that it had to be moved onward.

The house initially displayed early "Oregoniana" (pioneer mementos). In the mid-1930s, various civic organizations raised money to restore the house, and their sources included both the state and federal government. With some of the money, the association also moved the Forbes Barclay house next door. The house was made a National Historic Site in 1941, the eleventh in the United States. Today, the McLoughlin Memorial Association still operates the house.

Setting

Behind the house are the graves of John and Marguerite McLoughlin.

Exterior

The McLoughlins were wealthy, and the size of the house they built in 1846 demonstrates the size of their assets. It must have appeared a magnificent palace to the settlers, most of whom were living in crude log cabins. The neighboring Barclay house, constructed three years later, is small in comparison. However, despite the difference in size, the McLoughlin house cost about $4,500 to construct, while the Barclay dwelling cost roughly $17,500. The California gold rush had started when Barclay began building, and locals were forced to match the exorbitant rates that the clamoring miners to the south would pay for lumber.

John McLoughlin is believed to have designed his house, which has a symmetrical plan, hipped roof, and wide frieze below the cornice, all Georgian style elements. The door now facing the street, once the back entrance, has a transom, while the former front door has both a transom and sidelights, another characteristic of the style, as is the a similar front and rear entrance. Overall, the embellishment is restrained. Marion D. Ross, a University of Oregon professor, likened the architecture to that of early New England and eastern Canada; perhaps McLoughlin was trying to recreate in his home a design with which he was familiar from his boyhood in Quebec.

Interior

A Boston factory was the source of the doors, sashes, and moldings, and McLoughlin's own sawmill produced most of the other lumber for the house. Originally, the house was situated near the sawmill, making it convenient for John McLoughlin to check on his business. Before stepping outside, he would inspect his appearance in a mirror hanging in the hall.

The beaver hat hanging on the 1833 Scottish hat stand represents what drew John McLoughlin, the Hudson's Bay Company, and fur trappers to the Pacific Northwest: beaver pelts. Until the mid-1800s, a beaver hat was a sign of affluence. Changing fashion and a depleted beaver supply eventually made these hats outmoded, and their replacement, a silk hat, shares the hat stand. On the south wall hangs a Chilkat Indian ceremonial robe made of cedar bark and wild goat wool. To these Northwest Indians, the robe symbolized culture, power, and wealth; for McLoughlin, his house did the same.

The docent usually starts the tour by going through the dining room into a small adjoining room that serves as a trophy room. In a glass display case lies a medal from the Horticulture Society of London, which commemorates John McLoughlin's kindness to David Douglas, the Scottish biologist for whom the Douglas fir tree is named. (Unfortunately, the inscription spells his name wrong.) Nearby lies another medal, which McLoughlin received when Pope Gregory XVI designated him a Knight of St. Gregory the Great for his work in helping the settlers.

Also in the display case is the McLoughlins' silverware, imported from England, which bears the family crest, including a rampant lion. These refined implements contrast with the nearby crude long-handled pan used to cook food over an open fire at the fort. Other aspects of John McLoughlin's life are illustrated with the remaining articles in the room, including the Hudson's Bay Company flag and a copy of the Oregon City plat that he had filed.

Originally, this room and the one also just off the dining room were joined into one space that served as John McLoughlin's office. In here, he likely perused the profit statements from his enterprises, but he also wrote bitter correspondence questioning the Hudson's Bay Company's investigation of the murder of his son John, and letters to Oregon legislators promoting his donation land claim.

The combination desk and bookcase in the adjoining room held what was a "gentlemen's lending library" at the fort. The chairs and the table, which has leaves that allow it to seat up to twenty-four people, were used at the Chief Factor's house at Fort Vancouver.

The table extends to seat twenty-four
people, and was used at Fort Vancouver.

In order to accommodate the table, the room is outfitted as the dining room, but historians believe that the room now decorated as the parlor was originally used as the dining room because of the exterior door. The kitchen originally was located in an outbuilding, a typical arrangement of the time due to the unpleasantness of heat from the wood-burning stove in the summer and smoke problems year-round.

In the parlor stands an elaborate Chinese lacquer cabinet that has a hole in the center drawer that allowed the placement of a pocket watch. A clerk at the Fort, who later also rose to be the chief factor, gave the cabinet to Marguerite McLoughlin. With pieces such as this, it is understandable why the family's furniture was appraised at $1,000 after John McLoughlin died in 1857.

John McLoughlin kept his medical office in a space off the parlor, and because there was a doorway from the hall, it is likely that visitors seeking medical advice entered through the back door without disturbing the rest of the house. Today, the space is divided into two small rooms and used to display more modest bedroom furniture typically found in pioneers' homes.

On the second floor, four rooms are placed off the hall, but only three of these were used as bedrooms. The McLoughlin house was known locally as the "house of many beds," referring to the hospitality the family extended to visitors. When the bedrooms were full, guests likely slept in this hall.

The first bedroom on the right may have served as the McLoughlins' bedroom and it features John McLoughlin's hand-carved bed from Scotland. McLoughlin believed in sleeping in a sitting position, propped up by pillows, for heath reasons. Another beaver hat is appropriately included in the decor.

The second bedroom on the right features an 1850s spool bed. The McLoughlins' widowed daughter, who had three children, inhabited the house for several years, and historians believe that her children occupied this room. Resting under one chair is a foot warmer, in which hot coals were put in a pan. Near the bed is a chamber pot with a crocheted "silencer," which muffled the sound of the lid after use.

Opposite this bedroom is the sitting room. Men did not linger here, as it was intended for the women. John McLoughlin gave his eight-year-old granddaughter the rosewood melodeon, which stands against one wall. The center table has been called a pie crust table; fittingly, it is made of apple wood.

The last room features a large bed donated to the collection that once belonged to the family of Meriwether Lewis's mother. The bed features a navy-blue linen coverlet from 1790, and is the oldest piece in the house. The spread has an unusual stiffness, and was possibly starched with egg whites.

In the corner is John McLoughlin's oversized rocker, custom-built for a man of his large frame. Some visitors have reported seeing the rocker moving back and forth by itself. The McLoughlin house does have a history of possible visits by McLoughlin's ghost. The curator has heard the thud of heavy boots pacing the upstairs hall when no one was there; others have seen a tall silhouette duck through doorways. Another person on the grounds reported seeing McLoughlin's face peering out an upstairs window. McLoughlin died in the house in 1857 from complications of diabetes, so if his ghost remains in the house, perhaps he is pleased that his possessions and his memory have stood the test of time.

Rose Farm

National Register of Historic Places
Built: 1847
534 Holmes Lane
Oregon City
503-656-5146 (McLoughlin Memorial Society at the McLoughlin House)

Rose Farm sits in the middle of a residential area, although the surrounding houses were all constructed at a later date. As one of the first houses in the Oregon City area, it became the social and political center of the town, which was then the capital of Oregon.

Directions: From McLoughlin Boulevard, turn south on Tenth Street, cross the railroad track, and head up to Singer Hill. At the top of the hill, follow the street as it veers left and turns into Seventh Street, which turns into Molalla Avenue. At the signalized intersection of Molalla Avenue and Holmes Lane, turn right. The house is on the left at the corner of Holmes Street and Rilance Lane.

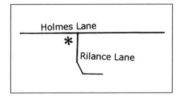

Open: Sundays, April through October
Hours: 1:00–4:00
Admission: $2.00 adults; $1.00 students
Tour: Guided
Entry: At the front door
Additional Attractions: Behind the house is the 1857 Dr. Daniel Stevenson house (viewable from the street only).

Also located in Oregon City are three other house museums: McLoughlin House (see page 23), Ermatinger House (see page 18), and Stevens-Crawford House (see page 36).

History

William and Louisa Holmes traveled over the Oregon Trail with their three children in 1843. Settling on a 640-acre claim on the upper level in Oregon City because of a fine nearby spring and the view of Mount Hood, they hastily built a two-room cabin. Four years later, they completed a house constructed with timber from the trees standing on their claim. However, their doors and windows were shipped from New England around Cape Horn.

Oregon City was then the meeting place of the provisional government, and since the Holmes's dwelling was one of the few finished houses in the area, it became a center of social and political events. Dr. John McLoughlin attended some of the many parties held in the second-floor ballroom. Later, Joseph Lane, the first territorial governor, delivered the news of Oregon's territorial status from the balcony.

The Holmes family grew to include seven children. Louisa Holmes grew pink roses on the grounds, and the house became known as Rose Farm. Descendants of the family lived in the house until 1919. The house became a rooming house, and then a rental house, until Ruth Powers purchased it in 1974. She restored the house, and then gave it in 1984 to

The Rose Farm has a recessed porch with unusual scalloped bargeboard.

the McLoughlin Memorial Society, which currently operates this museum along with the McLoughlin House (see page 23).

Setting

The area surrounding the house contains 1.9 acres, a fraction of the original 640 acres that comprised the Holmes claim. A well-landscaped yard separates the house from the street, and it includes a stately catalpa tree planted by the Holmes family.

Exterior

With its two identical front doors, the Rose Farm seems like a duplex, but it was constructed to be a single-family dwelling. (In the twentieth century, it actually was turned into a duplex, but has since been restored.) Each door opens up to a nearly identical room with a fireplace. For many double houses, the front porch served as a hall. This may have occurred at Rose Farm, although today the two front rooms, the parlor and sitting room, are connected inside the house.

The recessed porch and upstairs balcony flanked by two rooms distinguish the house, as does the scalloped bargeboard on the eaves. Historians believe that the family designed the house after their former Tennessee home. Despite moving to a new land, the Holmes family wanted .to live in a house that was familiar.

Interior

The first door opens directly into the parlor, a formal room reserved for special occasions or prominent guests. William, Louisa, and several of their children died in the house, and following the custom, they were "laid out" in the parlor. The custom of laying the body out shifted when embalming gained favor, and funerals moved from the family parlor to the funeral parlor.

Years earlier, Minnie Holmes, the eldest child, married Daniel O'Neill, who operated a worldwide shipping business, in the parlor. For their wedding trip, the couple sailed about the world and purchased furniture from three continents. The Chinese furniture in the parlor represents pieces they might have purchased. One piece actually owned by the family is the rosewood piano, which was shipped around Cape Horn in 1851 on the second ship carrying pianos to the Oregon Territory. Their piano would have been a welcome addition to the household, as square pianos

The ballroom on the second floor was used as a social center of Oregon City, and the balcony off the ballroom was the site of Territorial Governor General Lane's first address.

symbolized an upper-middle-class house. The design of square pianos remained unchanged for most of the second half of the nineteenth century, denoting permanence and timeless good taste.

If a piano made a parlor elegant, a fireplace made it cozy. Andrew Jackson Downing wrote in 1850, "All the perfection of the best system of heating and ventilating does not ... banish from our minds the desire for an open fire in the living room. ... We must have a little of the living soul—the glow of the hearth—there." Changing mantels on the Rose Farm parlor suggest the importance of the fireplace to the Holmes family. Although an irregularly cut stone mantel is now displayed, neighbor Roma Stafford remembered that it was of "stone cut square." Photographs dated 1902 show a wooden mantel in the parlor with a row of gray squirrels, which Stafford reported were painted by a cousin.

Small stoves fitted into the parlor and sitting room chimneys heated the upstairs bedrooms. To heat the bedroom off the parlor, the Holmeses placed a pan of live coals under the bed. One time the coals were left in the tightly closed room, and two daughters were overcome by fumes.

The two paintings in oval frames that hang in the sitting room once were positioned in a place of honor over the piano. The third child, Frances, also known as Frankie, used moss to create the lifelike three-dimensional greenery effect. She died in 1881, and the family bible states, "At Rose Farm after a long and painful illness, Frances E. Holmes in her 38th year."

The fireplaces in the Holmes's parlor and sitting room were important not only for heating the house but as a place to entertain their many guests.

Stafford related that "the family gathered and hundreds of friends were entertained" near the fireplace in the sitting room. Instead of a child's play area as is shown now, the nook to the right of the fireplace was originally a tiny closet where the Holmes family stored fireplace tools, wood, and kindling. In the early 1890s, following the fashion of the time, the door was removed, the walls were papered and decorated, and a seat was built in to create an inglenook.

The narrow winding stairway right of the nook was once the only way to the second floor. At one time, the Holmes family bathed in a copper bathtub that stood in a small room upstairs, and hot water had to be carried up the narrow steps. When the bather was finished, he or she would pour the water down a drain to a pipe that watered the roses.

The back of the house, where the kitchen and dining room are now located, has been altered several times over the years. Initially, the kitchen was in the rear of the house in a separate building shared with a washroom. The family later added a one-and-a-half-story kitchen to the main part of the house, and Minnie O'Neill used the half story for storage, which she called a "glory hole." Stafford related that O'Neill would "put on an old jacket, tie up her head in a silk kerchief, and slip into there with a candle and sort over her boxes of things."

A large porch housing the well was once located on the west side of the second kitchen. In hot weather, butter and meat were placed in the well to keep cool. Despite a screen cover, a mouse would occasionally get into the well, causing great excitement. The water had to be drawn out, a lantern lowered, and a person of slender build lowered in the bucket to scrub the walls. He or she had to hurry, for the spring replenished the well rapidly.

The current kitchen was installed sometime in the twentieth century, although it displays items from the nineteenth century. The Holmes family undoubtedly had a pie safe at one time, perhaps located on the back porch. Judge Samson of Clackamas County made the one on display in 1884 for his fiancée. Samson must have been a romantic man, for he punctured several hearts into the metal door panels.

After using the narrow staircase in the sitting room, the Holmes family undoubtedly welcomed the addition of the back staircase. In the upstairs hallways rests a seaman's chest from the Revolutionary War ship, the "Constitution," the world's oldest commissioned warship now afloat. "Old Ironsides," as it is called, is famous for its escape from five British ships in the War of 1812.

One of the rooms at the end of the hall displays Minnie and Daniel O'Neill's wedding clothes, which were at one time preserved in the red-painted family trunk now resting in the ballroom. The two other bedrooms off the ballroom served as changing rooms for out-of-town guests when balls were held. Overnight guests sometimes slept in the attic.

In 1848, five years after Oregon began operating under a provisional government, Joseph Meek traveled to Washington to petition for federal jurisdiction. He returned with General Joseph Lane, who addressed the large gathering from the Rose Farm balcony in March 1849. Lane, wearing his general's outfit, delivered the proclamation that Congress had established a territorial government in Oregon. Later that night, a barbecue of beef, venison, and bear meat was given in his honor and the participants danced in the ballroom until dawn. The members of the territorial government reportedly met for the first time in the ballroom on July 5th, 1849. Although Rose Farm was the Holmes family home for many years, it also was a significant site in early Oregon.

Stevens-Crawford House

Built: 1908

603 Sixth Street
Oregon City
503-655-2866 (museum)

The Stevens family wanted to have all the latest conveniences when they built their house in 1908. It now stands today as one of the first "modern" homes of Oregon's historic house museums constructed after the turn of the twentieth century.

Directions: From McLoughlin Boulevard, turn south on Tenth Street, cross the railroad track and head up to Singer Hill. At the top of the hill, follow the street as it veers left and turns into Seventh Street. After about two blocks, at the signalized intersection of Seventh and Washington streets, turn right. Go one block, and turn left on Sixth Street. The house is on the corner.

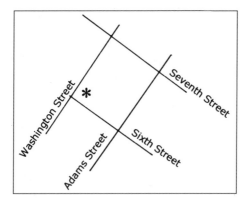

Open: Year around except in the last half of December and the month of January
Hours: Wednesday–Friday, 12:00–4:00; Saturday–Sunday, 1:00–4:00
Admission: $4.00 adults; $3.00 seniors; $2.00 children six to eighteen; $10.00 family up to five people
Tour: Guided
Entry: At the front door

Additional Attractions: The admission cost includes admission to the Clackamas County Historical Society's museum, located at 211 Tumwater Drive (call 503-655-5574 for information).

The Ermatinger House is located on the same block at 619 Sixth Street (see page 18). The Dr. John McLoughlin house is located two blocks northwest at 713 Center Street (see page 23).

Also located in Oregon City is Rose Farm (see page 30).

History

In 1862, at the age of fifteen, Harley Stevens left his home in New York state to join a military escort conducting an emigrant train across the plains. His future father-in-law, Captain Medorem Crawford, was in charge of the escort team. After being discharged from the Army in 1867, Stevens enrolled in a school for telegraphy, and was hired in 1870 to work for the Oregon & California Railroad Company as a telegraph operator in Oregon City. He later became a station manager.

Harley Stevens married Mary Elizabeth Crawford in 1871 at her family's farm in Dayton and the couple had two children, Harley Jr. and Mertie. Mertie Stevens never married, and lived in the house from the time it was built until her death in 1968 at the age of ninety-five. In her will, she provided a scholarship fund for Clackamas County students, and bequeathed her residence to the Clackamas County Historical Society, which still owns and operates the museum.

Setting

The Stevens-Crawford house is located on its original site on a corner lot.

Exterior

For their modern house, the Stevens selected a design without the heavy embellishment of the Victorian styles. Following the new design trends, the Classic Box style, also called American Box or simply Box, had restrained ornamentation. Few Classic Box houses existed before 1890, but by 1930 they were widespread across the nation.

Although the house has some projections, such as the enclosed side porch on the east side, the basic shape is rectangular, which gives the style its name. The wide overhanging eaves on the house and front and side porches provide a horizontal emphasis, another attribute of the style. Another common feature of the style is the hipped roof with a central hipped roof dormer.

Interior

Harley Stevens ran his stock, bond, insurance, and real estate business out of the front portion of the house. Just inside the front door is a foyer, where a hall tree like the one there now might have stood to hold clients' hats and umbrellas. The hall to the left served as the waiting area, while the room now used to collect admissions was Harley Stevens's office.

A copy of the wagon train military escort orders hangs on the wall in Stevens's former office, and it suggests how difficult the trip was. The orders state there was to be no furniture or extra baggage, and that the oxen team should not lose "flesh or spirits" for the first eight hundred miles. Furthermore, the captain "should also decide all quarrels or disputes … his decisions shall be final, whether right or wrong."

In the living room over the piano hangs a photograph of the Stevens family. They had wanted a modern home, but although the house was wired for electricity, then a new technology, they hedged their bets. The original chandelier in the room could use either electricity or gas. In the early days of electricity, the transmission was unreliable and gas lighting provided an emergency back-up source. The museum has installed a reproduction of an early bulb to demonstrate that turn-of-the-twentieth-

When the Stevens built their house, they wanted all the latest conveniences.

century fixtures gave off considerably less light than today's bulb. Generally, lamps and wall sconces would supplement the light from the chandelier.

The overmantel in the living room is from another Oregon City family, and can be seen in the photograph standing on the mantel. The photograph also shows a Victorian interior complete with a jaunty pair of antlers on one wall. No photographs remain of how the Stevens decorated their parlor, so the historical society must make decisions on the appearance of the house based on the items Mertie Stevens had in her possessions when she died. At that time, her house was so cluttered that only a trail ran through the ground floor rooms of the house.

To the right of the overmantel is a 1907 calendar advertising the insurance company in which Harley Stevens was an agent. The calendar lists the company's assets of $26.5 million, and boasts that its $2.8 million in losses for the 1906 San Francisco conflagration (and earthquake) were paid in full less than a year after the event.

The *Textbook on Architecture and Building Construction*, published in 1899, advised locating the dining room on the east side of a house instead of the west to avoid the setting sun during dinnertime. The Stevens followed that sage advice in the placement of their dining room, and added a step-saving built-in buffet that has every shelf and drawer accessible from the adjoining pantry.

Mertie Stevens enclosed the adjoining downstairs porch and used it as a bedroom in her later years when the stairs became too difficult to climb. The family's collection of wicker furniture once stood on the porch of their summer home located just across the Willamette River in West Linn. Wicker furniture gained in popularity in late Victorian times and remained so after the turn of the twentieth century, in part because of a movement advocating "sanitary" living. Wicker was easy to clean and permitted air circulation that was linked to good health. On the second floor, the Stevens built a sleeping porch, which also was advocated by the movement.

The utilitarian face on the pantry side of the buffet symbolizes the use of the room as a workspace. The room was also thoughtfully designed, with a place to hold the rolling pin and a shelf to organize recipes on note cards. The recipes, many handwritten with a fountain pen, are categorized under labels such as "Meat," "Meat Substitutes" (perhaps used during war rationing), and "Try."

The telephone at the entrance to the kitchen may originally have been located in Harley Stevens's office. The nearby three-story wood lift was used to bring fuel to heat the kitchen stove and logs for the living-room fireplace, as well as wood for stoves on the second floor. Another feature is the nook in the wall behind the wood stove, which allowed bread to rise without exposing it to cold drafts.

The parlor has a chandelier that ran on both gas and electricity.
The overmantel above the fireplace came from a Victorian
house in Oregon City.

Besides the pantry and the kitchen, the house has a number of other "working" rooms, such as the pot and pan closet, washroom, summer kitchen, and sewing room. On the floor in the washroom sits a large wicker basket to which the family had sentimental attachment. Harley Stevens was working at the train station the day he was to be married, but his relief was late. After his replacement finally arrived, he threw both his wedding clothes and the wedding cake (his responsibility) into the basket, hopped the ferry across the Willamette River, and caught a train to Dayton. He apparently arrived in time.

The Stevens used the back door as their primary entrance, and the hooks on the back stairway doubled its use as a closet. Upstairs, the middle bedroom is called the parson's room, although originally it was the Harley and Mary Stevens's room. When the parson stayed with the family, he slept in this room, and eventually the parents became tired of vacating the room and moved permanently down the hall. The couple bought Mertie Stevens the maple bedroom furniture in the room when they moved into the house. It once resided in Mertie Stevens's room down the hall.

Black and white photographs in the hall show Oregon City as a small town near the turn of the twentieth century. One shows the town's elevator, one of the few municipal elevators in the nation. A series of five photographs show 1912 Fourth of July parade entrants on Main Street. On the left side of the street is the four-story Masonic building that had just opened months before, and the local newspaper had reported that "in Oregon City it was a veritable skyscraper." It remains that today.

In Harley and Mary Stevens's room, a collar storage box lies on the bureau. Laundry was a chore, even after the turn of the twentieth century, and businessmen like Harley Stevens typically wore their shirts for several days. Collars, however, became visibly soiled and so men used detachable collars that could easily be cleaned with soap and water.

The tour ends by going down the front stairways into the former waiting room. Harley Stevens had an extraordinary collection of arrowheads, some of which are on display on the wall. His collection no doubt was helped by his newspaper advertisements that offered children a penny for every arrowhead they presented him. The Stevens-Crawford house, with its modern conveniences, is another testimony to the family's forward thinking.

Tigard House

National Register of Historic Places
Built: circa 1880
Canterbury Lane & 103rd Avenue
Tigard
503-639-2857 (museum)

Victorian homes preserved as house museums are generally behemoth structures, representing the extravagance of the times. The Tigard house, however, is small and compact. Despite its size, the family still deemed it worthy of decoration, and its embellishments distinguished it from the plainer houses in the neighborhood.

Directions: From Highway 99, turn south at Canterbury Lane. Travel about a quarter mile up to the top of the hill. The house is on the right.

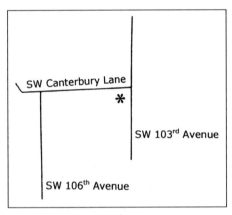

Open: Third Sunday of the month
Hours: 1:00–4:00
Admission: Donation $1.00 adults; $.50 children
Tour: Guided
Entry: At the front door
Additional Attractions: The center of Tigard, which was moved when the railroad station was established, is located approximately 1.75 miles north off of Highway 99 on SW Main Street.

History

John Wesley Tigard was born on Christmas Day, 1850, in Arkansas, and at the age of two crossed the plains with his family in a wagon train. After his family reached the Willamette Valley, they purchased land in present-day Tigard. John Tigard's father, Wilson, built the house for John and his wife Emma Ornduff as a wedding present. It was situated in the center of the town called East Butte (later Tigardville), at what is now Highway 99 and SW McDonald Street.

The couple had two sons and later divorced. John Tigard married Sophia Schmidler in 1892, and after she died in 1917, he married Ervilla Shaw a year later. Carrying a plate of cookies across Highway 99 from his house to attend a function at the Grange, he was struck by a car. He died three days later on April 7, 1931.

Ervilla Tigard continued to live in the house until her health failed in the early 1940s, and after her death, renters occupied the house. When the nearby interchange was being widened in 1978, local citizens banded together as the Tigard Area Historical and Preservation Association (TAHPA) to move the house to keep it from being razed. In the late 1980s, interested citizens again reorganized to restore the house, and today TAHPA owns and operates the house.

Setting

The house is now situated on what had been a vacant piece of land owned by the Tigard Water District. As a part of the house restoration, volunteers have tried to replicate the original landscaping with a white picket fence and the planting of five apple trees. In the fall when the trees are bearing fruit, volunteers give the apples to visitors.

Exterior

The house has Folk Victorian architecture, which is defined by Victorian embellishments added to the exterior of a simple folk form. On the Tigard house, the decorative elements are concentrated thriftily on the front facade. Square, diamond, and fish-scale shingles cover the gable, varying the appearance from the flush siding that covers most of the exterior. At the peak of the gable is a row of tiny spindles that mimic the finely detailed porch balustrade.

The compact Tigard house has its embellishment concentrated on the front façade.

Interior

Even though space was at a premium, the house includes a vestibule that served as a transitional area between the outside and the inner life of the house. This room moderated the temperatures, but it also served as a guest reception room. Since the house was built with no closets, the vestibule also provided a place for a hall tree to hold coats and hats.

Although a doorway leads to the kitchen, guests likely were steered to the parlor on the left. In larger homes, parlors were used primarily for guests, but because of the size of the house, it seems likely that the Tigards regularly used this room. In later years the room must have held a tragic memory for John Tigard. Sophia Tigard's skirts caught fire from the parlor stove and she died several days later. The floor remained scarred from the fire for years.

Charles Tigard, a younger brother, outshines John in local history. Charles, in addition to running the general store and local post office, was an Oregon legislator and president of the First Bank of Tigard. Several of the few family items in the house are connected with him, including the small table with the shell-shaped pull in the parlor. A neighbor recalled

The parlor is one of the original four rooms in the Tigard house.

that John and Sophia Tigard furnished their parlor with settee, a marble-topped table, and wine-colored oriental rugs.

A dry sink stands against one wall in the kitchen; a dry sink is one that has no faucet or drain plumbing, and must be filled by hand and drained into a container. The Tigards pumped water from their well by hand, although other farms in the neighborhood utilized windmills. Historians believe that the addition off the kitchen was plumbed in later years.

The bedroom now displays the family memorabilia, including a wooden box that Charles Tigard used for mail in the post office and a crudely built Windsor-styled chair built by the brothers' father. Originally, John Tigard's children likely slept in the attic, and used a ladder to the attic from the only bedroom. Perhaps privacy was not possible in such house, as the neighbor remembered that the bedroom was furnished with a high-back bed, marble-top commode, and white ironstone chamber and pitcher. Her memory of the color and material of the chamber pot suggests she must have seen it in its customary place under the bed fairly frequently.

Harlow House

National Register of Historic Places
Built: circa 1900

726 E. Columbia River Highway
Troutdale
503-661-2164 (museum)

The Harlows were one of Troutdale's leading families. The house, initially designed as a summer escape from Portland or a tenant farmhouse, has a "refined rustic" interior.

Directions: From Interstate 84, take Exit 18 and turn east, heading up the Sandy River. At the first stop sign, turn right and go across the bridge. Travel about half a mile to the house, which is on your left. A parking area is just past the house.

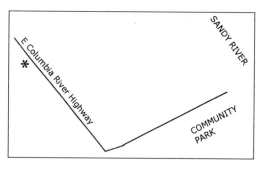

Open: June through September, Wednesday–Sunday; October through May, Saturday–Sunday
Hours: June through September, Wednesday–Saturday, 11:00–4:00; Sunday, 1:00–4:00. October through May, 1:00–4:00
Admission: $3.00 adults; children free
Tour: Guided
Entry: At the front door
Additional Attractions: The Harlow House includes a modern barn, which displays long-term exhibits relating to the history of the Troutdale area. Although the trail up the bluff is temporarily closed as of this writing, it leads up to acreage once owned by the Harlows that had been a pasture for settlers on the Oregon Trail who camped along the Sandy River before proceeding to Oregon City.

The historical society also operates the Railroad Museum in the former depot, located approximately one-eighth of a mile north on Columbia Street towards the center of Troutdale.

History

The Harlow House was built by Fred Harlow, the son of Captain John Harlow, who founded the town of Troutdale. John Harlow first settled in Portland in 1851, but twenty years later, he purchased land in present-day Troutdale, opened a store, and began operating a ferry across the Sandy River. Although an earlier post office in the vicinity was called Sandy, the captain called the area Troutdale after the trout ponds near his home. He died in 1883, and his third wife platted the town.

One of the captain's sons, Fred Harlow, built the house about 1900. After Troutdale incorporated in 1907, Fred Harlow served as the town's treasurer, in addition to operating a general store with his brother, Lou, and another partner. To further business growth in the town, the two brothers opened Troutdale's first bank; it failed in 1913, likely because Fred Harlow embezzled money. Family lore is that his brother Lou stayed to pay off the debts while Fred Harlow and his wife Minnie left town. After they divorced, Fred Harlow married a woman who later took care of him when his health failed, as well as of Minnie who came to live with the couple when she needed nursing.

Lou Harlow and his wife Laura, who had three sons, purchased the house in 1920. While living there, Laura Harlow served as Troutdale's second woman mayor in 1924. After Lou died, Laura Harlow sold the house to Lee and Mabel Evans, who had once lived next door to the Harlows and had remained Laura's friends. Mabel Evans was the town's piano teacher and was the first girl born in the newly platted town of Troutdale. After her death in 1979, the City of Troutdale purchased the property; the Troutdale Historical Society later acquired it.

Setting

The house is sited on top of a knoll to protect it from floodwaters, perhaps because an earlier flood in 1881 had affected the family fortunes. The captain had switched from raising trout to carp when the backwaters of the Sandy River and Beaver Creek crept up far enough to crest his ponds, allowing three thousand fish to escape into the Columbia River, where they multiplied. The carp had been worth five dollars each in 1880, but sold at five dollars a ton a dozen years later.

Exterior

Since the house likely was built as a summer home or as a tenant's farmhouse, it is no surprise that the exterior was not lavishly embellished. The basic form of the house is a two-story box with a one-story section on the west. The chief decorative feature is the long porch with latticework, which spans the entire front of the house. The green shutters on the windows that relieve the plainness of the white exterior were added at a later date.

Interior

Two nearly identical doors, one to the parlor, the other to the dining room, open to the front porch. The first door accesses the parlor, once a small room before the far wall was removed. Fir tongue-and-groove paneling and the open ceiling beams contribute to the room's rustic feeling. Although the room is compact, it feels larger with its eleven-foot-high ceilings.

Harlow house, built by the son of the founder of Troutdale, stands on a rise, perhaps to avoid flooding from the nearby Sandy River.

Fred and Minnie Harlow used the parlor in 1907 for the funeral of one of their two daughters, who had died at the age of ten of typhoid fever. Later, when Lou and Laura Harlow occupied the house, she created the hammered copper plate on the fireplace mantel. Flowery script spells out "salve," a Latin word meaning "welcome." Her prominent use of the word in her front parlor speaks to her education and disposition.

A Victrola rests on the built-in bench to the right of the fireplace. This was not owned by a Harlow, although it represents an aspect of Troutdale's history. In 1911, Multnomah County constructed a farm for the poor west of the town (now McMenamins Edgefield). Housed there were the infirm and elderly, as well as the destitute, who worked on the farm raising hogs and chickens and growing fruit and vegetables. At one point, the dining-room tables at the poor farm were divided into two classes: "meat" tables for those who worked and "mush" tables for those who did not. The Victrola, which appears carefully maintained, must have been a prized possession at the poor farm. Several other items from the farm, once meager possessions of the poor, are located throughout the Harlow house.

After her husband and all three children had died, Laura Harlow became too crippled by arthritis to climb the stairs, and she lived her last years in the house in the room adjoining the parlor in the back. For a short time, she and the Evanses lived in the house together.

Although the Evanses resisted painting the dark fir paneling in this room and the parlor, they did remove the dividing wall, probably to make room for Mabel's grand piano. From the mid 1940s throughout the 1960s, if a Troutdale child took piano lessons, they probably took them from Mabel Evans. The Evanses also replaced the double windows in this room with one plate-glass window.

Against a wall stands a cupboard once owned by the Harlows. According to lore, the wood used to make the cupboard had a part in Troutdale history. When the Oregon Railway & Navigation Company was building a railroad along the Columbia River, it initially had refused to build a station in Troutdale. The captain's response was to sail a brigantine up the Sandy River in a spring freshet, declaring the river to be navigable and demanding that the railroad company build a drawbridge. The railroad company decided it was less expensive to build a station. The wood for the cupboard reportedly came from the brigantine.

The pictures in the dining room show the house's former owners, including Mabel Evans at her piano. The kitchen is updated to the time when the Evanses occupied the house. The nickel and cast-iron woodstove was found in pieces in the basement, and likely was the original. It has, however, been modernized: when the left front burner is removed, electrical switches are revealed.

The wife of Lou Harlow, another son of the founder of Troutdale, hammered out the copper plate which says "salve," Latin for welcome.

The stairway paneling, like the kitchen, is painted white, but this gives way to wallpaper as one ascends the stairway to the four bedrooms on the second floor. One is outfitted as a nursery, another as a bedroom, and the third is used as an office for the Troutdale Historical Society. The fourth is designed as a sewing room. From this window, you can see the earthen outline of one of the captain's early fishponds.

Northern Willamette Valley

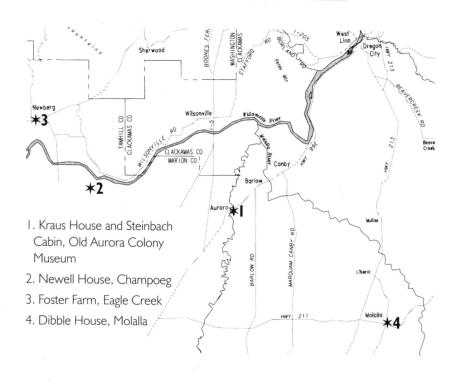

1. Kraus House and Steinbach Cabin, Old Aurora Colony Museum
2. Newell House, Champoeg
3. Foster Farm, Eagle Creek
4. Dibble House, Molalla

Kraus House & Steinbach Cabin

Built: circa 1875 (Kraus House), 1876 (Steinbach Cabin)

at the Old Aurora Colony Museum
15008 Second Street
Aurora
503-678-5754 (museum)

The Aurora Colony was the only Christian utopian society to settle in the Pacific Northwest in the nineteenth century. It endured for more than two decades, leaving in the town of Aurora an indelible mark that can still be seen today.

Directions: From Interstate 5, take Exit 278 and follow the signs to Aurora, which will put you on Ehlen Road heading east. In Aurora, Ehlen Road flows into Main Street. Turn left at Second Street, and proceed east, crossing Highway 99. The museum is on your right at the corner of Second and Liberty streets.

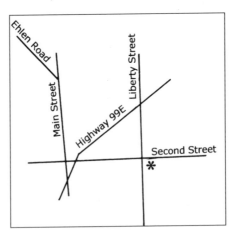

Open: March to mid-April and mid-October to December, Friday–Sunday; mid-April 15 to mid-October, Tuesday–Sunday
Hours: Weekdays and Saturday, 10:00–4:00; Sundays 12:00–4:00
Admission: $3.50 adults; $3.00 over sixty; $1.50 children ages six to eighteen
Tour: Self tour except for guided tour of the interiors of the Kraus house, Steinbach cabin, and summer kitchen.

Entry: Pay at the Ox Barn, where visitors can view a video about the history and settlement of the colony.

Additional Attractions: The 1862 communal Ox Barn is outfitted as a museum with artifacts, photographs, and displays that interpret Aurora colony life. The museum complex also includes the 1877 Will family summer kitchen, wagon shed, herb garden, and outhouse.

History

In 1836, William Keil, a twenty-five-year-old German immigrant, moved to the utopian community of the Harmonists in Pennsylvania. Keil, who had some knowledge of medicine, called himself a doctor, but also took up preaching. The charismatic leader soon started his own commune in Bethel, Missouri, in 1844. Within eleven years, it had grown to 650 residents and encompassed 4,700 acres, and Keil believed that a westward expansion was needed.

Scouts selected a new site in Willapa in present-day Washington, but Keil deemed the location too wet for agriculture and too far removed from roads. After wintering in Portland with some of his followers, he purchased land several miles south of Willamette Falls and west of the Pudding River. The community he founded there grew to include numerous houses and commercial structures, including a hotel, store, church, and bachelor-hall.

With perseverance and economy, the colony prospered. From spring to fall, the members planted and harvested acres of farmland and orchards. During the wintertime, they worked in mills and shops, producing clothes and implements. They also made furniture, some of which was sold. Contact with the outside world came through their hotel, which was well known by stage and later train passengers for its good food. One person reminiscenced, "Aurora cooking was famous all over Oregon. ... Why did trains stop for meals at Aurora when the Portland terminal was only twenty-nine miles away? Because the trainmen wanted the better meals that they could get at Aurora—better meats, better vegetables, better pies and puddings."

Like other nineteenth-century utopian societies, the colony's ideals were based on communal ownership. However, Keil guided his colony with an autocratic hand, and by the time he died in 1877, some dissatisfied members had already weakened the organization. With no charismatic leader to take over, the Aurora Colony was formally disbanded in 1883.

The Aurora Colony Historical Society acquired the Ox Barn in 1963, and three years later it officially opened as a museum. In 1967, George and Catherine Steinbach's log cabin was moved to the museum grounds "without losing a chink," according to the Salem *Statesman Journal*. The Steinbachs had occupied the cabin from 1877 to 1883 on their farm near the Willamette River.

In 1969, John Kraus and his two sons donated the Kraus house, which had stood about two blocks from the museum. George and Elizabeth Kraus, John's parents, had acquired the house in 1879.

Setting

The museum is located in the center of Aurora, now known for its concentration of antique shops. Many colony buildings still remain in the town and surrounding area.

Kraus House (circa 1875)

Exterior

Although the Kraus house is now part of the museum complex, it faces Second Street, giving a sense of how it originally looked when it was just another village dwelling. Originally, a colony house would have had more

The Kraus house has the characteristics of other Aurora Colony houses, such as a side-gabled roof and two interior chimneys.

yard area and shared its block with only one other house. This space was a necessity, as the homes usually had a small barn, a woodshed, a wash house/summer kitchen (the structure now located in back of the Kraus house is from the Will family), and often a shop building.

The Kraus dwelling has architectural elements typical of other colony houses, such as a side-gabled roof and two interior chimneys of different sizes on each end (the larger for the parlor fireplace, the smaller for the kitchen stove). Another characteristic of colony houses is the three front windows on the second story that are slightly smaller than those on the first floor and slightly lower than those placed on the side of the dwelling.

Colony houses generally lacked porches, although as in the Kraus house, many display porches that were added at a later date. The jigsaw-cut brackets on the porch posts contrast with the more utilitarian appearance of the dwelling.

Charles Nordhoff, a reporter roving the United States investigating utopian societies, noted in 1875 that houses in the Aurora Colony had an "entire absence of ornament" and "there is little room for poetry or for the imagination in the life of Aurora. … It was a droll illustration of their devotion to the useful to find in the borders of the garden … flowers alternating with lettuce, radishes, and other small vegetables." Perhaps because of the more extreme twentieth-century definitions of architectural "usefulness" and utilitarianism, the Kraus house now appears decorative.

Interior

One rule of Victorian etiquette was "never examine the cards in the card basket." In this case, however, inspecting the calling cards in the knitting basket by the door is a worthwhile exercise. One of the cards belonged to Frederick Keil, William Keil's son, its floral decoration indicating that such a design was not limited to women. In the social realm of the day, calling cards conveyed information like today's business card, but instead of relating rank, they communicated sentiments. For example, turning down the upper left-hand corner in some places meant felicitations, while turning down the lower right-hand corner was an expression of condolence.

The colony knitting basket containing the cards is a puzzle. Oral tradition is that primarily men made the colony's baskets, yet the census rolls of the time, which included occupations such as farmer and blacksmith, do not list basket making. One speculation is that basket making was considered a part-time home industry, and so the craft was not mentioned as part of the community's occupations. Another theory is that the colonists manufactured the baskets in the group's first colony in Missouri and

The settle in the Kraus' large parlor is a colony-made piece.

brought these durable items with them. Wherever it was crafted, the splint basket shares characteristics of baskets made in the colony: a double rim with "x" bindings, notched handles fixed to the inside of the basket, and a coiled bottom for stabilization.

The colonists also manufactured an array of furniture, including beds, dressers, tables, cupboards, chairs, and toolboxes. Like the Shakers, members of another utopian society that crafted furniture, Aurora's woodworkers used function and purpose as the key design elements. Visitors sometimes refer to the coat racks such as the one in the parlor to the left of the door as a Shaker rack. Some Aurora families actually had been members of the Harmony Society in Pennsylvania, which had extensive familiarity with the Shakers, and so the designs might have been influenced by personal contact. This piece, however, could properly be called an "Aurora Rack."

Nordhoff, writing about the colony house interiors, noted, "What is not directly useful is sternly left out. There are no carpets, even in Dr. Keil's house; no sofas or easy chairs, but hard wooden settles." The Kraus house appropriately has a colony-made settle facing the fireplace. Contrasting with the settle's hard surface, a red plush couch now against the wall provides upholstered comfort. Ironically, the couch converts to a daybed, a suggestion of daytime indolence that would go against the earlier colony work ideal.

Self-sufficiency for the colony was an important value, and the loom, spinning wheel, and sewing machine in the room give testimony to this ideal. Colony women made nearly all the members' clothing, although Nordhoff was not impressed with their appearance. "I suppose the lack of smart dress and finery among the young people on Sunday and at the wedding gave a somewhat monotonous and dreary impression of the assemblage."

The contemporary photographs of the descendants of George Kraus show no such restraint in finery. John Kraus, the older man in the 1976 Christmas photograph, is seen as a small boy in the black and white photograph on the adjoining wall left of the organ. In the kitchen hangs a 1974 picture of Kraus, holding a cup of coffee. The photograph shows the wagon wheel rug on the kitchen floor that still lies in the house today.

Nordhoff wrote that Keil's house had "an immense kitchen, in which women were laboring." While the Kraus house is smaller than Keil's, the kitchen occupies almost half of the first floor and served as a dining area. The woodstove, the focus of the room, bears a glazed tile with two nearly naked cherubs, one offering another a bunch of grapes. While cherubs connote a reward in the hereafter, their relaxed poise suggests that a respite from work might also be available in this world.

Oregon, End of the Trail reported that a visitor noted, "All this valley was like a province in Germany. Farming was carried on in the thrifty German way, and everywhere was heard the German tongue." A jar of sauerkraut stands on one kitchen shelf, appropriately representing the colony's farming, food preparation, and German heritage.

The kitchen cupboards underneath the stove chimney and the dish closet standing in the corner exhibit another distinctive characteristic of Aurora colony furniture, the knobs, which have interior pieces that function as the latch. The plank doors opening up to the central stairway, however, have simple, ingenious iron latches that lift the catch mechanism when the thumb piece is depressed.

The colony also was known for its spool furniture, as seen in the settle in the hall that could have doubled as a child's bed. In the room on the right, one of the spool beds has a trundle bed that could be pushed underneath the larger bed frame during the daytime. Spool beds were commonly labeled "Jenny Lind" beds after the Swedish soprano (renowned as the "Swedish Nightingale") who toured the U.S. in 1850-1852, at a time these beds were fashionable. Also in this room is a doll bed, crafted after full-size furniture, which also features a spool design.

Steinbach Cabin (1876)
Exterior

The Steinbachs constructed this cabin as a temporary home until they could build a house of milled lumber. Those responsible for the site selection had factored in the need for timber, and so the colony purchased densely forested land that already had a working sawmill. Although lumber was available when they arrived, the Steinbachs crafted this first house with logs that were hewed flat on both the inside and outside walls with a broad axe.

The cabin contains windows with each sash having six-over-six lights. Typically, windows were not aligned horizontally as they are on the cabin, but by placing the windows on their side fewer logs needed to be specially sized. On the front, the window on its side allowed the placement of the log rafters that support the attic.

The lean-tos on two sides were possibly built when the cabin was constructed, and likely enclosed at a later date.

Interior

The door height is only 5 feet 8 inches high, and the clear height of the ceiling is 6 feet 4 inches high. The limited height reduced the amount of construction labor, a factor in these "starter" homes. Perhaps it was also calculated to need less heat.

An eight-candle mold sits on top of the fireplace mantel, serving as a reminder of how the cabin was lighted. The cabin walls still bear traces of whitewash and newspapers, both of which lightened the interior.

Formally posed photographs of the George and Catherine Steinbach and their five children stand on the cabinet. All five children lived in this cabin, as did Frederick Miley, Catherine's father. Even with the lean-tos enclosed, the family clearly had less privacy than we are accustomed to today.

One clue that the Steinbachs may have expanded the original cabin is the step downward into the kitchen. Another clue is the chinking on what would have been the early cabin's exterior wall. Unlike that of the exterior face of the cabin, this chinking is original, since it was protected from the elements by the lean-to.

The kitchen implements on display generally are made either of wood or iron and have a practical design. A varnished wooden dough box, once owned by the Steinbachs, provided dough storage while the yeast rose; the lid supplied kneading space. The top on the iron Dutch oven is recessed to hold coals for baking bread.

Even though lumber was likely available, the Steinbachs built their first house out of hewn logs.

While the children slept in the attic now visible from the opening in the kitchen, George and Catherine might have slept in a spool bed at the far end of the cabin. Another spool bed is located in what was Frederick Miley's sleeping area. Unlike in other religious communities such as the Shakers, marriage was encouraged at the Aurora Colony, but the two-foot width of this bed would make remaining single a more comfortable option.

Historians believe that the grandfather's sleeping space was a separate room, which would explain the cabin's second exterior door. Possibly he reclined in a colony-made rocker with a rawhide seat like the one displayed. The footrest, donated to the museum by a member of the Miley family, is simply made with a ribbed bark and sapling frame, and shows ingenuity in design and construction.

The parlor stove is the "Bonanza" model made by a Portland company, indicating that upbeat product names are not recent advertising devices. The 1881 date on the stove is two years before the Steinbachs moved into a more substantial house.

Newell House

Built: 1956 (reconstruction of circa 1854 house)

8089 Champoeg Road N.E.
St. Paul
503-678-5537 (museum)

The house is a replica of the Newell home, which by the 1950s was in such poor condition that it could not be saved. The Oregon Society of the Daughters of the American Revolution rebuilt the house to the exact specifications. Today, it is difficult to tell from a distance that the house is a replica, except that buildings of that age would have leaned and settled over the years. This house, only about forty years old, still stands ramrod straight.

Directions: Although the house has a St. Paul address, its location actually borders Champoeg State Park. From the Interstate 5 freeway, take Exit 271, and head west. Follow the signs to Champoeg Park. The house is located just west of the main park entrance.

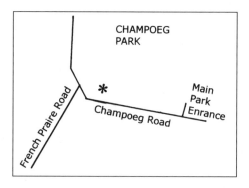

Open: March through October, Friday–Sunday
Hours: 1:00–5:00
Admission: $2.00 adults; $1.00 children
Tour: Guided
Entry: At the front door
Additional Attractions: The museum includes the Butteville jail and schoolhouse, both viewable only from the exterior
    Pioneer Mothers Memorial Cabin Museum, also operated by the Daughters of the American Revolution, is located in Champoeg Park.

(Despite its name, this museum, built in 1931, is considerably larger and grander than a typical settlers' cabin, which contributes to this building being designated a general history museum rather than a house museum.) The museum generally has similar hours to the Newell house (separate park admission & museum fee, call 503-633-2237). The Champoeg Visitors Center has displays that explain the area's significance (free with park admission, call 503-678-1251 ext. 302).

History

Robert Newell, a native of Ohio, was twenty-two when he joined the Rocky Mountain Fur Company as a trapper in 1829. Although he did not have medical training, his knowledge of simple operations and root and herb remedies earned him the nickname of "Doc Newell." His common sense and intelligence advanced him from the position of trapper to a trader with the Native Americans. In 1833, he married Kitty, the daughter of a Nez Perce subchief, who bore him five sons.

When the fur trade waned, the Newells with some trapping colleagues decided to settle in the West. They arrived in the Willamette Valley in 1840, and took up a claim on the Tualatin Plains. By the winter of 1842-1843, the Newells had moved to Oregon City, and traded the first claim for one along the Willamette River.

The death of Ewing Young, a wealthy pioneer who died without a will and known heirs, galvanized the settlers into forming the first governmental organization in the Willamette Valley after a close vote at Champoeg in 1843. Robert Newell became a member of the provisional government's legislative committee. Other public service came later, including that of state legislator in 1860.

Robert Newell also founded the town of Champoeg, soon after they settled on the claim along the Willamette. In 1844, Francis Pettygrove built a granary and warehouse there, but growth was slow. After Robert Newell returned from the California gold fields in 1850, the Newells started a store in the town. Pettygrove had discontinued his operations, and Robert Newell constructed a warehouse for wheat. The occasional flooding of the Willamette induced the Newells to leave their house on the bottomland adjacent to the town in 1854 and build a new house on higher ground about a quarter of a mile to the southwest. The act was fortuitous, as a severe flood in 1861 swept away the Champoeg houses, barns, storehouses, and mills.

Robert Newell's wife, Kitty, had died in 1845, and in 1846 he had married Rebecca Newman, with whom he had six more children. The Newells moved to Lapwai, Idaho, where he was appointed the Indian agent. In 1866, Robert Newell sold the last two hundred and three acres of his claim, which included the house and his interest in the Champoeg town site. Rebecca Newell died in 1867, and although Robert remarried again in 1869, he died November that same year.

Over the years, the Newell house had various owners until Henry Zorn sold it in 1955 with 2.37 acres to Ruth Powers, who in turn conveyed it to the Oregon Society of the Daughters of the American Revolution (O.S.S.D.A.R). The house was in such poor condition that the organization tore it down and constructed a replica on the site, using what original material they could salvage. The O.S.S.D.A.R. owns and operates the museum today.

Setting

The Newell house occupies a piece of the original Newell claim, which included parts of the present day Champoeg State Park lying to the north and east of the museum.

Exterior

The Newell house, like many buildings constructed in Oregon between 1840 and 1865, included elements of the Classical Revival style. The side of the house shows cornice returns, a feature that suggests a pediment, and six-over-six pane double-hung windows. The house also displays Gothic Revival features such as the steep gable roof and center gable.

Some differences did arise in the rebuilding. The Newells undoubtedly had access to a quality of timber that was long gone by the mid-1950s. The original house had a kitchen chimney, although this was not rebuilt. The house is sheathed in lapped aluminum siding, a modern invention.

Interior

Because they rebuilt the house, the O.S.S.D.A.R. did not have to deal with a common house museum problem: remodeling by subsequent owners. No vinyl floors needed to be ripped out, no cabinetry had to be removed. When they built the house to its mid-1850s specifications, they decided to wire the house for a minimum amount of lighting. The dim light in the parlor even in the daytime suggests the limited amount of natural light that the Newells had.

To the left of the front doorway is the oldest furniture piece in the museum, a tall case clock built in 1793. Although commonly called grandfather clocks, these timepieces did not acquire that name until 1876,

The house is a reconstruction of Robert Newell's circa 1854 house.

when a song entitled "My Grandfather's Clock" became popular. Robert Newell himself must have been a stickler for punctuality. While operating two bateaux (small flat-bottom boats) between the Willamette Falls and Champoeg, he ran an advertisement in the Oregon City Spectator which stated: "N.B. Punctuality to the hour of departure is earnestly requested. As time waits for no man, the boats will do the same."

Most of the parlor furniture is compressed in the center of the room to allow visitors to walk about it, although in the Newells' time some would have stood around the fireplace. Heat—or the lack of it—was an important consideration. In front of the rocker rests a wood and tin box foot warmer that would have been filled with coals. Standing by the fireplace is a brass bed warmer that held coals and would have been slid between the sheets.

The office located in the room off the parlor contains several items relating to Robert Newell. A crude wooden box with fifteen compartments to hold letters represents the time when Newell was postmaster of Champoeg. The snowshoes represent an earlier time in his life, when he was a fur trapper. Caroline C. Dobbs, a former historian for the Multnomah Chapter of the D.A.R., wrote in *Men of Champoeg* that unlike other trappers, "He never demeaned himself with debauchery, which was so common at the rendezvous, or lost the inherent instincts of a gentleman."

The next room on the south side of the house is outfitted as a guest bedroom. After the Willamette River flooded the town of Champoeg in

1861, many homeless families stayed with the Newells, whose house was a few feet above the high-water mark. The guests slept in the upstairs, the barn, and doubtless any other rooms that were available. The Newells lost their store and warehouse in the flood, but despite their own precarious financial position, they were hospitable to their neighbors. Many Champoeg residents were reported to say, "I do not know what I would have done had it not been for Doc Newell."

The sleigh bed dates from the 1820s to the 1850s, although new furniture sold today bears this design. In the Newells' bedroom on the other side of the parlor is an 1867 Renaissance Revival bed with its high headboard. Visitors reportedly find its more unusual design more desirable than that of the sleigh bed.

The Newells used the Great Room for both dining and working; here Rebecca Newell and the children would make goods for their Champoeg store, including knitting socks and braiding straw hats. The Newells also raised small animals such as piglets and lambs in this room. Today, part of the room is outfitted as a Victorian dining room. The cabinet that displays china, however, was likely used initially as a bookcase since the wooden back, now visible thorough the glass doors, was left unimproved because books would have hidden it.

The office includes mementos that refer to Robert Newell's life, including the wooden box that represents his position as a postmaster in the town of Champoeg.

The only Newell item in the house, a rocker, is located in the kitchen. Two other pieces of furniture, the pie safe and the dry sink, came from the Aurora colony (see Old Aurora Colony Museum, page 52). In the pie safe stands an M.J.B. coffee can showing the long-forgotten name of its maker, M. J. Brandenstein & Co. The nearby White Cross tea leaf container displays an early version of a product safety statement: "There are no dangerous ingredients used in White Cross tea." Adulterations in tea had a long history, not only in the countries of origin but also by wholesalers and storekeepers. Not only was the consumer bilked, but also some of the substitutes caused sickness or even death.

Upstairs, the Newell house is configured as museum space. The first room on the right contains Oregon's version of the Smithsonian's First Lady inaugural gowns. Here, the governor's first lady gowns range from Abernathy to Atiyeh. A sign appeals for the first lady outfits missing from the collection, although it does not list the suit that Frank Roberts wore during the swearing in of his wife, Barbara Roberts, in 1991, perhaps because he would technically have been "First Gentleman."

A collection of Indian artifacts is displayed in the next two rooms. Robert Newell was well respected among the Nez Perce. Even after his Nez Perce first wife died, he had such good relations with her people that they ceded him five acres when he was in Idaho. The land, now in the city of Lewiston, was the first to be granted to a white man by the Nez Perce.

The fine art of hand sewing is also displayed in the quilts bearing fanciful names such as "Drunkard's Path," "Flower Basket," and "Log Cabin." The oldest piece in the house, dating from 1728 to 1730, is the sampler hanging on the wall. A girl practiced her cross-stitch designs on this fabric, and then kept it as a reference in case she wanted to remember how to recreate a shape or lettering. The sampler speaks directly of its owner, as the girl stitched on it "Jane Smith is my name," but nothing more appears to be known about her.

Foster Farm

National Register of Historic Places
Built: 1883

29912 S.E. Highway 211
Eagle Creek
503-637-6324 (museum)

The house now standing on the Foster Farm was really the home of Egbert, Philip Foster's son. Philip Foster and his partner Samuel Barlow are renowned for building and operating the Barlow Road, an alternate route around the southern slopes of Mount Hood for those on the Oregon Trail. The Barlow Road ran in front of the Foster farm.

Directions: From Interstate 205, take exit 12/12A, driving east on Highways 212 and 224. When the two highways split, follow the signs to Estacada (Highway 224). At the junction of Highway 224 and Highway 211 in Eagle Creek, turn north on Highway 211 (at the blinking yellow light). The Foster Farm is just on the right after the turn.

Open: Mid-June through August, Friday–Sunday; September, Saturday–Sunday
Hours: 11:00–4:00
Admission: Donation
Tour: Guided

Entry: At the front door
Additional Attractions: The grounds include an 1860s Foster barn. In addition, the local historical society has built a replica of Philip Foster's 1850s store and a blacksmith's shop. During school visits, children wash clothes by hand, pack a wagon, and take part in other activities.

History

Philip Foster was born in Maine in 1805. His first wife died in childbirth, and he subsequently married Mary Charlotte Pettygrove, the sister of Francis Pettygrove, who would later flip a coin with Asa Lovejoy to determine the name of Portland. The Fosters and the Pettygroves sailed around Cape Horn, eventually arriving in Fort Vancouver in 1843 with $15,000-worth of provisions to sell. Philip Foster immediately went to work and within a week he and Pettygrove had opened a store in Oregon City. In 1844, Foster was elected the first treasurer of Oregon's provisional government.

Philip Foster entered into agreements with several business partners, including one with Samuel Barlow to construct a toll road around the southern slope of Mount Hood in 1846. The treacherous rapids on the Columbia River below The Dalles were a hazard to emigrants, and the new road offered an alternative for travel, although it was also arduous.

In 1847, the Fosters purchased 320 acres of a donation land claim at Eagle Creek, and then entered into a partnership to farm an adjoining 640 acres with two others. The farm, sited along the Barlow Road, was the first sign of civilization that later emigrants saw after many months' travel. The Fosters provided food and lodging for which, according to the pioneers, they charged dearly. One pioneer, Amelia Stewart Knight wrote she had to "buy feed for the stock, paid $1.50 per hundred for hay … eggs 1 dollar a dozen; onions 4 and 5 dollars per bushel, all too dear for poor folks so we have treated ourselves to some small turnips at the rate of 25 cents per dozen." Esther Belle Hanna wrote, "We have to pay $2.50 per day to stay here and sleep on your own blankets on the floor!"

In addition to the surviving son from Philip Foster's first marriage, the couple had nine children. Mary Charlotte Foster died in 1880. The Fosters built the present house on the family farmstead in 1883, and Philip Foster died a year later. Various ownerships continued to operate the Barlow Road until George Joseph presented it to the state in 1919.

Ruth Powers, a preservationist, restored the house in the late 1970s and donated it to the Jackknife-Zion-Horseheaven Historical Society, which operates the Foster Farm.

Setting

The Foster farm now has only two acres remaining from the original claim. The large lilac bush in the front of the house, the oldest in Oregon, played a significant part in Foster family history. Mary Charlotte Foster took a cutting from her tree in Maine, and carried it with her throughout her journey. She replanted it several times in Oregon City before finally moving to Eagle Creek. The Foster farm sells registered starts from the bush today.

Exterior

The Foster house is a simple form called gable-front-and-wing, and has only limited decoration. The architecture is in the Folk Victorian style, a catch-all category for houses less embellished than the Victorian styles which they are attempting to mimic. Generally, the principal ornamentation is located on the porch, gables, and brackets under the eaves. On the Foster house, the jigsaw-cut brackets on the porch are the most obvious decoration.

In this house, the entry that appears to be the front door actually opens into the dining room, not the parlor. The door to the parlor, located further down on the porch, is distinguished only by a transom. If the front steps are in their original placement, guests unfamiliar with the house would likely have knocked on the dining room door. When part of the Foster business was feeding Oregon Trail settlers, the dining room must have been a busy room. In 1883, however, selling meals was no longer a booming business.

Interior

Ruth Powers was instrumental in saving the Foster farm from deterioration in the 1970s, and some of her vast antique collection inhabits the house. Some of her opaque white glass (or milk glass) is displayed in a corner pie safe. The semi-opaque white glass, which looks like white porcelain, was usually made with tin oxide, although it was also made using the ashes of calcified bones. One of the most detailed pieces of the collection, which rests on top of the marble-topped server, consists of two hands cupped together as if they were receiving an offering. This suggestion has been subtly communicated to others since the hands sometimes serve as a depository for spare change.

An 1864 square piano, shipped around Cape Horn, dominates the living room. By the 1870s, the more compact and cheaper upright piano

The Foster house front steps lead to the dining room, not the parlor, which is located further down on the porch.

had surpassed the square piano in sales. Regardless of the style, the piano came to represent many things in the Victorian mind, including "medicine of the soul." Fittingly, the piano in the Foster house displays a book of religious songs. Entitled "Pure Delight Sunday School," the cover depicts four singing children, three of whom are following the words in the song book while the fourth gazes heavenward, seemingly enraptured.

On top of the piano is a small crazy quilt runner. Crazy quilts, which became popular after the 1876 Philadelphia Centennial Exposition, often included scraps of clothing from family members. Their design also allowed the quilter to display her expertise in the variety of stitches used to piece the fabrics together. Although quilts of all types are treasured today, they were also valued at the time they were made. Quilts were sometimes used as toll payment for the Barlow Road. In 1848, one quilt was valued at five dollars, the cost of one wagon to travel the road.

In the adjoining bedroom, a two-sided blue and white coverlet lies on top of the spool bed. The coverlet is called a Jacquard, after Frenchman Joseph Jacquard, who invented a loom bearing his name in 1801. The loom operated with a series of connected pasteboard cards with punched holes forming patterns that allowed an entire design to be woven without

The farm kitchen is simply furnished with a wood-burning stove and dry sink.

any adjustments by the operator. Because the patterns of the holes in the cards acted as a program for the loom, Jacquard is included in the list of significant names in the history of development of today's computers.

Philip Foster lived only a few months in this house. He collapsed in the kitchen after lunch on March 14, 1884, and died in this bedroom three days later. Only a few items of his remain in the house, and one of these is the simple bootjack, made out of a board, which is in the kitchen.

Two small bedrooms and a large hall are located upstairs. In the bedroom at the head of the stairs sits a folding rocker purchased at the St. Louis World's Fair in 1904. The cradle in the hall, the only piece of Foster furniture in the museum, came to Oregon with the family when they sailed around Cape Horn.

Dibble House

National Register of Historic Places
Built: 1859

616 S. Molalla Avenue
Molalla
503-829-5521 (curator)

The Dibble house is a rare example of a saltbox house in Oregon. Although few of the Dibbles' possessions remain in the house, the collection in the house includes a variety of artifacts from the Molalla area.

Directions: From the center of Molalla at Main Street and Molalla Avenue, head south on Molalla Avenue for approximately half a mile. The house is on your right.

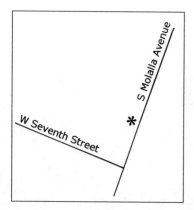

Open: March through December, Sunday or by appointment
Hours: 1:00–3:00
Admission: Donation
Tour: Guided
Entry: At the front door
Additional Attractions: The 1868 Von der Ahe House, which is used by the Molalla Area Historical Society as a meeting space, is located next door and has local history displays.

History

Horace Dibble was born in New York in 1815 and married Julia Ann Sturges in Iowa in the mid-1840s. In 1852, they immigrated to Oregon with three of their eventual eight children, settling about four miles from present-day Molalla. According to lore, Horace Dibble was hunting runaway oxen when he found a prairie knoll that he desired for a home site. The Dibbles purchased the 360 acres and hired a carpenter to build their house, paying him with their former homestead. It took three years, but by 1859 the house was completed.

Horace Dibble died in 1899, his wife in 1904. Over the next several decades the house was primarily a rental. In 1969, Ruth Powers, a force in restoring historic homes, purchased the house and then offered to sell it to the recently formed Molalla Area Historical Society. The historical society still owns and operates the house.

Setting

The Dibbles planted the apple trees still standing in the front and side yard of the house and sold the apples, in addition to wheat and other grain crops, to other pioneers and Northwest Indians.

The Dibble saltbox house, with its short pitched roof in front and long pitched roof in back, is rare in Oregon.

Exterior

The two-story Dibble house has a short pitched roof in the front and a long pitched roof in the back that extends to the first floor. This building type, rarely found in Oregon, is a New England architectural style called a "saltbox." The style evolved from a lean-to added to the back of a house that then was covered by an extension of the roof. In this case, the historical society believes that the house was constructed all at the same time.

The house was hand-made with axes and saws. The heavy timber frame was hewn with an adz, an axe-like tool which has a curved blade positioned at a right angle to the handle. Other pieces, such as the boards forming the corners and lap siding, were sawn. The front windows still display the original glass in the six-over-six panes.

Interior

The front door opens directly into the parlor. The fireplace, the central focus of the room, was important for heating this and the adjoining rooms. However, the narrow inner hearth must have required frequent attention to keep the fire stoked. Today, the bricks and mortar show damage suffered during an ill-conceived steam cleaning during the restoration.

Above the mantel are portraits of Horace and Julia Dibble in their later years. Formal photographs taken before the turn of the twentieth century generally show the subjects as stiff and formal, but humor still shows through in each of their faces, especially in that of Julia Dibble, who is wearing a pin bearing the family initial.

Very few of the family's possessions remain in the museum. The Dibbles did own the still-functioning clock standing on the mantel, and it was part of a modern-day petty intrigue. One day while the parlor was unattended, someone stole the clock. The historical society later received a call from someone who claimed to know its whereabouts but wanted a $100 reward for "facilitating" its safe return. As it was one of the few Dibble items, the society had little choice but to raise the money and pay the "reward." Today, the house is more carefully guarded.

The other furnishings in the living room came from other sources. The wine-colored sofa came from the Von der Ahe house now standing behind the museum. It has additional use as a daybed, as the back folds down and the one upholstered arm flips over to form a pillow rest. In the back of the daybed is a drawer that could be used for bedding.

Against one wall is a platform rocker displaying a needlepoint floral design on its upholstered arms, seat, back, and matching footrest. Women of the time were usually highly skilled in crafts such as needlepoint. Another

The portraits of the Dibbles are seen above the
mantle in the parlor.

example of fine craftwork is the intricately hand-sewn black wedding dress
with the velvet-edged hem and train. Black might seem a solemn color
today for a wedding, but darker colors allowed such garments to be worn
for other special occasions.

The kitchen also served as a place for eating and as a family activity
area. The placement of a freestanding woodstove several feet away from
the wall is unusual, although research proves this was the original location.
Today, the stove displays early-day "appliances": a waffle-maker, a teakettle,
and several flat irons, including one heated by hot coals and one by gas.

With no indoor plumbing, dishes were washed in a dry sink like the
one standing by the wall. Water heated on the stove was poured into the
sink, and afterwards, the hole was unplugged and the water drained to a
container. The pie closet on a far wall properly would stand on a back
porch. It kept food cool between meals and the screen doors prevented
flies from accessing the dairy products and other food.

The historical society believes that the Dibbles used the south room
off the kitchen for their bedroom, although some historians believe this
might have been a small sitting room. The room has the second fireplace
in the house. Like the one in the living room, this also has a narrow inner
hearth, and because it joins the main chimney, the brick mantle extends
into the room.

Another Dibble possession in the house is the coverlet made by Julia Dibble that lies on the spool bed. She handspun linen for the warp (the threads running lengthwise) and handspun wool dyed with walnut shells for the weft (the horizontal threads). On the wall next to the bed hangs a crazy quilt, a more common design of the period. The women from the Molalla Grange made this quilt in 1913, and in the spirit of the grange movement—whose members pooled their resources—the women contributed their squares to form the quilt. To retain their individuality, however, they each embroidered their initials or names on their square. Even if the date was not displayed, names uncommon today, such as Amelia, Gladys, and Clara, would have indicated the quilt's early origin. Although the colorful, irregularly cut fabric pieces grab one's eye, it is the quality and complexity in the stitching which make this quilt worthy of notice.

A second bedroom is located off the kitchen and the living room. W. A. Adams, a local furniture maker, made the cannonball-style bed. Like others in the furniture business, he supplemented his income by building coffins. This bed has rope for springs, although apparently this was insufficient for a later occupant who tried to install conventional box springs. Unfortunately, they would not fit without slicing off a piece of some of the bed posts. When the historical society restored the bed to its original rope springs, they asked a local woodworker to patch it.

The Dibble children slept on the second floor that is accessed via a narrow stairway off the parlor. A large bedroom is at the top of the stairway, while the smaller one to the right is outfitted as the children's room. The larger bedroom is dedicated to the fashions of bygone days. Two white cotton nightgowns are on display, each with a nightcap. On the far wall hangs a set of hoops that fastened around the waist and were worn under dresses. A smaller set for a girl hangs nearby, but since children have no defined waist, these hoops were designed to hang from the shoulders.

A peek into the attic of the unfinished walls and roof shows how the house was constructed. The mark of the adz is evident on the posts, and the attic clearly shows that this was a handmade house.

Hoover-Minthorn House

National Register of Historic Places
Built: 1881

115 S. River Street
Newberg
503-538-6629 (museum)

Oregon's strongest link to a U.S. President is with Herbert Hoover, who lived in Newberg for four years with his uncle and aunt, the Minthorns, before moving to Salem and eventually attending Stanford University. The house, typical in size and appearance of others of the same vintage around the state, suggests that extraordinary lives can be fostered in modest places.

Directions: From Highway 99, turn south on River Street at Hoover Park. Travel one block. The house is on your right at the intersection of S. River and Second streets.

```
┌──────────────────┬──────────────────────┐
│ Highway 99       │                      │
│                  │                      │
│                  │         HOOVER       │
│                  │         PARK         │
│              *   │                      │
│              ┌── S. River Street        │
│          S. Center Street               │
└──────────────────┴──────────────────────┘
```

Open: March through November, Wednesday–Sunday; December and February, Saturday and Sunday
Hours: 1:00–4:00
Admission: $2.00 adults; $1.50 seniors and students; $.50 children five to ten
Tour: Guided
Entry: At the front door
Additional Attractions: Hoover Park, located directly across the street, was once part of the Minthorn property, and today has picnic facilities.

History

Herbert Hoover was born in West Branch, Iowa, in 1874. His father died when he was six, and his mother two years later. Midwest relatives took care of him and his two siblings, but in 1885 his uncle, Dr. Henry John Minthorn, inquired whether Hoover wanted to come live with him. Minthorn was serving as the superintendent of the Friends Pacific Academy, a Quaker school in Newberg. He and his family were living in this house, which had been built by one of the founders of the new town of Newberg. Minthorn and his wife, Laura Miles, who also taught at the academy, had two daughters but had lost a son in the winter of 1883. (The couple would have another daughter in 1887.) At the age of eleven, Hoover boarded the train to come west.

The Minthorns and Hoover stayed in Newberg until 1889 before moving to Salem so that Henry Minthorn could become president of the Oregon Land Company, a venture that promoted the sale of real estate to Quakers. Hoover worked as a clerk in the office. In 1891, the newly formed Stanford University held entrance exams in Portland, and although Hoover excelled in mathematics, his other marks were not good. He was advised to come to California for tutoring over the summer and in the fall he was able to gain admittance.

At the university, Hoover studied geology and mining, and met Lou Henry, then the only woman geology major at the university, who would later become his wife. After graduation, he managed and reorganized mining properties in Western Australia, China, and elsewhere, becoming a millionaire by the time he was forty. He then turned to humanitarian work, assisting the return of thousands of Americans from Europe after the outbreak of World War I and then aiding war-torn Belgium. After the United States entered the war, he headed the Food Administration, which sought to curb wartime profiteering on the food supply. He then served as the secretary of commerce between 1921 and 1928 under Presidents Harding and Coolidge.

His 1928 presidential nomination overwhelmed residents of West Branch, although a Portland relative was more laconic, telling an *Oregon Journal* reporter, "we feel pretty good about it." President Hoover had only a few months of economic prosperity before the 1929 stock market crash, and the rest of his term was spent dealing with the social and economic conditions of the Great Depression. Communities of the homeless disparagingly became known as "Hoovervilles." In the next election, the Democrats promised prosperity, and Franklin Roosevelt was elected.

In 1948, Dr. Burt Brown Barker, a boyhood friend, led the efforts to restore Hoover's boyhood residence. This work included removing a cupola, reopening the front porch, rebuilding the back porch, and restoring the woodshed to its former position. The work was finished in 1955, and Herbert Hoover attended the dedication on his 81st birthday. It was a big celebration in the state, with the three television networks broadcasting the event live.

Hoover died in 1964. The National Society of Colonial Dames of America now owns and operates the house.

Setting

The Nellis pear tree in the center of the yard dates from the time Hoover lived in the house. According to the story, on the day he arrived in Newberg his aunt was making pear butter and invited him to sample the fruit, which he had never tasted. They were so delicious he ate until he was sick, and it was years before he had another pear.

The landscaping of lawn and simple plantings is a late Victorian style popular when Hoover lived in the house. Elizabeth Lord of Lord and Schryver, Oregon's first female landscape architectural firm, crafted the plan. She ensured that all roses on the grounds were in existence before 1850.

President Herbert Hoover spent four years of his boyhood in this modest house.

Exterior

The Hoover-Minthorn house, like many modest houses of its vintage in small towns across the state, displays a few details in the Italianate style: a hipped roof, interior chimneys, and decorative brackets under the eaves. The L-shaped house has tall, narrow windows, another characteristic of the style.

The shed that extends south of the house is not aesthetically pleasing, though it was eminently practical, since wood for the stoves could be chopped and hauled into the house without exposure to rain or snow.

Interior

The house has two doors that open up to the main porch. While first-time visitors presumably knew at which door to present themselves, modern-day guests are directed to enter through the door leading to the dining room.

Three pieces of furniture in the parlor once belonged to the Minthorns. The couch, which originally came from Hoover's birthplace in Iowa, was used in Henry Minthorn's office at the Pacific Academy. The two platform rockers, a popular piece of furniture in the late nineteenth century, stood in the parlor while Hoover lived here. Platform rockers (also called patent rockers) have a stationary base designed to guard against wear on rugs. A 1955 photograph on the wall of the parlor shows Hoover relaxing in one of the rockers.

The parlor rug originally lay on the stage under a grand piano in an Oregon City opera house. When Dr. Burt Brown Barker was scouring antique dealers for the proper floor covering, one called him offering the 1880s rug recently salvaged from the building before it was destroyed. Ironically, since theaters were generally termed "opera houses" to make them sound more respectable, perhaps the Quaker Minthorns would have shuddered at the rug's former life.

One wall exhibits a painting of Hoover at fifteen, revealing the young man's high cheekbones and intelligent eyes. A portrait of Henry Minthorn hangs on an adjoining wall. Despite his position at the Pacific Academy, Minthorn kept his medical practice, and even saw an occasional patient in the small office located off the parlor. When a patient visited, the door between the dining room and the parlor could be closed to separate business from the family.

The dining room table once belonged to Joel Palmer, an Oregon pioneer of 1845 who, among other positions, was Superintendent of Indian Affairs for the state in 1853. Evangeline Martin, one of Hoover's Sunday school teachers, once owned three of the dining room chairs. Sunday school attendance was an important part of Hoover's religious training. In later years, whenever he was in the state, he invariably called on Martin. According to Barker, Hoover "has been known to keep Oregon's most prominent citizens cooling their heels outside while he visited with his old Sunday school teacher."

The silver cup and saucer on the table were given to Henry Minthorn when he left the Pacific Academy. The china in the tealeaf pattern was not part of the Minthorn collection, but was popular during Hoover's time. According to Barker, acquiring such an extensive collection of this china pattern took luck as antique dealers reportedly told him that the pattern would be impossible to find because it was heavy and people discarded it when the lighter grades of china appeared. However, an acquaintance invited Barker to go through his house to see if there was anything that could be used to furnish the Minthorn house. Barker, accompanied by a friend knowledgeable about antiques, found nothing worthwhile until they went into the dining room where they spied the china, which Barker's

One of the Minthorn family's platform rockers rests in the parlor.

friend called "the most perfect collection she had ever seen." The donor was reluctant to part with it. Barker made a list of the items in the house, though "his china was the only thing we really wanted." About a month before the house officially opened, the donor told Barker that he would send him six settings, but the package arrived containing many more pieces. After the man died a few months later, his heir told Barker that he thought "we got all the china as there was none left when he inherited the house."

The stand with shelves in the corner, called a whatnot, is so named because of the endless varieties of articles which were displayed on it in Victorian homes. The Minthorn whatnot displayed seashells that remained in the possession of a relative who later returned them to the house. On the day of the house's inauguration, Hoover spotted the seashells, placed one by his ear, and said, "It sounds just as it did when I was a boy."

The kitchen is separated from the main part of the house by a step. One of Hoover's jobs was to keep the kitchen stove woodbin full, and he spent many hours splitting wood in the shed located off the back porch.

A narrow stairway leads up to the second floor. The three Minthorn girls likely shared the room at the head of the stairs, and the bed on the right belonged to Mary, the youngest child. In the hall left of the doorway, a photograph shows Hoover, usually seen in formal poises, smiling while holding his dog.

The Hoover-Minthorn kitchen includes a cabinet, which was popular before built-in cupboards.

The Minthorn parents shared the larger bedroom. The room has a complete bedroom toilet set, with a chamber pot by the bed to reduce nocturnal visits to the privy. The wash basin on the dresser holds water for shaving and washing, and the slop bucket on the floor is the receptacle for the used water. This set displays a grape pattern, connecting nature with natural functions.

Hoover's bedroom is filled with furniture that he used and a fishing pole that he asked specifically to be placed there. The room is small, tucked under the sloping roof. In this room, it seems hard to believe that he could ever have dreamed that his life's journey would lead to the White House.

Brunk House

National Register of Historic Places
Built: 1861

5705 Salem-Dallas Highway (Highway 22)
Rickreall
503-371-8586 (museum)

The Brunk house was part of a pioneer farm that remained in the family for three generations. Brunk items as well as local history artifacts are displayed throughout the house.

Directions: Although the museum brochures have a Dallas address, the house is located in an unincorporated area closer to Rickreall. From downtown Salem, follow the signs to Dallas via Highway 22. The house is located on the right about eight miles from Salem and about one-quarter mile beyond the Highway 51 turnoff to Independence.

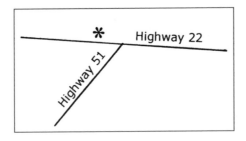

Open: June to September, Saturday–Sunday
Hours: 1:00–4:00
Admission: Donation
Tour: Guided
Entry: At east side door
Additional Attractions: The 1.6-acre museum includes some Brunk outbuildings such as the granary, outhouse, storage house, and potting shed. A shed displays vintage farm equipment. The museum also has herb and vegetable gardens, as well as an old rose garden.

History

In 1849, Harrison Brunk, his wife, and their children left Troy, Missouri, and traveled on the Oregon Trail and Barlow Road to Polk County. Harrison Brunk, who was born in 1812, had married Emily Waller in 1838. Family lore is that upon his mother's death in 1847 the Brunks had inherited part ownership of several slaves, but slavery was repugnant to them, and they decided to come west. Once in Oregon, the family took up a donation land claim on what is now the Baskett Slough National Wildlife Refuge. Possibly because the land was swampy, in 1856 the Brunks bought the claim of Harrison's distant cousin, Hugh McNary, and two years later purchased adjoining property from A.C.R. Shaw. They lived in a log cabin until a neighbor, Thomas H. Pearce, constructed the house for $844 in 1861.

The farm at one time included about eleven hundred acres with livestock and an orchard. The couple's twelve children likely helped with the chores. In 1888, Emily Brunk died at the age of sixty-eight, and three years later Harrison sold the farmhouse and acreage to his son, Thomas, and his wife, Clara. Harrison Brunk died in 1895.

Thomas and Clara Brunk had six children, although one died as a baby. The oldest son, Thomas Earl Brunk, or Earl, inherited the house. He never married and worked at a bank in Salem, where he bestowed a bouquet of sweet peas on a different coworker every day. He was killed in 1974 after being struck by a car while on his morning walk along the Salem–Dallas highway that runs in front of his house. He left the house and several outbuildings to the Polk County Historical Society, which operates the museum today.

Exterior

The Brunk home is a variation of a folk form called an I-house, which has a plan of two rooms wide and one room deep. A central hall with a staircase usually divides the two rooms. In the Brunk dwelling, each main room was subdivided so that two small rooms were created on each end of the house. As with other I-houses, the Brunks later extended the structure by adding a kitchen on the back of the structure.

When Earl Brunk bequeathed the house, the porch had been altered from two stories to one. The historical society has restored the porch, including jigsaw-cut brackets, to how it appeared in an 1880s photograph.

Interior

After entering the kitchen, visitors are escorted to the central hall, where docents pause to show photographs of three generations of Brunks. Earl Brunk, who bequeathed the house to the Polk County Historical Society, is the studious-looking boy just left of his father in the family photograph.

The tour next goes into the parlor. The word "parlor" derives from the Old French parler, "to talk," and this room evolved into the best space in a dwelling to have formal social calls and special events such as weddings and funerals. In the Brunk house, Sunday services were occasionally held in the parlor.

During Harrison and Emily Brunk's later years, they used the parlor and the adjoining two bedrooms as a separate suite. Emily Brunk is believed to be one of the four women on the front porch in the photograph hanging on the parlor wall. Porches, besides being a place of leisure, were also workspaces for such tasks as shelling peas or shucking corn. In this photograph, three of the women are sitting, indicating a period of relaxation, but they were not so long from their chores nor was the portrait formal enough for two of them to remove their aprons.

Thomas and Clara Brunk's 1889 bible lies open on a parlor table. As was the custom, the births and deaths of their six children are recorded in it, and some unknown hand has written the 1974 date of Earl Brunk's death. Besides this family history, the bible features a page dedicated to "Family Temperance Pledge." Numerous reasons are given to influence

The Brunk house served as a
farmhouse for three generations.

one to sign the page, including Number 7, "For the Bible pronounces that no drunkard shall enter heaven," and Number 12, "Intemperance obstructed civilization, education, religion, and every useful reform." Despite these compelling reasons, none of the Brunks had deemed it necessary to sign the pledge.

Thomas and Clara Brunk acquired the platform rocker in the room shortly after they were married. By that time, Americans had long considered rockers to be "the best seat in the house," and even President Lincoln sat in one at the Ford's Theater the night he was shot. The platform rocker, with its stationary base, allowed an honored guest to rock without adding wear to the carpet.

The tour then goes upstairs where more Brunk furniture is located. Harrison and Emily Brunk's twelve children slept upstairs in the two large bedrooms, similar to a dormitory setting. In the first room, believed to be the "girls' room," stands a crudely made bed and dresser likely made by the Brunks or another local carpenter. The design of the handmade furniture appears to be in the Renaissance Revival style, which ironically was mass-produced in factories.

Other items of various Brunk family members are on display in the second bedroom. Following a tradition, Earl Brunk for many years carried a pearl-handled knife given to him by his father, and he eventually acquired a similar one owned by his grandfather Harrison. Loving female hands must have made the shaving kit for Thomas Brunk, which has space inside for a brush, razor, soap, and a mug. Harrison Brunk's spectacles, made in Scotland in 1705, traveled with him on the Oregon Trail when they were already old.

A notebook that Earl Brunk used to sketch bird heads, beaks, and claws for his college ornithology class lies on the desk in the first-floor sitting room. One of the rooms off the sitting room initially served as the bedroom for Harrison and Emily Brunk. A wall in the room now displays two shotguns, and underneath the display a typewritten note cryptically reads, "First gun [hanging] on the prison wall at Oregon State prison," and explains that a "cowboy came by a flock of sheep and they wouldn't move so he shot some of them. The farmer then used this gun to blow the cowboy out of his saddle." This anecdote, representing the war between cattle ranchers and sheep herders, suggests that its writer likely sided with the sheep herders.

The historical society is uncertain when the kitchen was added to the back of the house. Not everyone agreed that a farm kitchen should be located in the rear, as one farm wife wrote in 1863 in the *Genesee Farmer* magazine that "the kitchen may be wherever there is room for it, with a view from curtainless windows of barnyard or wood-pile. ... No wonder

One of the upstairs rooms has a
number of Brunk family items.

women look careworn." Gradually over the years, some consensus grew
that kitchens in farmhouses should be placed away from a view of the
farm outbuildings and towards the road, where the woman could have a
view and contact with passersby.

When Earl Brunk died, the house had a bathroom off the kitchen
(since removed) and a sink with running water in a pantry. The house
never had a tub, and it is likely that Earl Brunk bathed himself in a tub
placed in the middle of the kitchen for most of his life.

One Brunk item standing in the kitchen is the wooden 1880s sugar
barrel, and an 1870s flour bin stands on the porch, large enough that it
could easily be mistaken for a wood box. Earl Brunk compiled an album
chronicling his family's life, which included these items, and showed that
he was proud of his family history.

Bush House

National Register of Historic Places
Built: 1878
600 Mission Street S.E.
Salem
503-363-4714 (museum)

Because Sally Bush wanted to keep the house as her father had furnished it, today the museum has the original wallpaper and the family furniture, both features that are unusual in Oregon's house museums. Sally Bush, the daughter of a wealthy man, was also atypical for her generous heart, which is evident in the stories about her.

Directions: From Interstate 5, take Exit 253 and head west about two miles on Mission Street S.E. A parking lot in Bush's Pasture Park is located along Mission Street, and a short walk up the hill leads to the house. Another parking lot, located closer to the house, is accessed by turning left on High Street S.E. Opposite Bush Street is a short road leading into the park and the parking lot.

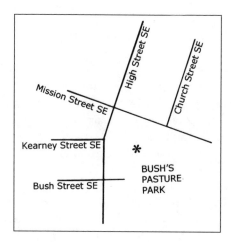

Open: Year around
Hours: May through September, Tuesday–Sunday, 12:00–5:00; October through April, Tuesday–Sunday, 2:00–5:00 (last tour begins at 4:30)

Admission: $4.00 adults; $3.00 seniors and students; $2.00 children
Tour: Guided
Entry: Ring front doorbell
Additional Attractions: Adjacent to the house is an extensive old rose garden with over one hundred beds. The Bush Barn Art Center, located in the family's former barn, features monthly exhibits and a gallery (separate hours, 503-581-2228).

Deepwood Estate, another historic house museum, is located at 1116 Mission Street S.E., within walking distance (see page 97).

Mission Mill Village Museum, which includes the Lee, Parsonage, and Boon houses, is located at 1313 Mill Street S.E., about one mile northeast (see page 105)

History

Asahel Bush II was born in Massachusetts in 1824, and came to Oregon in 1850. He started the *Oregon Statesman* newspaper in Oregon City, then the state capital, but when Salem was chosen for the state capital, he moved with the newspaper office and plant. He married Eugenia Zieber, the daughter of his printer, in 1854.

The couple had four children, Estelle, Asahel III (also called A.N.), Sally, and Eugenia. In 1863, a year after bearing her last child, Eugenia Bush died of consumption, and Asahel sold the newspaper to spend his time raising the children. He reentered the business world in 1869 when he formed a partnership with William Ladd of Portland to open the first bank in Salem, Ladd and Bush. Eight years later, he became the sole owner and president.

That same year, with his children off at college, he began construction on the house on land he had purchased in 1860 from David Leslie. The January 13, 1878, *Oregon Daily Statesman*, his former newspaper, reported that "Mr. Bush's taste as shown ... his home is simple but elegant. ... During the coming summer, Mr. Bush will lay out and improve his grounds, which when completed, will give him an elegant home surpassed by none in the state."

After graduating from Smith College in 1882, Sally Bush returned to Salem and became mistress of the house and a hostess for her father. The Bushes had a gentleman's farm on their one hundred acres and kept cows, horses, and goats. Asahel Bush died in 1913, but Sally continued to live in the house. In 1944, A.N. Bush, who had deeded the city fifty-seven acres of the eastern half of the property in 1917, approached the city to ask if they were interested in the remaining acres. The city put the matter to the voters, and although the measure to buy the property for $175,000 passed, the levy to raise the money failed. A second bond issue was approved in 1945, and the city purchased the property with Sally and A.N. Bush retaining a life estate. Sally Bush died in 1946 at the age of eighty-six, while A.N. died in 1953 at age ninety-five.

The Salem Art Association agreed to operate the house as a museum and purchased the original furnishings from the family on a contract. The Association initially operated an art gallery on the second floor of the museum, but the gallery moved to the barn when it was remodeled after a 1963 fire. Today, the city of Salem owns the house, while the Salem Art Association operates the museum and the nearby art gallery.

Setting

Bush's Pasture Park is appropriately named, as it was pasture for the family's Jersey cows that supplied all the milk, cream, and butter for the house. After the milking, the buckets were brought to the basement of the house, where, according to Elizabeth Lord, "the cream was so thick and heavy it had to be taken off with a special skimmer."

Anna Powell, whose father was the Bushes' physician, remembers roaming the fields, gathering flowers and climbing fences with her godmother, "Aunt Sally," who had a special affinity for children and animals. The highlight of the outing was a visit to the barn, which Powell described as "large and dusty, and fragrant with hay and animal smells; just right for horses and a goat or two. There was always time to pat and speak to each animal."

Another Bush building is the greenhouse, believed to be the oldest in the state. Asahel Bush had it constructed for Eugenia, and gave her fifty potted flowers for it. Eugenia Bush may have tended the flowers, but Sally arranged the dining table centerpieces, which reportedly "brought forth exclamations of surprise from the guests." The greenhouse is still open to visitors.

The house sits on a grassy knoll. Although the Salem Parks Department takes care of the landscaping today, when Sally Bush ran the house, she ordered that the front lawn was not to be mowed until after the spring flowers had faded and dropped their seeds. Powell said that she had a photograph of Sally Bush standing in the tall grass and "smiling as though pleased to find herself in its midst."

Exterior

Asahel Bush built his house in an understated Italianate style, which had been popular since the 1840s. So many houses in towns across the nation displayed the style that it was also called the American Bracket style, or simply the American style. As the name implies, decorative brackets located under the eaves were among of the main characteristics of the style, and these are found on the Bush house.

The Bush house displays other characteristics of the style, such as tall, narrow windows with segmental arches on the second floor and "flattened arches" on the first floor. Many Italianate styled houses have hoods above the windows, but the Bush house is decorated with surrounds highlighted with contrasting colors. This surround design is incorporated in the doorway on the porch; even the attic vents mimic the shape.

Before the City of Salem could repaint the house in 1999, workers first had to remove seventeen coats of paint. The colors chosen were "dove gray" on the body with "mojave red" and "blue wing" for contrast. Dove gray paint was originally on the house when it was completed in 1878, although the January 13, 1878, *Oregon Daily Statesman* seemingly did not appreciate it, calling it a "light mouse color."

Although towers are sometimes added as a decorative feature to Italianate style houses, the tower in the back of the Bush dwelling contained

Despite his wealth, Asahel Bush chose a house with relatively understated design that was the centerpiece of the Bush farm.

a water reservoir that furnished running water to the kitchen, bathtubs, water closets, and sinks in the bedrooms. Later, after city water was available, A. N. Bush installed an elevator in the house, and the machinery was placed in the tower. Another change in the back of the house involved the one-story wood shed, which initially stored wood for the house's two stoves (one in the basement), ten fireplaces, and wood-burning central heating system. Now it is storage space.

Interior

Like other Italianate style houses, the Bush house has a central hall and a stairway with a single flight of stairs. In this case, the long staircase with twenty-three steps needed to be braced in the 1950s to prevent sagging.

Victorian guests would leave their calling cards in a tray resting on the hall tree's marble shelf when the family was not able to receive them. In later years, after the practice of calling cards disappeared, change was kept on the hall tree shelf. Sally Bush, who ran the house, had a sympathetic heart, and the money would be given to the destitute who knocked at the door. She also routinely provided meals at a side door, and although Asahel Bush disliked the commotion, he allowed it because it made Sally happy.

Since the house remained in the family and was essentially unchanged since it was built, the Bush house has been preserved rather than restored. Most of the furniture in the museum was owned by the family, including items in the hall: the table, the hall tree, and the chair that holds gloves in the seat compartment. Personal items are also part of the museum collection, including Asahel Bush's straight cane with the ivory handle that stands in the hall tree, and on a hook above, A. N.'s worn wide-brim black hat.

The house attracts wallpaper experts from around the world since it still retains the original late 1870s wallpapers. Although she could have afforded remodeling, Sally Bush kept the house unchanged over the years as a tribute to her father. The wallpaper in the parlor shows an Asian influence. Fittingly, on the mantel rest two ginger jars that echo those in the design of the border above.

Ten marble fireplace mantels, nine of which came from Italy, also distinguish the house. Of the ten, the parlor mantel, costing $125.00, was the most expensive, understandably, since it includes a delicately carved girl, kissed by the bird perched on her shoulder, and flanking alabaster scenes, one of a boy fishing, the other hunting.

The wooden valances are also embellished. Like the mantel, the centers of the valances display a woman's head, giving an additional human expression to the room. Stylized wooden faces from the great classical

The original wallpaper and the Italian marble mantle with the delicate carving embellish the parlor.

civilizations also are found on the burgundy furniture, both in the medallions on the crest rail and on the arms.

Asahel Bush purchased furniture to go with the new house. The prevailing style at the time was Renaissance Revival, and the Bush house has the largest collection in this style of all the museum houses in the state. For the parlor, he purchased a set of matching furniture: sofa, two armchairs, and four parlor chairs. Also in the parlor is a marble-topped table on which rests a box of Allegretti chocolates, a particular favorite of A. N. He ordered many boxes of this candy, described as "very bitter dark chocolate with an indescribable cream center, " and gave them to friends and colleagues.

A.N. Bush and his male descendants had a personal connection with the marble statue depicting a boy perched on a stool reading. Scratched on the base is "Bush as a good boy," and the figure was held up to the Bush males as a model of behavior. The importance Asahel Bush placed on reading can no doubt be traced to his journalistic background. The alabaster figure on the mantel in the sitting room also shows a cherub-like boy reading a book on a pillow, the slip fastened by four bows.

The gilded mirror above the mantel was one of two that Asahel Bush purchased from a New York firm for $235.00 (the second is in the dining room). While much of the furniture was freighted by railroad from the East, the mirrors were too fragile to undergo such a journey. Instead, they were packed in floating oil and sent by ship around Cape Horn in 1881.

To the left of the mantel mirror is a metal extension arm from a gaslight, the only available lighting technology when the house was built. Although this fixture was not converted, the Bushes added electric wiring to many of their gas chandeliers when the new technology became available.

However, they kept the gaslight system operational after wiring the house, as a backup because of the frequency of power outages.

The Aeolian Orchestrelle player organ, purchased by the Bushes in 1900 to celebrate the turn of the twentieth century, represents another technological advance. This organ can be operated both manually and with rolls similar to a player piano. Apparently the Bushes favored the latter method as the nearby cabinet holds about one hundred forty rolls. Some of these tunes have been long forgotten, such as the "Spring Maid Selection" or the "Yale Varsity Two Step," although the music from operas such "La Boheme" (1896) and "Madame Butterfly" (1904) has endured.

While the Bushes played music in the sitting room, they generally relaxed in the library. Asahel Bush, describing the house in a letter to Sally when she was at college, wrote, "We live mostly in the library." After Sally Bush returned to Salem in 1882, she paid bills and browsed seed catalogues while seated at the desk placed against the bay window, which allowed her to view the garden.

Her sister Estelle's portable desk now lies on top of Sally Bush's desk. After Estelle Bush married, she and her husband adopted a girl whom they named Eugenia. Powell remembers her mother relating that when Eugenia was attending an exclusive girls' school, Estelle would stand behind bushes and watch her play. Estelle explained that it would upset her daughter if she knew her mother was spying on her, but she loved to watch her. Eugenia died in 1918 at twenty-one, and Estelle's husband followed in 1923. Estelle lived another nineteen years as a widow.

Near one of the three bookcases in the library is an 1890 map of Salem. On the right side, near the illustration depicting the Pacific Nursery & Residence of C. N. Potter, the Bush house is visible in the trees along Mission Street. At the southeast corner of Commercial and State streets stands another piece of Bush real estate, the Ladd and Bush bank.

The library has an exterior door that leads to the porte cochere. Initially, it provided a covered area to alight from carriages and it continued to be used when the automobile became popular. According to Powell's recollection, Asahel Bush had a "shining, silvery-gray" Rolls-Royce sedan. A speaking tube separated the passengers from the driver, Jacob. The automobile, however, was not Bush's only "car." He also maintained a private railroad car, described as having "shining brass and sumptuous comfort," at the Portland rail yards.

After an evening of lingering in the library, Asahel Bush would retire to his adjacent bedroom. He was fifty-four when he constructed the house, and a first-floor bedroom was convenient as he got older and found the staircase difficult to climb. He slept in the Renaissance Revival bed still

Prison labor constructed the large stove in the Bush kitchen.

standing in this room, which has pillow shams displaying the letter "B." Asahel Bush died in this room, and his last words were, "Is everything all right?", a question that indicated he may have been thinking about his responsibilities at the bank when he died.

Asahel Bush's bedroom was located next to the one downstairs bathroom, a wonder in a time of outdoor privies. It amazed the neighbors, and children would knock at the front door and ask to see the "indoor outhouse." Perhaps after examining the water closet, they were equally amazed at the claw-footed tub with its insert of white painted copper to keep the water warm.

The large French Range in the kitchen, which rests on bricks, originally had a boiler in the back that provided the hot water in the house. Its other amenities include a separate broiler for meat, and copper warming shelves. Prison labor constructed the stove, but once it was in place, the "labor" was not finished. Iron stoves must be blackened daily to avert rusting, and the large Bush stove must have been a major chore.

In a small room off the kitchen stand two pie safes, one of which belonged to the family. Before refrigerators came into use, the Bushes also had an icehouse built with twelve-inch-wide sawdust-filled walls to keep their food cool. (Today the gardeners use this building.) The kitchen has two pantries, one for final food preparation and the pass pantry where dishware was stored. From the utilitarian kitchen and pantries, today's visitors go into the formality of the dining room, just as the servants did.

Elizabeth Lord, landscape architect and daughter of Oregon Governor William Lord, was a frequent guest at the Bush table. She recalled that the table setting was of the best linens, silverware, and china, simple in design but rich in quality. Powell's parents were frequently invited to dine with the Bushes along with governors Geer and Lord, and Powell's mother also spoke about the quality of the china, crystal, and silver, and noted that the meals were always delicious. While Sally Bush was a vegetarian, she still provided guests with meat for the main entrée, although there were always plenty of vegetables.

Powell's reminiscence includes a story that gives insight into Sally Bush's character. One morning when Powell's mother came into the dining room, she found Sally Bush looking at a piece of slightly burned toast. A maid approached Sally Bush, inquiring whether it was all right, and Sally told her is was just the way she liked it. At her Powell's surprise, Sally Bush whispered that the maid was new and very nervous, and that she was trying to save her from an embarrassment. Unfortunately, from then on for every breakfast, the toast was slightly burnt.

The dining room is notable for its marble fireplace mantel, the only one in the house that came from Vermont, and for the Lincrusta wallpaper, which became popular during the 1880s. Frederick Walton, who had invented linoleum in 1863, developed the process in 1877 of embossing semi-liquid linseed oil backed with heavy canvass or waterproofed paper. As the paper was just invented a year before the Bush house was completed, the Lincrusta paper must have been another source of wonder to guests.

A maid playing a music box in the hall like the one resting on the table there called the family and guests to dinner. Above the music box is a portrait of Asahel Bush painted when he was eighty-eight years old. This is the fourth attempt by the painter, as the family rejected the first three. From the painting, Asahel Bush's eyes seem to follow modern-day guests as they go up the steps to the second floor.

Today, a caretaker occupies the back section of the house, and several rooms, including the two bedrooms for servants and a second bathroom, are not open to visitors. The first bedroom at the top of the stairs, which was a guest bedroom, is filled with donated Victorian toys and a Renaissance Revival crib, an appropriate style which matches the rest of the Bush furniture. A photograph on the wall shows the front porch of the house filled with Sally Bush and neighborhood children. Sally Bush was known for celebrating local children's birthdays with parties featuring ice cream and cake, and the events were such a success that some claimed to have three birthdays in one year.

The grand dining room features one of the two mirrors
that was shipped around Cape Horn floating in oil.

Asahel Bush brought the tall case clock in the hall back from his family
home in Massachusetts, which had been occupied by Bushes from the
seventeenth century. A depiction of that house is seen above the mirror
hanging in the hall. Below is a hand-carved cherrywood chest of drawers
created by Asahel Bush's cousin.

The northern bedroom, initially shared by Eugenia and Sally Bush,
now displays period apparel that is changed with the season. The room
across the hall was another guest bedroom, and it features the original
Renaissance Revival bedroom set. Like the other rooms, this room had
hot and cold running water, which likely was another source of amazement
for the guests. From this room, a guest could gaze out to the front lawn
and see the uncut grass that Sally Bush favored, a wild contrast to the
civilized interior of the Bush house.

Deepwood Estate

National Register of Historic Places
Built: 1894
1116 Mission Street S.E.
Salem
503-363-1825 (museum)

Deepwood was named after the children's book *The Hollow Tree and Deep Woods Book* by Albert Bigelow Paine. Not only the unique name, but the gardens and respectful changes to the house over the years demonstrate that this unique Queen Anne style dwelling was well loved.

Directions: From Interstate 5, take Exit 253 and turn right to travel west on Mission Street S.E. At Twelfth Street S.E., turn south, go one block to Lee Street and turn right. The parking lot entrance is on your right; a short path leads to the Deepwood Estate.

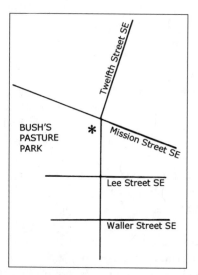

Open: October through April, Wednesday, Thursday, and Saturday (Tuesday and Friday by appointment); May through September, Sunday–Friday
Hours: 12:00–5:00 (tours start on the hour)

Admission: $4.00 adults; $3.00 students and seniors; $2.00 children six to twelve, under six free. Access to the gardens is free from dawn to dusk
Tour: Guided
Entry: Ring the front doorbell
Additional Attractions: Deepwood Estate includes extensive gardens, several of which were designed by Lord and Schryver, the Northwest's first female landscaping architectural firm (see *Setting* below). Near the modern greenhouse (open to the public) is the start of the Rita Steiner Fry nature trail, which winds its way along Pringle Creek.

The Bush House, another historic house museum, is also located within walking distance in Bush's Pasture Park at 600 Mission Street S.E. (see page 87). Near the Bush House is the Bush Barn Art Center, which has a gallery and exhibit space (separate hours, 503-581-2228).

Mission Mill Village Museum, which includes the Jason Lee House, the Parsonage, and the John D. Boon house, is located at 1313 Mill Street S.E., about half a mile northeast (see page 105)

History

The Deepwood estate involves three families, the first being the Ports, who built the house. Luke Port, born in England in 1834, immigrated to the United States with his family in 1844. On arrival, he met Lizzie Walsh, and they married in 1857. The Ports had a daughter, Flora May, in 1860, who was subsequently renamed Alpha when the couple had a son in 1865 whom they called Omega.

Luke Port, who was listed in the 1870 Census as a "retired physician," traveled around the United States with his family looking for investments. In 1884, after living in places such as San Diego and San Francisco, the Ports arrived in Salem, and were soon dividing their time between the state capital and Vancouver B.C. Upon hearing that their son was lost at sea in 1887, the Ports left Salem to seek more definite news. They eventually returned in 1893, purchased six acres and hired architect William Knighton to design the house. It was completed in September 1894, but the Ports lived in it only sixteen months before selling it to the Binghams.

George Bingham, a district attorney in 1895 and later a judge, bought the property for his wife Willie. The couple had just lost their three-year-old son, and the new home was for the couple and their baby daughter Alice. Alice Bingham left the house at age fifteen to board at a school in Tacoma, and at twenty she married Keith Powell. After her parents died in 1924 and bequeathed the house to her, Alice Bingham Powell sold the house to Clifford Brown, whose parents had been acquainted with the Binghams.

Clifford Brown, a successful hop and wool broker, also had business holdings in a cannery. At the time his family moved into the house, he and his wife Alice had two sons, one who was ten years old and the other fifteen. In 1927, Clifford Brown drowned in an accident in British Columbia. Alice Brown continued to live in the house as a widow, and in 1929 she commissioned Elizabeth Lord and Edith Schryver, the Northwest's first female landscape architectural firm, to design new gardens. By 1930, Alice Brown was calling the house and grounds "Deepwood" after the children's book *The Hollow Tree and Deep Woods Book*, a favorite of one of her sons.

In 1945, Alice Brown married Keith Powell, the widower of Alice Bingham Powell at a ceremony at Deepwood in the Scroll Garden. The couple lived in the house until 1968 when poor health forced them to move. After Alice Brown Powell died in 1971, the City of Salem acquired the property. The Friends of Deepwood were organized to manage the property, an arrangement that continues today.

Deepwood is considered to be among the best Queen Anne-style houses in the state

Setting

A significant part of Deepwood's charm is its masterfully designed gardens by Lord and Schryver. For a schematic of the gardens and insightful information, obtain a brochure entitled "Historic Deepwood Gardens" at the house or at the Salem Convention & Visitors Association at 1313 Mill St. S.E. (1-800-874-7012).

The majority of the gardens are south of the house and adjacent to the carriage house, whose tower complements that of the house. A large yew tree with a hole in its trunk once stood in a grassy expanse in the rear of the house. Alice Brown called it the "hollow tree" from *The Hollow Tree and Deep Woods Book*. The tree gradually died and was removed in the mid-1980s.

Lord and Schryver designed the gardens now called the Great Room, Spring Garden, Tea House Garden, and Scroll Garden. They envisioned them as a series of outdoor rooms enclosed by devices such as fences or hedges. Schryver told a 1930s garden club audience that "enclosed gardens, attached and closely related to the house whenever possible, form an outdoor room in which we may have privacy and intimacy for work and relaxation."

Part of their strategy to "lure the curious on," as Schryver once said on a radio talk show, involved using paths, gates, furniture, and art. The garden art added by Alice Brown includes a wrought iron gazebo from Portland's 1905 Lewis and Clark Exposition in the Great Room, a fence made of cresting, a decorative metal roof strip, from Portland's Davis Building in the Scroll Garden, and a column fragment from Oregon's 1876 Capitol, which burned in 1935, that now stands in the Shade Garden. The house's restored spring house gazebo also is in the Shade Garden.

Exterior

Deepwood is cited as among the finest Queen Anne style houses in Oregon. The style is recognizable by its profuse design elements, and Deepwood has features such as a recessed second floor balcony, a series of gable and hipped roofs, and a tower with a bell-shaped roof topped with a finial.

Queen Anne houses also exhibit varying textures, and Deepwood has both lap and shingle siding. In contrast to the siding, the stone block foundation rises between one half and one story high at different points on the house. Imparting a visual sense of the base material rising up the side of the house, the stone work is also used in the chimney. Inserted into the chimney is a glass window, providing a delicate contrast to the hefty stone.

Another major feature adding to the house's asymmetrical appearance was the porte cochere, the covered porch that angled away from the house. When Alice Brown converted the porte cochere to the solarium, the driveway, which had encircled the house, was removed. Today the solarium, outfitted with wicker furniture, conveys a sense of the languidness Alice Brown must have enjoyed there.

Interior

In the 1870s, architects and builders began advocating that the ideal home should be a personal statement, symbolizing the owner's values. The Ports selected the Povey Brothers of Portland to furnish stained and beveled glass windows for their two front doors and transom, thereby declaring very early to visitors that opulence and good taste were part of the Ports' standards. Povey Brothers, called the "Tiffany of the Northwest," had been in business just six years when the Ports commissioned them to create these and the other decorative windows for their house. The brothers, who came from a long tradition of English stained-glass craftsmen, had advertised in the telephone directories of many Pacific Northwest cities; they also targeted the religious market by advertising in the *Catholic Sentinel* weekly newspaper. Their commissions included a number of Portland churches, as well as the Elsinore Theater and the Supreme Court Building, which are both in Salem.

Not only did Victorians perceive the home as a place of self-expression, but it was also seen as a place of nature. Birds and dogwoods are featured in the stained-glass windows in the hall. David Povey, the designer among the three brothers, added beveled diamond-shaped clear-glass inserts in the center of the windows, which allowed views of nature outdoors. The insert in the middle window was also practical, as one could see who was alighting from carriage or car in the porte cochere.

The Povey Brothers' stained-glass windows are one of the notable features of the Deepwood Estate.

The focal point of the front parlor is the ornate

fireplace with another Povey Brothers window above the mantel. This window is believe to be a memorial to Omega, the Ports' only son, who had been lost at sea in 1887. The three Ports—Luke, Lizzie, and their daughter Alpha—are represented as the three roses, while Omega, whose life was cut short, is represented by a single bud.

The only significant item once owned by the Ports that is still in the house is an English painting of a fisherman and two women. It hangs to the right of the fireplace and was acquired during the Ports' two years of travel in Mexico and Europe, where they attempted to gather information about Omega's tragic death.

On one wall is an enlarged photograph of Luke Port taken from a "carte de visite" about 1870. Carte de visites, portrait photographs mounted on cards measuring two and a half by four inches, were first introduced in Europe in the 1850s and then became the rage in the United States. These photographs were the first to be affordable, and portraits of friends and relatives were soon assembled in householders' albums. "Cartomania" eventually gave way to the cabinet portrait, a larger photograph that was so named because it could be propped up on a cabinet.

The *Statesman Journal* frequently reported on the construction progress of the house. The September 27, 1893, *Statesman Journal* noted, besides its opulent features, that the house "would be supplied with every convenience known to the house builders of today." Salem had electricity in 1886, and the house was wired for it when it was constructed. A wood-burning boiler in the basement provided central heating. Interior louvered shutters, like the one seen on the parlor window, could be raised and lowered to block the light as needed.

About 1932, Alice Brown added bookcases to the back parlor, although to make them fit, the pocket doors that had divided the two parlors were removed. Alice Brown's remodeling indicates her sensitivity to the original character of the house, as the new woodwork mimics the old in the paneling and bead molding.

In Victorian times, a woman demonstrated that she was cultured by playing a piano or organ. The Edison cylinder player in the back parlor, which created music simply by turning the crank, represents a technological shift to machine-made music. The player piano, although still in the shape of a piano, also represents a new technology. By 1910, almost every piano manufacturer also was making an "automatic piano." The Gulbransen-Dickinson Company advertised that "All the family will quickly become expert … without long practice! All the joy without hard work!" The advertisements also began showing men at the piano; they had been discouraged during Victorian times from an active role in creating music

The fireplace has a Povey Brothers stained-glass window that is believed to be a memorial to the Ports's son, who died tragically.

at home. Since no skill was involved in pumping the bellows, there was nothing "unmanly" about working a machine.

Alice Brown also converted the ground-floor bedroom off the back parlor to a library by installing glass-covered bookshelves. A guest or a reader would have been equally pleased with the two sets of Povey brothers' windows in the adjoining bathroom. The toilet, still operable, has a good view of the windows.

The Povey Brothers advertised "bent" glass in 1893, and it is possible that the curved glass windows in the dining room were from their firm. Historians believe that the firm supplied the window for the porch door off the dining room since it is similar to those in the front door. The door allowed fresh air and nature to be let into the dining room, and the porch, which wraps around the house from the front door, created an "outdoor" room.

Alice Brown must have had a sense of fun. At a 1932 New Year's Eve party, guests were given crayons to draw on the walls in the dining room, back parlor, butler's pantry, and kitchen before these walls and the ceilings were refinished. Alice Brown's sister Vivian drew her own version of Duchamp's "Nude Descending a Staircase" on the east dining room wall.

Knighton had designed the placement of the butler's pantry just as the *Textbook on Architecture and Building Construction*, published in 1899, advised. "On no condition," it stated, "should the kitchen be permitted to open directly into the dining room." Furthermore, the pantry doors dividing the two rooms were not to be placed opposite each other so as to avoid a view of the kitchen every time both doors were open. The butler's pantry served as a place for the dishes and the dumb waiter (later removed by Alice Brown), as well as an insulator against noises and smells from the kitchen. One of the noises that diners were sure not to hear was the sound of the opening and closing of the ice box, and later the refrigerator, since both of these once stood on the porch next to the kitchen.

Alice Brown installed a back staircase, but the best way to journey to the second floor was via the main stairway in the hall. The decorative archway in the second floor hall is another feature of the house, and the room Alice Brown designated as the children's bedroom has more curved windows like those in the dining room. Apparently she was not concerned about "rough housing" by her teenage sons.

This room shares a half bathroom with the back bedroom, which might have been the maid's quarters. Also in the back of the house is what could have been George Bingham's study. Above the desk are portraits of Alice Bingham's 1913 graduating class from Miss Head's School of Young Ladies in Berkeley. Two years later, she married Keith Powell in front of the Omega window in the front parlor. Although she inherited the house, she soon sold the house to the Browns, and Keith Powell did not have the opportunity then to live there. After his wife died 1941, Keith Powell received a second chance to occupy the house when he married Alice Brown in 1945.

In the closet between the east bedroom and the sitting room is another Povey stained-glass window, a statement that even the humble spaces should have surprising beauty. Alice Brown's 1930s bedroom set in the bedroom and sitting room display a floral motif, while the ivy wallpaper and the green painted light fixtures also suggest a connection with nature. Above the vanity is a photograph of Elizabeth Lord and Edith Schryver, the landscape architects she hired. When Alice Brown purchased the house, it was already nicely connected to nature, but in the years she lived there she strengthened those ties.

Lee House
Parsonage of the Methodist Mission
Boon House

National Register of Historic Places
Built: 1841 (Lee), 1841 (Parsonage), and 1847 (Boon)
Mission Mill Museum
1313 Mill Street S.E.
Salem
503-585-7012 (museum)

The former buildings of the Thomas Kay woolen mill, one of the few mill museums in the Pacific Northwest, comprise most of the structures at the Mission Mill Museum. Both the houses and the mills can be toured with or without a guide, but a docent is particularly helpful for understanding the mill process.

Directions: From Interstate 5, take Exit 253 and travel west on Mission Street S.E. After about two miles, take the exit for Willamette University and City Center. Stay in the right lane, following the sign to Twelfth Street and state offices. Once you are off the off-ramp, get in the right lane. In about one block, turn right on Mill Street S.E.; the museum is on your left.

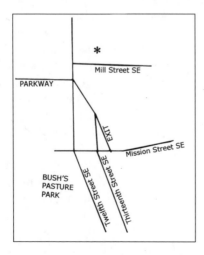

Open: Year around, except holidays
Hours: 10:00–5:00
Admission: $6.00 adults; $5.00 seniors; $4.00 youth (six to eighteen); $20.00 family
Tour: Guided and self-guided
Entry: Pay admission at the tour desk
Additional Attractions: The Mission Mill Museum also includes the Thomas Kay woolen mill, founded in 1889, and the 1853 Pleasant Grove Church. The Marion County Historical Society Museum in located on the northwest corner of the Mission Mill (call 503-364-2128 for hours and admission).

Deepwood Estate (see page 97) and Bush House (see page 87), two other historic museum houses, are located in Bush's Pasture Park, approximately one mile southeast of Mission Mill Museum.

History

In 1833, a story circulated that four Nez Perce Indians had traveled to St. Louis seeking religious instruction. Three weeks after the account was published in the newspaper, Dr. Wilbur Fisk, president of Wesleyan University in Massachusetts, submitted a communication to the Methodist mission board urging establishment of a mission to the Nez Perce. Rev. Jason Lee, his former pupil, was selected for the undertaking; along with nephew Daniel Lee, also a missionary, two teachers, and an assistant, he joined a fur-trading caravan for an overland trip in April 1834. After consulting with John McLoughlin, Chief Factor at the Hudson's Bay Company outpost at Fort Vancouver, Jason Lee founded the mission in the Willamette Valley, about ten miles north of present-day Salem.

Jason Lee began a school for Northwest Indian children, but the results were not successful and marred by tragedy. Carey noted in the *General History of Oregon* that "it has been estimated that out of fourteen children received into the home the first year, five died, five ran away, and of the remaining four, two died the second year." The results were as dismal the next year. Jason Lee, finding that his time was spent with building, farming, and taking care of the sick, wrote that he needed additional help. The first group, which set off in 1836, included Anna Maria Pittman, who soon married Jason Lee but died in childbirth in 1838 along with her newly born son. Jason Lee, who was back East to persuade the mission board to allow him to continue his work and to convey a petition for United States government protection over the Oregon Country, heard about the death of his wife by a messenger.

In 1840, Jason Lee and his new wife, Lucy Thompson, accompanied a group of more than fifty to Oregon on a chartered ship, the *Lausanne*. This "Great Reinforcement" included Rev. Lewis H. Judson, a cabinetmaker, and Rev. Josiah L. Parrish, a blacksmith. Daniel Lee had already started a mission in present-day The Dalles, and some of the group was dispersed there and to Nisqually, Clatsop, and Willamette Falls. Jason Lee soon moved his mission from its initial site to Chemeketa, now Salem, because, as he explained in a letter, "The Bugs having fairly driven us out....I left my things with the Bugs, and have no house where to lay my head, but still think the [Northwest Indian] children must first be provided for. "

The Methodists had brought with them on the *Lausanne* machinery for a sawmill, and the first building to be erected with the lumber was a multifamily dwelling (now called the Lee House), which served as the headquarters of the mission. Some distance away, construction also started for the Indian manual training school, and the parsonage for the school's director, Rev. Gustavus Hines.

John Hussey in *Champoeg: Place of Transition*, called the Methodist mission "the center of American interest and activity in the Oregon Country," and the missionaries logically were involved in the preliminary discussions about a provisional government. The February 1841 death of Ewing Young, a former trapper who died without a will and had a considerable estate, provided further motivation to settlers to organize the functions of government. The second meeting about the matter convened at the Lee house, and the third at the parsonage. The vote for a provisional government took place at Champoeg on May 2, 1843.

The mission board, however, became concerned about expenditures and the low number of conversions of the Northwest Indian population. The board removed Jason Lee as superintendent and sent Rev. George Gary to liquidate the holdings. Jason Lee, learning about his demotion while in Honolulu, returned to the East and cleared his name with the organization. Shortly thereafter, he died on March 2, 1845, at the age of forty-two.

After George Gary arrived in 1844, he sold all the other property at Chemeketa except the parsonage, and it became a boarding house for Methodist circuit riders. The Lee house had a different fate. After several ownerships, John McClane acquired it, but when he left to visit the East Coast, John Boon "jumped" his claim, asserting that McClane had been away from the land more than the allowed time. The two eventually settled their lawsuit.

John Boon, who with his family had occupied the third house now on the museum site, had come to Oregon in 1845, and became involved with the mission's former sawmill and gristmill operations. He served in the Territorial Legislature and was a territorial and state treasurer from 1851 to 1862.

In 1953, the parsonage was moved onto the Thomas Kay woolen mill property (the mill was still working); the Lee house was moved to the mill site in 1963. The museum was formed to include the woolen mill in 1964. In 1972, the Boon house was given to the Marion County Historical Society and then became part of the museum.

Setting

The three buildings form an L shape on the eastern edge of the former mill grounds.

Lee House (1841)

Exterior

The Lee house displays folk architecture, a term which describes relatively simple construction built for only basic shelter, with no pretense of following a style of architecture. The house was the first structure built entirely from lumber sawn at the Methodist mill, and was home to four families the first year. Several alterations to the structure have occurred over the past one hundred sixty years. Historians believe that the windows once had nine-over-six lights, instead of the six-over-four lights now displayed. The central doorway is likely not original, but was added when the inside hall was built sometime in the 1880s. Instead of the present two chimneys, possibly all the stoves were connected to one central chimney.

The façade with the two-story porch now facing the grassy area was originally the back of the house. Historians are unsure whether the double porch is original, although an 1858 drawing of the house shows it at that time. If the house did have a porch, it would have been a place of work. A wooden wash tub and wash board would have been stored there. Washed clothes, after being hand wrung, would have hung on a line on the porch or been laid on nearby bushes to dry during warm weather. A vegetable garden would have been nearby, as well as a wood pile and trash heap.

The Methodist missionaries used the Lee house as the dwelling for four families in 1841.

Interior

Instead of the central hall and staircase there today, historians believe that the original staircase might have been outside the house or in the room now designated as the Parrish apartment. The Parrish apartment, on the right, housed Rev. Josiah Parrish, his wife, and their two children.

Each apartment had a small stove for heating and cooking. Meals for the missionaries were often plain, from a "dinner pot" with a boiled dish of salt beef or pork and vegetables such as cabbage or turnips. Occasionally, other meat was eaten, such as salmon, duck, venison, or chicken. Lieutenant Charles Wilkes, who along with his men was surveying for the U.S. government, ate at the missionary, and recorded in his journal that he "dine[d] a la Methodist on salmon, pork, potted cheese, and strawberries, tea & hot cakes. ... The meal was eaten by us all in brotherly love, but hunger assisted me or I never should have been able to swallow mine."

The missionaries used dishware that they had brought with them or purchased at the Hudson's Bay Company store at Fort Vancouver. Wooden ware, such as bowls, paddles, scoops, mashers, strainers, and buckets for water, milking, and hauling garden produce, was an important part of the kitchen. While some wooden ware was manufactured, many pieces were made by hand with a knife and other hand tools.

The missionaries also brought some of their clothing and furniture with them from the East. The June 7, 1839, *Christian Advocate and Journal* reported, "Those who go on this mission are advised to furnish themselves with clothing for at least two years, and those who have families, with beds and bedding, and household furniture." The Parrishes transported the sleigh bed in this apartment with them on the *Lausanne*.

Like the Parrish apartment, the Lees' part of the house had a cook stove (the fireplace mantel now displayed was added at a later time). Jason Lee and his second wife occupied this apartment until her death during childbirth. A photograph of Jason Lee hangs on one wall, while a picture of their daughter, Lucy Anna Maria, hangs on another wall. Named after both of Lee's wives, she grew up to become a teacher at Willamette University.

The two upstairs apartments each are divided into two rooms, and historians believe that the ground-floor apartments were similarly designed. Even with two rooms, however, the Judson apartment on the second floor was crowded. Rev. Lewis Judson and his wife had four children, one of whom was born in these quarters. Although the settlers usually had rough carpentry skills, Lewis was a cabinetmaker, and he brought his tools with him on the *Lausanne*. A wooden box by the bed displays the tools he might have used; the baby chair he built for his youngest son exhibits his skill. A portrait of the child grown to manhood hangs on the wall above the chair.

On the nearby table rests a writing box, which belonged to Lewis's sister, Adelia. Writing boxes, which were generally miniature chests, provided a smooth surface for writing letters, and had compartments for paper, inkpots, and quill pens. Adelia's desk also provided a protective place for the mirror affixed to the inside of the lid. Other portable furniture is located in the adjoining room. The unpainted chairs there were designed as kits to save cargo room on ships, and were assembled at their destination.

William Raymond and his wife originally occupied the fourth apartment. William Raymond, originally a farmer, worked at the sawmill. Almira Raymond wrote to her parents in 1843 about her missionary work, noting that "here is work enough for our hearts and hands." She likely had no idea that she would leave William twenty years later, charging him with domestic violence and prolonged infidelity with another female missionary who had been part of the 1840 reinforcement. (Lewis Judson's second wife would also charge domestic abuse in her 1858 divorce petition.)

Parsonage (1841)

Exterior

Historians believe that the parsonage, completed just weeks after the Lee house, was originally located where the woolen mill water tower now stands. Like the Lee house, this structure has folk architecture. However, the Lee house is narrow in width, making it seem tall, while the parsonage is better balanced, with more classical proportions. Jason Lee wrote to the mission board that Rev. Gustavus Hines, who first occupied the parsonage, felt deserving of congratulations for a "noble looking house."

Interior

Many of the current furnishings in the parsonage date from the period 1840 to 1860. Standing in the parlor is a chest of drawers that George Abernathy brought with him on the *Lausanne*. Abernathy served as the steward of the mission, and after it disbanded, he acquired the Methodist store and inventory at Oregon City. When he had difficulty making change due to the paucity of circulating money, Abernathy showed his ingenuity by devising a form of currency from pieces of flint rock left by the Northwest Indians, who had fashioned arrow points and spearheads. On

Rev. Jason Lee wrote that Rev. Gustavus Hines felt deserving of congratulation for a "noble looking house."

each chip issued by Abernathy was affixed his name and face value of the "change." George Abernathy went on to be Oregon's only governor under the provisional government, serving from 1845 to 1849.

A rag rug lies in front of the chest of drawers. Rag rugs, generally of wool, cotton, and linen, were woven on a narrow loom about thirty-six inches wide. Homeowners sometimes wove rag carpets themselves, but they were also available commercially. Until broad looms were available, rag carpet would be sewed together to enlarge the width, as was the carpet in the dining room, which was made in three sections.

The dining room table is more formally set than during the mission period, although on the wall hangs an engraving depicting Christ's Last Supper, an appropriate choice for a parsonage.

The room adjacent to the parlor in the back of the house is outfitted to portray a classroom of the Indian manual training school, since historians believe that the parsonage was used temporarily for instruction until the main school building was completed. In 1844, the trustees of the Oregon Institute, a school for pioneer children, purchased the building, and the school became the forerunner of Willamette University, located directly west of the museum site.

The next room is furnished with cooking stove, dry sink, and worktable, the basic components of early kitchens. Dried herbs hang on the wall, signifying their importance in cooking, curing sickness, scenting clothing, and controlling insects. Based on evidence found in journals, a small herb garden is recreated today behind the parsonage.

Upstairs in the first bedroom is Adelia Judson Turkington's cowhide leather trunk with the letters "A T" displayed on the lid. The inside is lined with 1832 newspapers from Danbury, Connecticut, where she lived when she was first widowed. After she learned that her brother Lewis Judson was traveling to the Lee mission on the *Lausanne*, she decided to come along, and at the last minute married James Olley, a member of the party. Their marriage was not to be a long one, as James Olley drowned in the Willamette River in 1842 trying to get logs out to build a cabin, leaving Adelia a widow once more.

The museum staff has decorated the next room as a minister's study, complete with a writing desk and collection basket. The original wallpaper was in a Gothic design. The colors faded over the years, and the room now displays reproduced wallpaper in the original tan and violet hues with white highlighting.

The last room has walls which display the construction of the house, which consisted of planks (one twenty-two inches wide) laid horizontally. Hamilton Campbell, who was believed to be the architect of the house and initially lived here, was eloquent in his application to the mission board. "The missionary cause I am well aware is one of the greatest causes. First to consider the immense value of immortal and never dying Souls and Secondly to consider the many thousands that are destitute of a Knowledge of heaven or the plan of Salvation and are daily falling into Eternity without it." Campbell apparently was adept at prose as well as architecture.

Boon House (1847)

Exterior

The diminutive folk style Boon house is believed to be the oldest remaining single-family dwelling in Salem. Its simple design, relatively easy to build, was reproduced throughout the Willamette Valley. However, the size of these houses became a detriment to their existence, and they have been demolished to make way for larger homes.

About 1867, an ell was added to the back of the house, and the kitchen was moved to this section. The addition is easy to spot, because the board and batten siding contrasts with the lap siding.

The modest Boon house once served as the living quarters for nine people.

Interior

There is no vestibule, and the front door opens directly into the parlor, a traditional floor plan for early houses. In the parlor is a tufted sofa upholstered in horsehair. The hair, forming the weft, comes from the horse's tail, the only fibers long enough to weave without spinning. The warp was usually of cotton or linen. Horsehair cloth is smooth and slick until the hairs start to break, and then it becomes a very scratchy surface on which to sit.

The print above the sofa, "The Peaceable Kingdom" by American folk artist and Quaker minister Edward Hicks, is one of his dozens of variations of this picture, and represented the biblical prophesy that the lion shall lie down with the lamb. Some variations like this print included a scene of Quaker William Penn signing the treaty with the Indians.

One bedroom is located off the parlor, and another one is located off the dining room. In the dining room, a framed cutout in the wall reveals the rough-hewn planks that form the Boon house.

When John Boon "jumped" the claim, he and his family moved into the Lee house. A panorama of Salem in 1858 includes a picture of the Lee house, calling it the "Home of J. D. Boon." Apparently, the Boons were eager to move to a larger house, but in the settlement they had to move out again.

Settlemier House

National Register of Historic Places
Built: 1891

355 N. Settlemier Avenue
Woodburn
503-982-1897 (museum)

The Settlemier house is an exuberantly decorated Victorian house on its exterior, but the interior reflects a fine remodeling in the Arts and Crafts style.

Directions: From Interstate 5, take Exit 271, heading for city center. About one mile from the freeway, turn south on Settlemier Avenue, a signalized intersection. Travel south four blocks; the house is on the right at the intersection of Settlemier Avenue and Garfield Street.

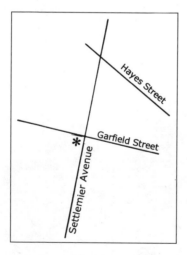

Open: March through December, first Sunday of the month
Hours: 1:00–4:00
Admission: $3.00 adults; $2.00 children
Tour: Guided
Entry: Ring front doorbell

History

In 1849, when Jesse Settlemier was nine, his family left Illinois for the West. While the family was in California mining for gold, his mother and one of his brothers became ill and died. George Settlemier, his father, and the rest of the eight children then traveled by ship to Oregon, and spent time in Oregon City before George took a claim in the Waldo Hills near Mt. Angel and started the first nursery in Marion County.

When he was older, Jesse Settlemier and his brothers started a nursery near Tangent in Linn County, but this venture was dissolved shortly after he married Eleanor Cochran in 1862. The couple purchased land in the French Prairie at a sheriff's sale, and started a nursery in 1863. However, the title to their land was defective, and after losing a legal battle that went all the way the U. S. Supreme Court, the Settlemiers were forced to repurchase the property.

When the Oregon & California Railroad Company was constructed through his property, Jesse Settlemier platted the four-block town of Woodburn in 1871. His nursery business had spread to one hundred acres by 1889, and he served a market extending into California, Utah, Washington, Idaho, and British Columbia. The August 1889 *West Shore* magazine related that 450,000 trees were budded there that summer.

The Settlemiers had six daughters and one son, Frank. Eleanor Settlemier, the mother, died in 1879, and a year later Jesse married Clara

Jesse Settlemier, the founder of Woodburn,
built this lavish house as a badge of wealth.

Gray, who died just thirty-one days later. Jesse Settlemier married a third time to Mary Woodworth, who bore him another son, Jesse Jr. In 1891, Jesse and Mary Settlemier constructed the house, which was designed by C. S. McNally of Salem, and moved in early 1892. About the time the house was completed, Jesse Settlemier retired from the nursery business, turning it over to Frank.

Frank Settlemier had been born in 1873, and married Mable James in 1893. When his father died in 1913, he inherited the house and reportedly most of the family assets. Frank Settlemier was apparently not possessed of a pleasant disposition. Aletha Miller, Mable's goddaughter, related in the March 24, 1989, *Statesman Journal* that Frank Settlemier was a cross man, "but he owned half the town, so why not?" Jean Koch, another Woodburn resident, remembers hearing that Settlemier shot boys who took chestnuts from his trees with his pellet gun loaded with rock salt. "One year, we were told we could pick up chestnuts ... if we asked permission first and then brought our nuts to Mrs. Settlemier, so she could take half of them."

After Frank Settlemier's death in 1951, the house was brought by Kilian and Hazel Smith, who understood the architectural significance of the house and largely maintained it. After being widowed, Hazel offered the house to the French Prairie Historical Society, which purchased the house in 1972. When Hazel forgave the last $10,000 of the original $45,000 sale price, the historical society had a mortgage-burning celebration. Part of the entertainment was a song with lyrics beginning with, "Then a group of lovin' people/ Bought the house of many dreams/ They fought hard to keep it standin'/They came up with many schemes."

Setting

The house is located on a spacious, park-like parcel in a residential neighborhood. Many of the older plantings came from the Settlemier nursery.

Exterior

Tucked away from Woodburn's main street, the Settlemier house is distinguished from its neighboring more recently built houses by its size and lavish embellishment. Settlemier, who was nearing retirement, built the mansion as a badge of his wealth. The house was so noteworthy that the *Woodburn Independent* followed its construction progress in 1891, boasting at least twice over the year that the house cost $7,000.

Jesse and Mary Settlemier chose the Queen Anne architectural style for their house, following a trend which veered away from the more rigid regularity of classical styles and instead advocating ebullience in shape and design. Varying roof shapes are characteristic of the style, and the Settlemier house exhibits gable and hipped roofs as well as a conical roof on the tower. The two-story porch, which forms almost a quarter circle from the northern to the eastern façade, adds to the irregular plan, as does the tower above it.

While the ornamentation might initially appear to be placed on the house in a whimsical manner, themes allow the exterior to look cohesive. The balustrade and porch posts on the first and second story are similar, and another balustrade is suggested in the embellishment on the tower above. The base of the tower, just below the roof, flares outward, as do the north and east gables above the second-floor windows. Floral-like accents are located on the first-floor porch posts, flanking the northern chimney, and in the northern gable ornament. While the January 2, 1892, *Woodburn Independent* touted that "this beautiful residence is a place for home comforts, not for impressive show," the house still inspires awe.

Interior

The January 2, 1892, *Woodburn Independent* noted that the "front entrance opens into a large hall, which is handsomely finished with panel work of redwood, oak, ash, cedar, sugar pine and manzanita, highly polished." These varying woods, which must have pleased the nurseryman in Jesse Settlemier, can still be seen in the wood molding and the curving central staircase.

The newspaper boasted that the Settlemiers' new home was "the best arranged ... in Marion County." One of the features the reporter was writing about could have been the curved closet located underneath the staircase. Near the center of the far closet wall, all by itself, is a single drawer measuring eight by twelve inches. Perhaps when coats were stored here, it was a handy place to put gloves.

Although the newspaper praised the house in 1892 as "furnished in that style which shows good taste and unlimited means," by 1911 Frank Settlemier had remodeled the interior of the house. At about the time the house was built, the arbiters of design and taste had begun declaring the Victorian house too ornate, with too many rooms cluttered with too many things. One of the new styles the critics began favoring was Arts and Crafts, which stressed simplicity and craftsmanship. Ironically, while Frank Settlemier had the interior of the house substantially changed in 1911, the exterior of the house continued to display the Victorian features decried by the critics.

The interior changes began in the entry hall, where the extension of the staircase into the hall was diminished so that it occupied less room. In addition, a single French front door replaced two entry doors. The double doors into the living room, which replaced pocket doors, match the French front door.

An article in the February, 1906, *Art in Architecture* suggested that "in reconstructing an old house there is often an opportunity for throwing together rooms that are too small for use by themselves and forming one large living room." Frank Settlemier did exactly that when he removed the dividing wall and pocket doors between the front and back parlor, creating the large room there today. Part of the new thinking was that instead of individualized spaces, one living room would be a multipurpose space. In addition, built-in furniture was advocated, as it minimized the clutter that designers saw as the sin of Victorian decoration. The built-in bookcases on either side of the tile fireplace not only saved space but also created a horizontal emphasis, another element of the Arts and Craft style.

The five-shelved whatnot along the living-room wall was among the furniture pieces that the Arts and Crafts advocates decried. In Victorian times, the whatnot would be full of articles reflecting the homeowner's sophistication and artistic ability. This whatnot contains two family photographs of the Settlemiers, one showing Jesse Settlemier and his third wife Mary, their son Jesse Jr., and Jesse Settlemier's seven children from his first marriage.

The curving staircase in the house is one of the reasons the January 2, 1892 *Woodburn Independent* called it "palatial."

Jesse Settlemier's father, George, is seated in the center of the second photograph. On the organ is a copy of the music sheet "Of What is the Old Man Thinking," which was written by a grandson and based on a poem recited at George's 83rd birthday. The lyrics tell the story of his journey to Oregon by way of California.

In the library stands a square piano, which was considered a necessary part of an upper-class home and represented years of practice for the pianist to attain levels of skill. On the opposite end of the spectrum, the Gem Roller Organ resting on the table, popular from the 1880s through the turn of the twentieth century, only required that the operator crank the machine to produce music. The 1909 Sears, Roebuck and Co. catalogue advertised it as "so simply constructed that even a child can operate it." Each roller played a song, and Sears offered sacred music such as "Nearer, my God, to Thee" and popular tunes such as "Why Did They Dig Ma's Grave So."

The *Woodburn Independent* reported that "every luxury that tends to make life easy is found in this residence." One of these luxuries was a buzzer on the dining-room floor, which would summon the help to serve the next course or remove dishes. Frank Settlemier apparently saw no reason to remove this convenience, as the 1911 plans still show this in place. The housekeeper in Frank Settlemier's employment apparently had a difficult job, as she had to do the washing in the basement and then carry the loads up three flights to the attic to dry, because Frank Settlemier believed that it was improper for his washing to be out on the line for everyone to see. To iron the clothes, she then had to carry everything back down to the basement.

Arts and Crafts elements are also evident in the dining room, including the dark oak ceiling beams and high wainscoting with a plate rail. The *Woodburn Independent* noted that it had a large china closet with a "fireproof safe for silverware." The dark oak built-in buffet likely was altered in 1911 to match the rest of the dining room. Although it does not have a fireproof safe, it does have secret drawers located behind the glass doors. The bottom shelves are raised about two and three quarter inches to provide space for hidden drawers.

The house has two kitchens, although this is not how it was initially constructed. When the Settlemiers owned the house, they used the south room, which is now outfitted with the woodstove. Hazel Smith moved the kitchen to the room adjacent to the dining room, which had been used as two pantries. The pass pantry was closest to the dining room, and the kitchen pantry was beyond, next to the porch. The 1911 architectural drawings show that the kitchen pantry was outfitted with an icebox and a cold closet, the latter cooled by a cold water coil.

Upstairs, the *Woodburn Independent* specially noted that there was a large hall. Among the major changes to the house that Frank Settlemier undertook in 1911 was to eliminate the hall by building closets in that space. Thereafter, to travel from the front to the back of the house on the second floor, one would have had to travel through bedrooms (awkward if occupied) or use the main staircase to access the front two bedrooms and the servants' staircase for the back two bedrooms.

The master suite on the south side of the house was originally constructed with an adjoining sitting room. In the largest Victorian homes, husband and wife slept in separate rooms with a connecting door. The woman's bedroom often had a private sitting room or "boudoir" where she would sew, write letters, and entertain her closest friends. While the sleeping arrangements of Jesse and Mary Settlemier are unknown, the secluded sitting room is another feature of what the newspaper called a "palatial" house.

The small built-in bench by the fireplace suggests the influence of the Arts and Crafts movement while the flamboyant Renaissance Revival set in the adjoining bedroom is representative of the type of furniture Arts and Crafts reformers advocated against. Such furniture was considered as part of what critic called "that fatuous craze for the crudely ornate."

One of the house's three bathrooms adjoins this bedroom. The *Woodburn Independent* even described a bathtub in the house, saying it was "large copper, zinc lined." The earliest bathtubs affixed to the floor appeared during the time of the Civil War, and were individually fabricated from sheet metal—lead, copper or zinc—and encased in wood. After the turn of the twentieth century, magazines began campaigning against germs and disease, and the bathroom was a special target. Cast-iron bathtubs on legs allowed the floors to be easily cleaned. An advertisement in the May 1915 *Good Housekeeping* insinuated that even these were obsolete, and that a built-in bath (with no legs) was "far superior in sanitation and convenience to the bath on feet."

The bathroom has a built-in tub and a bidet, called a "seat bath" by advertisers of the time. It was often pictured as part of the well-furnished bathroom, and was similar in size to the portable tubs which had stood in the middle of the kitchen on Saturday night. In 1888, one advertiser suggested that a bidet was "most useful ... in serving a double purpose, as it is equally well adapted for use as a Foot Bath."

In the back bedroom on the south side hangs a picture of Frank Settlemier sporting a modified crew cut. On the desk lies an 1878 copy of the *Illustrated Historical Atlas Map of Marion & Linn Counties Oregon*. On page 33 is a map showing the Jesse Settlemier's lands and, in the corner, a map of Woodburn.

Southern Willamette Valley

Monteith House

National Register of Historic Places
Built: 1849
518 Second Avenue S.W.
Albany
541-967-8699 (museum)

The Monteiths were among the early founders of Albany, and the tradition is that this house was the first frame house in the town.

Directions: From Interstate 5, take Exit 234/234b. Following the signs to city center/historical districts, travel west about two and a quarter miles on Pacific Boulevard S.E. Take the city center/Corvallis/Hwy 20 exit, which will place you on Lyon Street, a one-way street. Turn right on Third Avenue S.W., and travel five blocks to Calapooia Street, and turn right. Go one block, turn right on Second Avenue S.W. and go a half a block. The house is on your right.

Open: Mid-June to mid-September, Wednesday–Saturday
Hours: 12:00–4:00
Admission: Donation $2.00 per person
Tour: Guided
Entry: At the front door

Additional Attractions: Albany is noted for its many historic homes. Pick up a guide at the Albany Visitors Association at 300 Second Avenue S.W.

History

In 1848, Walter Monteith, formerly of the Albany area of New York, paid $400 and a Cayuse pony for a land claim at the confluence of the Calapooia and Willamette rivers. His brother, Thomas, took up a claim directly east of his property. The brothers constructed a log cabin straddling their claims that same year. After a profitable visit to the California gold fields, they returned in 1849 and finished constructing a frame house. Instead of facing Second Avenue as it does today, the house stood on Washington Street.

In the early 1850s, the brothers operated a general store in the house, and they were also partners in the Magnolia Flourmill. In 1854, Thomas Monteith went back to Iowa to marry Christine Dunbar. A year later, Walter Monteith married Margaret Smith and they constructed another dwelling in Albany. Thomas and Christine Monteith continued to live in this house until they constructed another home in the 1860s. Walter Monteith died in 1876, and Thomas died thirteen years later.

At some point, the house was moved from its Washington Street frontage to a site on Second Avenue, perhaps so that the corner lot would be available (a commercial structure now occupies this property). A subsequent owner eventually divided the house into three apartments. In 1974, the City of Albany purchased the house, and today the Monteith Historical Society operates it as a museum.

Setting

Although the house was one of the first buildings in Albany, today it is sandwiched between a commercial structure and another dwelling.

Exterior

The Monteith house has a symmetrical box-like shape, and was originally built with minimal decoration. One exception is the cornice returns on the gable ends, a feature of the Classical Revival style.

A distinguishing feature of the house is the rebuilt double porch that runs across the front of the house. While a porch on the first floor suggests an outdoor workspace for chores such as washing clothes, the second story, located off the bedrooms and the hall, implies leisure. Those reclining on this level could view the street, but were separated from it.

In the early 1850s, Walter and Thomas Monteith
operated their store out of their two-story house.

Interior

In the early 1850s, the Monteiths operated their general store in their house. Today, the historical society has furnished the room to the right of the front door as a general store, complete with a counter from which the proprietor would serve customers. (Self-serve grocery stores did not become popular until the 1930s.) Barrels in the room represent the bulk containers from which foods such as crackers, dried fruit, pickles, chewing tobacco, and cereal were sold. The barrels stood open or were loosely covered, allowing the customer to inspect the goods before purchasing. Not until the Civil War, when foodstuffs had to be transported to the troops, did individual packaging begin to replace bulk food.

A brick of still fragrant tea lies on the counter, so compressed that it looks like a block of iron. The tea was sold in chunks, and the merchant broke off smaller pieces as the customer required. Also on the counter is a cone-shaped sugar loaf. Sugar in early days was a luxury, and many families sweetened their food with honey, molasses, and maple products. Sugar loaves required a tool no longer used in contemporary culture today, the sugar hammer. Genteel ladies knew the art of breaking pieces from the loaf with a hammer, then cutting the pieces into lumps. Although the loaf has long disappeared from grocers' counters, many mountains in the United States, including one in Polk County, are called "Sugarloaf" because of their shape.

Photographs of Thomas and Christine Monteith hang on the wall in the parlor, along with pictures of Walter and his wife, Margaret. When Walter Monteith got married, the *Oregonian* printed his wedding announcement, and the editor wrote

> *Our old friend Walter has been captured at last. He was (as we supposed) an incorrigible "old batch" but has surrendered to calico. We had supposed Sebastopol might be taken [city in Ukraine which sustained an eleven-month siege during the 1853-1856 Crimean War], but Walter, never. No matter, we won't write what we think. Allied forces "can do something as well as others."*

On another wall hangs a striking portrait of Minnie Monteith, the daughter of John, a third brother. As part of a leading family in town, Minnie Monteith scrutinized her suitors carefully, finally settling on one. The couple owned a hotel in Albany, but eventually moved to Portland. They became estranged, but continued to live in the same house. According to the story, on a hot August night in 1905, after Minnie had strolled around the city with a friend, they returned to her house to drink her

One of the rooms in the museum potrays the time when the Monteiths operated a general store in the house.

home-brewed ginger ale. Minnie took the first sip, informed her friend not to drink the ginger ale, and went to the kitchen to rinse her mouth. She dropped dead of potassium cyanide poisoning, and the mystery was never solved. Her husband died three months later of natural causes.

Hanging on another parlor wall is a copy of a portrait of George Washington by Gilbert Stuart, one of America's premier portrait painters. Stuart made over a hundred likenesses of Washington, although the president was not an easy subject. According to Stuart, "an apathy seemed to seize him, and a vacuity spread over his countenance most appalling to paint."

Whether the Monteiths owned this painting of Washington is unknown, but they did own the chairs covered with now faded green upholstery in the parlor. Other Monteith items are scattered around the room, such as Thomas's sword from the Fifth Regiment of the Oregon Volunteers that stands by the fireplace. It was in this room that the volunteers assembled, answering the call to aid Union soldiers during the Civil War. Unlike the Democratic Hacklemans, the other founders of Albany, the Monteiths were staunch Republicans, and this parlor was also the place where the Oregon Republican Party was born.

The fireplace in the parlor is about thirty-eight inches high, but the one in the kitchen, which would have been the main source for cooking,

The Monteiths, staunch Republicans, organized the Oregon Republican Party in their parlor.

Margaret Monteith kept a number of dresses that are now part of the museum collection.

is only thirty-two inches high. Historians are unsure why the kitchen fireplace is smaller, since cooking would have necessitated a larger opening than the one in the parlor, which would have been used for heating.

A map on the wall of the kitchen depicts Walter and Thomas Monteith's claim. In 1948, Lottie Monteith Pipe, a daughter of Thomas, reminisced about the house in the Albany *Democrat-Herald*. The house originally stood on Washington Street, and Pipe related that the line between Walter and Thomas Monteith's claims ran through the house, allowing the brothers to live together yet still occupy their respective claims (a condition to acquire ownership). The dining table, according to Pipes, was affixed to the floor so that each could eat his meals on his own property.

Three bedrooms are located upstairs. The 1850 census shows that the Monteith bachelors, another family with three children, and Samuel Althouse all lived here, although the sleeping arrangements are now unknown. The first bedroom open to public inspection has no doorframe, and illustrates the single-wall construction dividing the rooms. In the larger bedroom, a dress that was in the possession of Margaret Monteith is displayed. She kept a collection of her own dresses long after they had gone out of style, and, on occasion, she and the town women would hold soirees and dress up in these garments. When she died, a neighbor asked for the collection, which in turn was given to the museum.

Moyer House

National Register of Historic Places
Built: 1881
204 Main Street
Brownsville
541-466-3390 (Linn County Historical Museum)

The Moyer house is one of the few house museums featuring stenciled and painted ceilings. It also has painted transoms and panels above the bay windows, all of which contribute to this house's distinctiveness.

Directions: From Interstate 5, take Exit 216 and head east on Highway 228, following the signs to Brownsville, about four miles. Once in Brownsville, turn north on Main Street. After crossing the bridge, look for the house on the left.

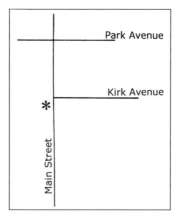

Open: Weekends year around
Hours: Saturday, 11:00–4:00; Sunday, 1:00–5:00
Admission: Donation
Tour: Guided
Entry: At the front door
Additional Attractions: Brownsville includes the Linn County Historical Museum, located in a complex consisting of a former railroad station and several freight cars at the 101 Park Avenue (call 541-466-3090 for hours and admission).

History

John Moyer, who was born in Pennsylvania in 1829, came over the Oregon Trail in 1852. A carpenter by trade, Moyer was helping to build the house of Hugh Brown, the founder of Brownsville, when he met Brown's daughter, Elizabeth. They married in 1857, and settled on a 160-acre tract outside of Brownsville. The Moyers moved into Brownsville after the town was formally platted, and eventually moved to North Brownsville, at the time a separate town just to the north. (North Brownsville and Brownsville are now merged).

After several failed business ventures, John Moyer found success operating the North Brownsville sash and door factory, and became involved in a local woolen mill. He eventually left the operation of the sash and door factory to his sons, and went on to establish the Brownsville water works, to organize an Albany woolen mill, and to incorporate the Bank of Brownsville, where he became president.

The Moyers began planning this house in 1878. The December 19, 1878, *Brownsville Advertiser* used John Moyer as an example to its readers that year when it noted, "Mr. Moyer has built a new walk from his door to the front gate, and has made other improvements. Mr. Moyer is always neat and tasty about his place, and we wish all our citizens were, we would have a much nicer looking town than we have." An October 20, 1882, Albany paper bragged in 1882 that "Mr. J. M Moyer lately completed one of the finest, if not the finest, residence in this upper part of the Willamette Valley."

The couple had six children, although only the two sons who ran the sash and door factory survived early childhood. John Moyer died in 1904. Elizabeth Moyer continued to live in the house until her death in 1921. A local banker then purchased the house and its furnishings. Over the following decades, several families occupied the house, and at one point it was even divided into apartments. In 1962, the Linn County Historical Society acquired the house. Four years later it was transferred to Linn County, which still owns and operates the museum.

Setting

The house sits on a portion of the original Moyer property, which once included the family's sash and door factory. Local residents used the hill behind the house for recreation, and the Brownsville Brass Band performed on an elevated stage there.

Exterior

The house displays elements of the Italianate style with decorative brackets on the frieze near the roof and tall, narrow windows with elaborate hoods. Some architectural historians have categorized the house's style as Italian Villa style, which was modeled after vernacular Italian farmhouses. One of the features of Italian Villa structures is a tower or cupola, as on the Moyer house. The original cupola reportedly had seats with which to view the town, appropriately lofty for one of the town's prominent families. The current cupola, a reconstruction, is not accessible.

Italian Villa houses were originally constructed in masonry, but the availability of timber in Oregon dictated the use of wood. Nevertheless, the front facade has flush wood siding imitating stuccoed masonry. But the corner boards on the Moyer house with their jigsaw-cut design refute any suggestion that this dwelling is anything but wood.

Among the house's many distinctive features are the windows, including the bay windows on the north, east, and west sides. Even the more regular rectangular windows are distinguished by heart-shaped designs on the trim. The period paint scheme, a putty color with trim painted in accent

The Moyer house is distinguished by its tower, cresting, and jigsaw-cut ornamentation.

tones of tan and chocolate brown, emphasizes the jigsaw-cut designs. Although the house cresting is now wood, it was originally of iron.

Two entry doors were initially located off the front porch, but the one on the south wall has been enclosed. The current front door, which was the more embellished of the two, was designed for guests and opens into the hall. In case any of the local townspeople may have forgotten who owned the house, "J. M. Moyer Residence" was painted on the front door transom.

Interior

Elizabeth Moyer, described in Charles Carey's *History of Oregon* as "a lady of culture and refinement," owned the elegant black umbrella with the copper handle standing in the hall tree. It bears not only her name, "Mrs. Jo. Moyers," but also "Brownsville, Oregon," suggesting perhaps that she was fearful of losing it in another community or proud of her identification with the town. Whatever the reason, a personal item of hers left where she would have put it conjures up the thought that any moment she may appear.

The Moyer house is one of the few museum houses in the state still displaying stenciled and painted ceilings. Ceilings became increasingly decorated in the 1880s as critics labeled plain ceilings as unseemly. To further embellish their ceilings, the Moyers also had medallions installed above the hanging light fixture.

Photographs of the Moyers hang over the fireplace in the room now called the living room, while on the south wall hangs a photograph of John Moyer's brother David and his wife. David Moyer was apparently not attached to the family name, because when his future father-in-law thought that "Moyer" sounded too English, he obligingly became David Myer.

The room to the south, now called the sitting room, could have been the formal dining room. Pocket doors once closed off this room, and access to the kitchen is possible through the closet, which then would have been a butler's pantry. Today, this room is furnished as a music room.

A scene believed to be of the Three Sisters mountains graces the panels above the bay window in this room. In the parlor at the north end of the house is a fruit and flower design, a scene more likely to be found in a dining room. This design was repeated in the ceiling of the room now designated as the dining room, although the Moyers possibly used this room as a breakfast room because of its size and northern light.

The rough boards on the ceiling in the western end of the dining room show that this room, like the kitchen, was expanded. The boards

The Moyer house has the original stenciled ceilings and ceiling medallions.

show bits of blue wallpaper, the same as that hanging on the unremodeled walls of the kitchen, indicating that these boards were removed from the kitchen and reused in the dining room expansion.

In the kitchen, *The White House Cookbook* stands among the row of cookbooks on the table. Rather than listing the ingredients and then describing the process as contemporary cookbooks do, this 1924 edition presents the recipes in paragraphs. Confirming the old saying that for pork one uses "everything but the squeal," the cookbook includes recipes for both head cheese and pickled pigs feet. For those who prefer beef, instructions are also included for "Boiled Beef Tongue" and "To Roast Beef Heart."

When the light is on in the kitchen, a person standing in the hall can see one of the original painted transoms over the kitchen door. Originally, painted transoms were above the interior doors throughout the house.

The stairs to the second floor are steep and curving, with the serpentine balustrade rail requiring several pieces of wood to achieve the twist. The sheer drop in one section, however, must have discouraged any child from sliding down the banister.

At a small landing the staircase splits, with one set of stairs leading to the Moyers' bedroom. In this room is the greatest concentration of their possessions: the Eastlake-style bed, bureau, and commode. A chamber pot is tucked under the bed. For several years, the household members used an outhouse located just south of the southern porch.

On the other section of the hall are another bedroom and a door to the Moyer sitting room, which was also accessed from their bedroom. Also off the hall is a door to the deck. Here they could survey and be seen, be visible yet remain remote.

Morse House

National Register of Historic Places
Built: 1936
Morse Ranch Park
595 Crest Drive
Eugene
541-682-5380 (museum)

This little-known house museum is tucked away in a park in south Eugene. Although its supporters have just started collecting furnishings for the interior, the museum gives insight into an important senator in Oregon's political history.

Directions: From the downtown at Willamette Street and Seventh Avenue, head south on Willamette Street. At the next signalized intersection after 29th Avenue, turn right, staying on Willamette Street. Go one block, and turn right on Crest Drive. Follow Crest Drive up the hill, and look for the park on your right. The house is near the parking lot for the park.

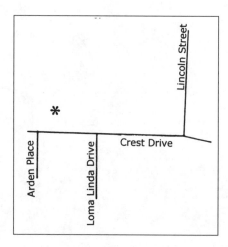

Open: Wednesday–Friday, except holidays
Hours: 2:00–5:30 or by appointment
Admission: Free; donations accepted by the Wayne Morse Historical Park Corporation

Tour: Self-guided
Entry: At the front door
Additional Attractions: The land around the house is designated as a park, and has a picnic shelter and a fenced off-leash area for dogs.

History

Born in October 1900, Wayne Morse grew up on a farm outside of Madison, Wisconsin. He attended the University of Wisconsin where he met and married Mildred Downie in 1924. After graduating from the University of Minnesota with a law degree in 1928, he accepted a position as associate professor at the University of Oregon Law School. In the fall of 1929, the Morses made their first visit to the South Hills area of Eugene looking for a home site, but the young couple lost their savings in the October stock market crash. In 1936, the Morses began to acquire property in the area. They then asked a friend and University of Oregon architecture professor, Wallace S. Hayden, to design the house and outbuildings.

In 1931, Wayne Morse had become the youngest dean of an accredited law school in the country, but in 1937 he took a leave of absence to head a U.S. Attorney General study. During that year, he settled a labor dispute within the Justice Department, and began work as a labor arbitrator. In 1942, President Roosevelt appointed him to the War Labor Board, a panel

A University of Oregon architecture professor designed the house on the Morse ranch.

charged with settling strikes to maintain production during the war. After resigning from the panel and from his university position, Wayne Morse campaigned for and won the 1944 U.S. senatorial election.

Although Morse was a Republican, he began to disagree with the philosophy of his party. In 1952, as a second term senator, he publicly cast his vote for Democratic presidential candidate Adlai Stevenson. One week later, he resigned from the Republican Party, becoming the sole Independent in the U.S. Senate. During that time, he made a record-breaking speech against a bill that would have allowed state rather than federal control of offshore oil. The speech lasted a marathon 22 hours and 26 minutes, and he stood the entire time.

After Wayne Morse changed his party membership to the Democratic Party, he won a third term as senator, the first person in United States history to be reelected after switching parties. In his third term, he began using his influence to pass education bills, including the Higher Education Facilities Act of 1963, which provided two billion dollars for colleges. He later helped push through the bill that created Upward Bound and Head Start, and the Elementary and Secondary Education Act, which distributed $1.3 billion to schools with low-income students.

During his forth term, Wayne Morse began his vocal opposition to the Vietnam War. In 1966, he gave sixty-seven speeches against the war in twenty-one states. That same year, President Johnson asked him to settle an airline machinists' strike and a railroad workers strike, but Morse's settlement angered some labor groups. The loss of labor support and his anti-war efforts were significant factors contributing to his defeat in the 1968 Senate race. Wayne Morse ran again for the Senate in 1972, but was unsuccessful. While campaigning again in 1974, he was suddenly admitted into the hospital, and died a few days later.

In 1975, Mildred Morse expressed her desire for the ranch to become a public park. State and federal funds purchased the home, and the ownership was transferred to the City of Eugene. The Wayne Morse Historical Park Corporation develops the historical, educational, and interpretive resources at the park.

Setting

After purchasing their first twenty acres, the Morses erected a fence, although it was not to keep people out or to proclaim the land as their property; it was to contain about one hundred Angora goats that busily began to eat the overgrown foliage. The Morses sold the goats later at a profit. With the white fence running along Crest Drive, the park still appears like a ranch.

Exterior

The white house with its shingle siding and the matching garage and stables look much like they did when the Morses lived there. Wallace Hayden designed the house in a Colonial Revival style. Characteristics of the style are the side-gabled roof, the double-hung multi-paned windows, and the sidelights around the front door. Colonial Revival houses are generally symmetrical, but Hayden tilted the south wing, which gave the senator a view of his Devonshire cows from the breakfast nook each morning.

Interior

The front door brass knocker's horse head and horseshoe shape symbolize the former use of the land and the Morses' love of horses. Inside, on the left wall in the hall, a black-and-white photograph shows the family in an intimate moment. Wayne Morse is reading "Blaze and the Forest Fire" to the three daughters draped on and around him while Mildred Morse listens, seated in a nearby chair. This idyllic, intimate family moment captured in a photograph raises speculation over who took the photograph, and why it is of such good quality. According to a former Morse aide and a board member of the Wayne Morse Historical Park Corporation, the photograph was likely a posed political shot. (Mildred Morse probably already knew the story.)

The Morses' spacious living room was used for entertaining politicians, law students, and fellow horse aficionados.

The best place to start a tour of the house is in the living room, where grazing deer occasionally can be seen through the picture window. The four-section couch and ottoman is from the Morses' "Brown Period," a time in the 1950s when the couple were spending considerable amounts of time in Washington, D.C. Mildred Morse redecorated the house in brown tones so that the furnishings would be practical for ranch life.

In the evenings, when not entertaining politicians, horse lovers, or university law students, the family would listen to radio programs or read books. Currently on the bookcase to the right of the fireplace is a trophy won by Spice of Life, Wayne Morse's Arabian, which played a part in the 1944 election. While on the campaign trail around the state, Morse rode Spice of Life in central and eastern Oregon towns such as Prineville and Pendleton, and later called it "the horse that won an election."

Folding doors separate the living room from the dining room. When Wayne Morse and his friends played poker, the doors would be shut, and his daughters relate stories of sneaking down the steps from their bedrooms to eavesdrop. The 1930s chandelier is aptly suited for brightly-lit card games or dimly-lit dinner parties.

By the time the state purchased the house, much of the Morse furniture had already been sold, although the caretaker found in the garage the sideboard now standing in the dining room. The table in the kitchen nook where Wayne Morse looked at the livestock while he ate is gone, but the built-in features of the kitchen still reflect Mildred Morse's plans when the house was built. Morse, who had graduated from college with a home economics degree, had input into the kitchen's design and function. For example, the kitchen has ample cabinet space, at a time when many kitchens were built with less storage. An upper cabinet by the nook contains a folding ironing board—not an uncommon feature—but the bottom cabinet face swings out to support the board. The pantry is really a "cold closet" as it vents to the outside. When the door opens, a light turns on automatically, and the Morse girls reportedly spent many of their childhood hours trying to determine precisely when the light went on.

Off the main hall, steps lead down to a room with changing exhibits. This room originally was the garage, although it was impossible to drive straight in as the garage makes a jog in order to align this section with the main part of the house. The garage placement also allowed drafts of cold air into the house, and so the Morses converted it to a rumpus room for the girls shortly after the house was built.

A separate hall off the front door on the first floor leads to Wayne Morse's memorabilia-filled study. Mildred Morse initially had used this room, placing her desk against the front window so she could monitor the girls playing in the yard while she worked. She was an adept seamstress,

Wayne Morse's study displays mementos that he had
in his Washington D.C. office.

as demonstrated by the slipcover covering the loveseat. She also made the
dresses that she wore to White House dinners.

The black-and-white photographs of the family adorning the wall above
the couch were once located in Wayne Morse's office in Washington,
D.C. The room also includes professional photographs of the presidents
and other politicians he knew. By the window rests a photograph of
Kennedy on which the president wrote, "to a great Senator who helps
keep the West free."

On the other wall hangs an undated photograph of Lyndon Johnson,
with whom Wayne Morse clashed ideologically over the United States'
involvement in Vietnam. Johnson wrote on the photograph, "Now who
will be chairman who draws the black bean," likely referring to the failed
1842 Mier expedition, in which the Mexican army executed the seventeen
of the one hundred seventy-six captured American soldiers who had drawn
the black beans from among a jar of white ones. Perhaps Johnson was
referring to his 1966 appointment of Wayne Morse to settle the airline
machinists' and the railroad workers' strike, knowing that it would probably
kill Morse's political career.

The file cabinet still holds papers from Morse's 1974 campaign. On
the desk lies one of the daughters' appointment books from that year. It
lies open to July 22nd, and the words "Daddy died" are written on that
day.

Shelton-Mcmurphey-Johnson House

National Register of Historic Places
Built: 1888
303 Willamette Street
Eugene
541-484-0808 (museum)

While many houses are named after the original family who occupied the house, the Shelton-McMurphey-Johnson house commemorates the three families that were instrumental in shaping the house. Local residents also refer to the lavishly decorated house as the "Castle on the Hill."

Directions: From Interstate 5, take Exit 194b and travel west. Get off at Exit 2, the downtown/Coburg Road exit, and follow the signs to the downtown, which will place you on Coburg Road. Get in the right lane, and after you cross the Willamette River bridge, watch for a small highway sign for Third Avenue. Turn right, go two blocks, turn left on High Street. Go one block, turn right on E. Fourth Avenue, go one block and turn right on Pearl Street. Turn left on E. Third Street, and follow the road a short distance to the house.

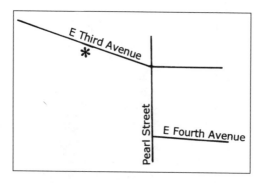

Open: Sunday, Tuesday and Thursday, year around except holidays
Hours: 12:00–4:00
Admission: $3.00 adults; $1.00 children under twelve
Tour: Guided tour
Entry: Ring front doorbell
Additional Attractions: Skinner Butte, a public park, is located behind the house and has an overlook and hiking trails.

History

In 1873, Dr. Thomas Shelton, his wife Adah Lucas, and their baby Alberta moved to Eugene. Thomas Shelton was a prosperous physician and druggist, but soon involved himself with investments such as the city's first water utility and real estate. In 1883, the Sheltons began purchasing portions of Skinner Butte, acreage that had been part of the homestead of Eugene Skinner, the founder of the city.

The Sheltons hired Walter Pugh, a Salem architect, to design a house situated on a level terrace with a panoramic view of Eugene and the surrounding hills. Shortly before the house was completed, a mysterious fire burned it to the ground. Years later, a disgruntled workman on his deathbed, who had been angry at being fired, confessed to arson. The house was rebuilt according to the original plans, and the Sheltons moved in late 1888.

Although railroad tracks separated their land from the downtown, for years the Sheltons pursued an extension of Willamette Street across the tracks. Willamette was then the main commercial street, and perhaps the family wanted the prestige of it extending to their property. While the street never officially crossed the railroad right-of-way, the house kept the Willamette Street address, even after carriage access was moved to Pearl Street.

After Thomas Shelton died in 1893 at the age of forty-nine, Adah moved to Portland and Alberta and her new husband Robert McMurphey lived in the house. Robert McMurphey, involved in insurance and real estate, soon became involved in the Eugene water works, the enterprise his father-in-law had started. Alberta McMurphey, who had completed studies in 1886 at the University of Oregon's School of Music and who had worked as a music teacher and photographer's assistant before her marriage, became involved in civic affairs. She participated in the beautification of the train depot grounds (which were in view from her house), and served as the president of the school board.

The McMurpheys had six children. Robert McMurphey died in 1921, and Alberta lived in the house until she died in 1949. Dr. Eva Johnson then purchased the house. Born in Pendleton in 1889, she had grown up just blocks from the house. She graduated in chemistry at the University of Oregon, the only woman in her class, and then attended medical school in Chicago, where she met her future husband, Curtis Johnson. They practiced medicine in Madison, Wisconsin for twenty-five years, and raised four children.

In 1951, Eva Johnson returned to Eugene, and she later related, "on the second day I was here I bought the McMurphey House—all by myself."

I loved it. I had to go back East to get my husband. My friends back there thought I was crazy." Eva Johnson began a counseling practice in the house. Her husband displayed his Asian art collection and military artifacts in the attic tower room, and spent considerable time there playing solitaire. He died in 1967. The couple had rented portions of the house to college students, a practice Eva Johnson continued after his death. Since her children were not interested in inheriting the house, Eva Johnson, who died in 1986, bequeathed the house to the Lane County Pioneer Museum. Today, the City of Eugene owns and maintains the house.

Setting

Originally, a carriage drive and a flight of wooden steps from E. Fourth Avenue led to the property. Today, steps and a path diagonally traverse the hillside.

Skinner Butte was a treeless grassy knob when the house was built, and the Sheltons started an ambitious tree-planting program. A barn stood to

Although the house burned to the ground shortly before it was completed, the Sheltons rebuilt it to the exact same specifications.

the east on the site of the present-day apartment tower, while just to the south was a vegetable garden. The McMurpheys used the property as a "gentleman's farm," and Robert McMurphey and the children maintained the yard, aided by a hired man in the spring when the tall grass was waist high and had to be cut with a scythe. Eva Johnson later had a dog kennel, greenhouse, chicken coop, and goat house on the property, all of which have been demolished.

Exterior

Up close, the house can appear overwhelming with its profuse decoration. The Victorian age was a time of exuberant embellishment, aided by machines churning out mass-produced decorative pieces which had just started being shipped by railroads around the country. Pugh designed the house in a Queen Anne style with an irregular plan, various roof shapes, differing wall surfaces, and a long porch.

The various projections and indentations cast shadows that give the house a three-dimensional effect. To highlight these distinctive surfaces, Victorian houses were typically painted a variety of colors, but even with its principal mint green color, the decoration of the Shelton house still seems abundant today.

One of the distinctive features of the house is the tower. Its roof was altered in 1915, but the Johnsons reconstructed it in the mid-1950s, and also installed windows so that Curtis could look into the front yard when he was in the tower room. Eva Johnson later related that "my husband went up there to play solitaire about eleven one night. ... I hunted all over for him and finally went to bed. The next day, I'd done two tubs of washing by the time he came down. [Since the door had no inside handle] he had to dismantle the door with a pocket knife to get out."

The entry balustrade curves inward to guide a visitor up to the front doors. Niches flank each side of the entry, and the sunburst pattern below each is repeated on the double doors. The doors once had frosted glass with a floral pattern like the glass transom above, but the City of Eugene removed them to install safety glass.

Interior

A portiere, or doorway curtain, once hung in the hall and shielded the stairway from view. In the last quarter of the nineteenth century, these curtains gained popularity as a way to prevent drafts and as another place to display needlework skills. Portieres usually hung in the doorways of public rooms (although one separates the sitting room and bedroom in this house), and since they were visible from both sides, each side had to fit in with the décor of the room it faced.

A portiere properly would have hung between the hall and the parlor. Henry Seidel Canby, remembering his 1890s home in "God Bless Our Home," wrote that while the hall was "Main Street, meant for traffic," the parlor was "decorum. It was the largest room in the house, and the least used, with the most massive tables, the biggest pictures, and the showiest chairs. ... [and] the piano which, when used for practicing, admitted the only disorder allowed in that room." In the Shelton house, the parlor properly served as the site of Alberta and Robert McMurphey's wedding in July 1893. A formal photograph in the bay window shows the couple standing there with plants filling the space behind them and vines strung overhead. Today, draped plastic ivy commemorates the event.

The photograph on the floor shows Alberta Shelton and her new husband standing in the bay window during their wedding. Today, the draped plastic ivy commemorates the event.

Robert and Alberta McMurphey's six children had to attend meals three times a day in the dining room. In dining as in gardening, the family primarily relied on themselves. Elsie McMurphey, one of the children, later wrote, "our meals were served family style by Papa. Daughters cleared the table, passed the dishes to the hired girl, crumbed the table and brought in the dessert."

The house was built with gas lighting; the current light fixtures date from the time when house was wired for electricity. In the dining room and other rooms, the fixtures can still be turned off individually at each light. In addition, interior shutter panels in the windows could be raised and lowered depending on the level of light desired.

The McMurpheys used the sitting room as the center of family activity. Henry Seidel Canby wrote that the sitting room was "smaller, cozier, with easier chairs, bookcases, a tall brass lamp. ... Here the family sat and friends were entertained (company went into the parlor). Here were the magazines, the books to be read, the cat, the dog, and the children studying after supper." Elsie McMurphey remembered, "We would do homework or read, frequently out loud, in the sitting room by the warm fireplace. Sometimes we would eat corn that had been popped over the coals in the furnace, and Papa would peel apples, handing a slice to each in turn."

A photograph on top of a desk shows Eva Johnson seated at the same desk, perhaps examining a file. In her last years, she allowed tours in the house while she remained in bed in the adjacent room. The Shelton furniture now standing in the room was handed down through the various ownerships of the house.

In 1919, with Robert's health deteriorating, the McMurpheys decided to move his insurance office to the house. They expanded the conservatory on to the porch, added a door between the conservatory and the bedroom, and installed the outside door to the porch, which allowed clients to call without entering the front door. Alberta McMurphey still went from house to house to collect premiums.

The bedroom off the sitting room contains the original Shelton family furtniture.

The McMurphey children slept upstairs, as did the live-in servant. The servants' quarters typically are separated by a back stairway, but in this house a narrower set of stairs off the main staircase lead to the servant's chambers. Although the other bedrooms have closets, the servant's room had a simple open bar on which to hang the clothes.

Maintaining the house in a historical style was important to the Johnsons, even when they rented rooms to tenants. Eva Johnson reportedly preferred University of Oregon architectural students because she believed that they would be sensitive to the original design of the house. Nevertheless, two architectural students that rented the servant's quarters lowered the twelve-foot ceiling by building a loft in the mid-1970s. It still remains in the room, now the director's office.

In 1912, the McMurpheys added a sleeping porch over the back porch, now accessible from the director's office and the second-floor hall. Fresh air was considered healthy, and the whole family began sleeping here. To keep warm during the winter, they heated bricks in the oven, wrapped towels around them, and placed them by their feet. In the 1950s, Eva Johnson installed a kitchen there for the tenants and added an outside stairway.

The McMurpheys created a sewing area in the far end of the central hall. Each child learned to sew, mend, and darn. According to Elsie McMurphey, "this was a boon to my older brother Robert, who, during (his army service in) World War I, became the company tailor and made a considerable amount of extra money."

The boys used the bedroom opposite the staircase, while the girls occupied the bedroom on the other side of the staircase. The bedroom under the tower was reserved for guests, including Adah Shelton when she visited from Portland. From her window, in the house she had built, she could see Eugene's growth over the years.

Lower Columbia River

Flippin House

National Register of Historic Places
Built: 1900
620 S.W. Tichenor Street
Clatskanie
503-728-3608 (museum)

The Flippin House is grand enough to be called a castle by local residents. To Thomas Flippin, building this house represented his moving up in society as a prosperous lumber man, but to his wife Florence, who had also worked in their lumber company, it represented a refined way of life that she disliked. After living there only three years, the couple moved out, and then separated.

Directions: From Highway 30 within Clatskanie city limits, watch for a small highway sign. Turn south on S.W. Tichenor Street. The house is on the right about a block past the intersection of Tichenor and Fourth streets.

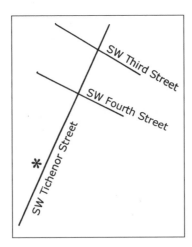

Open: Wednesday–Friday; year around, except holidays

Hours: 10:00–2:00
Admission: $3.00 per person
Tour: Guided
Entry: At the front door
Additional Attractions: The Clatskanie senior center cafeteria is located in the building basement, and it serves lunch at 11:45 a.m. For those under sixty, the fee is $3.75; for those sixty and above, the donation is $2.50.

History

As a teenager, Thomas Flippin had a low-status job in a lumber camp in Columbia County during the 1880s. He eventually met and married Florence Elliott, who came from a lumbering family, and the two filed claims on adjacent 160 acre tracts of timberland about five miles from Clatskanie. They then purchased two hundred more acres of timberland, which included a mill dam and the frame of a sawmill. With borrowed money, they began West Oregon Lumber Company.

Florence Flippin, with her background in lumber, was an ideal partner in a lumber company. Years later, a former workman told her son, Thomas Flippin Jr.,

I remember your mother well. In the afternoon she would put you down in the sawdust pile for your afternoon naps and relieve the fireman while he cleaned up under the mill. Than she would go to the filing room and work on our saws. I would rather work with saws filed and set by your mother than any professional filer I ever knew.

The Flippins lived in the cookhouse at their lumber company, but when their two children grew to school age, the couple decided to move to Clatskanie. They purchased the property adjacent to the school and began building the house. In late spring of 1900, they left the rough life of a lumber camp and moved into their opulent new home. Tom Flippin Jr. later recalled, "From my father's viewpoint, progressing from a skidgreaser on a bull-team skidroad at the age of seventeen to a home like this (with a backlog of money to support it) at about the age of thirty-five was a tremendous accomplishment. He was proud of it."

While Thomas Flippin enjoyed the status of an upscale house in town, Florence abhorred it. Instead of working at the lumber camp, living in town meant that she now had the responsibilities of running a house and formal entertaining. To cope, she relegated much of the housework to servants and spent most of her time outside landscaping the yard. After living in the house for only a short time, the Flippins moved, and then separated shortly thereafter.

The house sold several times, and at one period was rented as apartments. George and Anne Salmi purchased the house in 1959, and for some years opened it for tours. Even after they discontinued the practice, people still came to the door asking to see the inside. The Clatskanie seniors, the current owners, purchased the house in 1979.

Setting

The Flippin house is located on a knoll above the street in a residential area. From the lawn, the visitor has a view of the surrounding Clatskanie hills, and can glimpse Highway 30 snaking its way through the far trees.

Exterior

The twin towers flanking the house initially do make the house look like a castle, albeit one of wood rather than of stone. The house has other castle-like allusions. Under the front steps is an arched opening, and although obscured by bushes, it suggests that the visitor must cross a moat to get to the front door. The tall concrete foundation is formed to look like blocks, alluding to the stone exterior of a fortress.

The house has both Colonial Revival and Queen Anne features, typical of its time. The house's symmetry and modified Tuscan-like columns are

The Flippin house is so grand that local residents call it a castle.

Colonial Revival elements, while Queen Anne details are shown in the different roof types such as the bell-shaped tower roofs and pyramidal roofs on the dormers. Another Queen Anne characteristic is varied wall surfaces, such as the octagonal and diamond-shaped shingles. Thomas Flippin's brother, Will, painstakingly sawed the shingles, and Thomas Jr. later wrote that he "never looked at the Castle without thinking of the enormous amount of labor and the artistry that went into that shingle siding."

The intent of the blue-gray designs rendered by the shingles on each side of the house remains a mystery. On the north side, six large diamonds are depicted with a background of wavy shingles. A former owner of the house speculated that the diamonds represent square-rigger sails, with the background shingle pattern forming waves. On the south side of the house, the design is more complicated. The boy on the moon and the five-pointed star suggest a heavenly allusion, but the cone shape on the left remains perplexing. The former owner believed it is the nose of a rocket, but that would have implied considerable futuristic thinking.

Interior

Instead of opening up to a narrow hall, the front door opens up to a large room. The historical tradition of this room is the medieval "great hall," which could be another castle reference. The elegant fireplace, with glazed tiles imported from Italy, still suggests that this was a significant space. However, Henry Seidel Canby, remembering his home in the 1890s in "God Bless Our Home," noted that "fireplaces had not yet come back except as tiled ornaments for the hall where, of course, no one ever used them."

If the Flippins entertained in this room, the black walnut pump organ donated by a local family and now standing by the staircase is appropriately placed. Anyone who knows how to operate the organ is welcome play it. The instrument originally cost $27.50, and traveled west via a covered wagon on the Oregon Trail. Because of the difficulties of the route, it is surprising that there apparently never came a time when its owner decided that it was better to drop it off and travel more lightly.

The expansiveness of this hall and the adjoining rooms provides space for contemporary functions. After the seniors acquired the house, the town's chief of police noted that "If you have a castle, you should have a king and queen." In 1981, the seniors crowned the Salmis, the former owners of the house, and for several years continued to select a king and queen. Today, however, one docent reported that the seniors have difficulty finding a king because the men generally lack enthusiasm for the job.

The organ, which can be played by visitors, was reportedly transported over the Oregon Trail.

The room on the left is furnished as a dining room, but the Flippins likely used it as the parlor or sitting room. A similarly elaborate fireplace to the one in the hall graces one wall. Both mantels were crafted elsewhere, and their detailed embellishment contrasts with the simpler locally made woodwork elsewhere in the house. Nevertheless, the lumber for the house was carefully chosen. According to Thomas Flippin Jr., "My father regarded the sawyer as the 'key man' in a mill and did all his own sawing. When a choice log came through the mill, he would cut out a little lumber for the house and barn. Every bit of lumber in the Castle is his handwork and his choice."

The fine workmanship in the house is exemplified in the adjacent tower. No joint shows in the white concave ceiling, making it difficult to gauge the ceiling height. Gentlemen initially smoked cigars and played cards in this area, shielded from the rest of the house by a heavy drape. Perhaps admiring the ceiling was one of their pastimes.

The house currently can be rented for weddings, but hopefully the receptions are different from the one portrayed in the engraving, "A Scottish Wedding," which hangs on a wall in the dining room. By the broken crockery and the drunken pose of one of the participants, it appears that the wedding celebration is well along. A server in the picture is providing more libations; the frame decoration of grapes intertwined in leaves further emphasizes the drinking theme.

In the kitchen stands a "kitchen queen," the predecessor of built-in cupboards and countertops. In one cabinet, a compartment with a small sifter at the bottom held the flour, and on the other side was a jar for sugar. On this door, a "Daily Reminder" suggests a shopping list of items such as beets, bluing, and buckwheat, and a small cork strip allowed pins to denote which provisions were needed. The kitchen queen includes a slide-out shelf for additional work space.

The kitchen in the cookhouse at the lumber camp was the setting of a family story that reveals insight into Florence Flippin's hearty character. In that kitchen, a ladder ran through the attic to the roof, which had a trapdoor to allow good ventilation. One day while her father-in-law was sitting in the makeshift parlor reading a book, Florence Flippin, who was boiling the wash on the wood stove, looked up and saw the roof was on fire. She quickly filled a ten-pound bucket, grabbed an ax from the wood box, and climbed the ladder to the roof and chopped out the burning roof section. Since burning pieces of the roof had dropped into the attic, she stomped out the hot coals and sprinkled water on the other burning debris. After she had come down for another bucket of water and returned to ensure the fire was out, she came into the parlor covered with ashes and cinders, her hair singed, and with burn holes in her clothes and shoes. When she related what she had just done, her father-in-law said, "That was good. I've always thought what a fine thing it is to have a resourceful woman in the house." He then went back to his reading. Accustomed to such a rough life, Florence Flippin understandably felt out of place in a more refined house.

The Red Room is off the kitchen, but evidence suggests that this originally served as the family's dining room because of the built-in buffet. The bedroom located adjacent to this room held a strong memory for Thomas Flippin Jr. when

> *the carpenters were still working on the door and window trim in the first floor bedroom.... Here was a paradise for two little kids. The room became our headquarters. The floor was littered knee deep with yellow fir shavings that were so curly, so adaptable; that smelled so good and felt so good after playing so long in sawdust and bark chiggers. When the carpenters were through and started to clean up the shavings, there was a big howl from the kids. Mother told us to take all the shavings up to our playrooms in the second story off the round towers. We were generous to ourselves and never did give up our shavings as long as we lived there.*

The second ground-floor room with the tower is now called the Music Room because of the square piano residing there. The parlor furniture includes a burgundy armchair, generally called a "gentlemen's chair," while its peach-colored mate is a "ladies' chair." The latter is slightly shorter, has a wider seat, and is without arms, allowing for the voluminous hoop skirts of the 1850s and 1860s. The lack of arms on the chair also allowed a woman the freedom to move her forearms when doing handwork.

The furniture in this room once belonged to Dr. Otto George, to whom the room is dedicated. Dr. George once worked in Alaska and painted the two Alaskan pictures on display. He was known locally for developing a salve for burns, and although it was never officially approved, local people for years testified to its effectiveness. One disadvantage was that it smelled like cod-liver oil.

In the upstairs hall, black-and-white photographs show early logging camps, economic mainstays of the Clatskanie community. Some of the photographs are from the lumber camp of Simon Benson, a Norwegian immigrant who became wealthy through his business acumen. The bedroom at the end of the hall on the left is dedicated to another prominent person in Clatskanie, Dr. James L. Wooden. The room includes his well-used obstetrics bag that doubtless aided him in delivering an estimated two thousand babies between 1907 and 1957. Dr. Wooden also opened a small hospital in Clatskanie above a storefront, which consisted of two rooms with two beds each. According to a newspaper clipping, one room was used for the men, who were frequently involved in logging accidents, and the other for women, who were generally there for maternity. Patients were not always so fortunate as to make it to the hospital, and sometimes by the glow of an oil lamp the pioneer doctor had to perform "kitchen table surgery."

Thomas and Florence Flippin used the bedroom with the tower on the north end of the house. The space under the tower is now outfitted as a nursery, although it still contains a kitchen sink from the time the house was divided into apartments.

The local quilting society now uses the room in the center, believed to have been Thomas Flippin's billiard room, and a reminiscence by Thomas Jr. suggests that the room accessed through the billiard room was the children's bedroom. Wherever the billiard and playroom were located, the Flippins used them for only three years. The house was a dream for part of the family, but not for all.

Caples House

Built: 1870

1915 First Street
Columbia City
503-397-5390 (museum)

The house occupies its original site facing the river. From the porch and small second-story balcony, the Caples could see boats stopping at what is now Pixie Landing Park. The river was a source of fish and water, and lumber for the house was transported up the river from Longview.

Directions: After entering Columbia City limits from Highway 30, turn towards the Columbia River at I Street. The house is on the northwest corner of First and I streets.

Open: March through October, Friday–Sunday and holidays
Hours: 12:00–4:00
Admission: $2.00 adults; $1.00 children
Tour: Guided
Entry: Ring bell at the house front porch.
Additional Attractions: A former washhouse has pioneer tools and the carriage house is a doll museum.

History

Accompanied by his widowed father Joseph and his brother and sister, Charles Caples traveled west over the Oregon Trail in 1844, when he was twelve. After spending time in Salem and Portland, Joseph Caples filed a 320-acre claim in present-day Columbia City and began building a log cabin. Charles Caples went to the California gold fields in 1848, and then returned to claim 320 acres next to his father. He cleared his land by selling the cut wood to passing riverboats that needed fuel.

In 1855 Charles Caples married Lucinda McBride, and began to study medicine under a doctor in Portland. He established his practice in the area between Columbia City and Longview. He and Lucinda had five children: Margaret, Willie Louise, Dell, Frederick, and Byron. Charles Caples died in 1906, but Dell continued to live there. In 1959, at the age of eighty-nine, Dell Caples presented the house to the Oregon State Society Daughters of the American Revolution after she moved to a nursing home. She died in 1969, just a year before the house opened as a museum.

The Caples house, which stands a block from the Columbia River, remained in the family for eighty-nine years.

Setting

The house sits on the southern end of a block that includes the Knapp Community Center, which was built as a fundraiser to support the Caples Museum. The site includes about seventeen trees that were part of the Caples orchard. Along First Street stands a 130- to 150-year-old bigleaf maple.

Exterior

The house is based on a simple folk form called a gable-front, based on the gable facing the street. The jigsaw-cut brackets gracing the porch posts relieve the utilitarian facade. A one-story kitchen is in the back of the house.

Interior

Despite the availability of modern stoves, for years Dell Caples cooked her food on the wood-burning stove in the kitchen. The stove also heated her water. The house was connected to the local water system, but the only outlet is a spigot located outside the kitchen door. On the pantry wall hangs a yoke fitted for a child. It allowed the balancing of two filled water buckets in the days before the availability of piped water. A former caretaker related that following a boy with a switch was one way to obtain "running water."

Dell Caples had the house wired for electricity in 1929, but there were few outlets in the house. Instead of a vacuum cleaner, she might have used a "vacuum sweeper" like the one standing by the stove. It was a "new-fangled" appliance when it was introduced. On the bottom of the sweeper, someone has affixed the yellowed directions, which start out by advising, "Push the machine forward and backward."

Another early implement is the iron gopher trap hanging on the wall behind the stove. The two rings would be clipped together, and the trap would be shoved down the hole. The gopher, burrowing along, would stick its neck between the two rings, release the catch, and the springing separation of the two rings would slice its head off.

Charles Caples used the small room located off the kitchen warmed by the stove as a birthing room. Today it displays Indian baskets and Frederick Caples's treasures from his geological excursions in Alaska and Canada.

A picture of Dell Caples sitting on the porch in her dress is located on the bottom shelf of a display case in the room that her father used as a doctor's office. A photograph of Charles Caples, wearing his Pioneer

Association ribbon proclaiming that he crossed on the Oregon Trail in 1844, hangs on a wall. Caples was not only a doctor, he was also a woodworker, and he crafted the corner cabinet where he kept his medicines.

He also made the combination bookcase and desk in his doctor's office. It has a vertical piece that could be raised and, if supported by legs since removed, was used as a writing surface. In the course of practicing medicine, Caples also performed the services of a dentist, and the various implements displayed on the shelves indicate that extraction, not repair, was the solution to tooth pain. Doubtless the nearby black couch frequently came in handy.

The esteem for Abraham Lincoln felt by nineteenth-century citizens is suggested in the Currier and Ives print hanging on the wall which states, "The Nation's Martyr." The Civil War saber mounted on the fireplace mantel in the parlor is from a Union soldier. The largest item in the room, the square Curtiss piano, was not brought into the house easily. Both it and the settee traveled from the east coast around Cape Horn, eventually ending up at what is now Pixie Landing dock. They were freighted by wagon up to the house, but the front door was too small for the solid

Charles Caples ran his doctor's office in this room, and built the combination bookcase and desk.

cherry-wood piano. The two front windows had to be removed in order to get the piano into the house.

Charles Caples made the furniture in the bedroom near the head of the stairs, where the two boys slept. A picture in the room, entitled "The Doctor," suggests a pose that Charles Caples might have assumed when tending to sick children in the area. Hanging in the nearby girls' room are two portraits that Dell Caples painted of her sisters. Obviously sharing the small room did not induce sibling rivalry, as both girls, each clutching a flower, are depicted as sweet and innocent.

In the display case in the hall hang several coverlets made before the turn of the twentieth century. One, crafted in Switzerland, traveled to the eastern coast of the United States and then came to Oregon in 1853. Another survived the rigors of the Oregon Trail, although its creator did not.

In the nearby bedroom is a bed, reportedly made of wood from the Black Forest in Germany, that was used by the Caples family. Dell Caples owned the foot-powered sewing machine standing in the room, and took sewing classes at the Oregon Agricultural College (now Oregon State University). Her sewing book, with O.A.C. appropriately stitched on the cover, rests by her machine and contains samples of her work.

The Caples house, like several other house museums, has been the location of ghost sightings. The former caretakers reported seeing the apparition of an older woman standing at the wood stove. Perhaps it is Dell Caples, still doing housework.

Coast

Flavel House

National Register of Historic Places
Built: 1885
441 Eighth Street
Astoria
503-325-2563 (museum)

Captain Flavel, a wealthy businessman, loved luxury, and his retirement home was to convey his financial success in life. Polly McKean Bell, a friend of the Flavels' daughters, called it a "fairy story castle."

Directions: From Highway 30, which is Marine Drive for those heading eastbound through downtown or Commercial Street for those heading westbound, turn south on Eighth Street. The house is just behind the county courthouse at the intersection of Eighth and Duane streets.

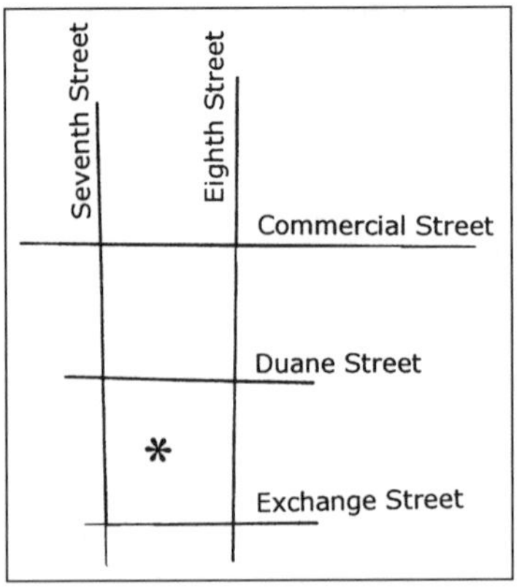

Open: Year around, except holidays
Hours: May through September, 10:00–5:00; October through April, 11:00–4:00
Admission: $5.00 adults; $4.50 seniors; $2.50 children
Tour: Self-guided
Entry: At the side door that faces Duane Street

Additional Attractions: The Clatsop County Historical Society also operates the Heritage Museum at 1618 Exchange Street and the Uppertown Firefighter Museum at 2986 Marine Drive (call 503-325-2203 for hours and admission).

History

George Flavel was born on November 17, 1823, but his place of birth has been cited as Ireland, New Jersey, or Virginia. Little else is known about his life until he left Norfolk, Virginia, in command of the brig *John Petty* and sailed around Cape Horn in 1849 with cargo for the California miners. Finding the market overstocked, he went on to Portland and sold his goods there. He eventually began piloting the *Goldhunter*, which ran between San Francisco and Portland, and became one of the first licensed bar pilots crossing the Columbia River.

In 1854, at the age of thirty, he married Mary Boelling, the fourteen-year-old daughter of Conrad Boelling, a hotel owner.

George Flavel formed a partnership with Captain Asa Meade Simpson in 1857 to expand his bar piloting business. With the purchase of the barkentine *Jane A. Falkenberg*, he conducted a profitable shipping operation. Under another captain's command, the *Falkenberg* beat all previous records to Honolulu when it crossed the Pacific in less than thirteen days. Flavel invested in a tugboat operation and real estate, in addition to serving as the county treasurer in 1872 and school board director in 1873. In 1885, he was president of the First National Bank of Astoria and a Clatsop County commissioner.

That same year, he was completing the construction of his house, which was designed by architect Carl Leick. The February 10, 1885, *Daily Astorian* boasted that "Captain Flavel and Col. Taylor, two of our oldest residents, are building new private residences that will be ornaments to the city." He and Mary Flavel moved into the house with their two unmarried daughters, twenty-seven-year-old Nellie and twenty-one-year-old Katie. The oldest child, also called George, had already married.

In 1893, George Flavel died; Mary continued to live in the house until her death in 1928. When Nellie Flavel died in 1933, the house became property of her grandniece Patricia Flavel, who donated it to the city for public use. In 1936, the city manager suggested the building be razed and a park established on the site, since Astoria was without funds to alter the structure. After public debate, the city returned the dwelling to Patricia Flavel, who then gave it to the county, and the house became a museum for Clatsop County Historical Society in 1951. Today, the historical society owns and operates the house.

Setting

The Flavels began landscaping the block several years before construction of the house. Polly McKean Bell, a friend of the Flavel daughters, related that when they started building "no landscaping was necessary. It was a case of finding enough clear ground for the foundation. Afterwards choice shrubs and trees were added."

The grounds, which encompass one city block, were not just for strolling in the garden. Bell recalled playing tennis and archery on the lawn, and in an arbor south of the house, a "trim maid in cap and apron waited upon us. For many of us who lived in a simpler manner, this was altogether a festive affair."

The Flavel property also includes a two-story carriage house built in the style of the house. When it was constructed, the July 22, 1887, *Daily Astorian* related that "Capt. Flavel is finishing what when completed will be one of the finest and handsomest stables and carriage houses in the state." The July 28, 1887, *Daily Astorian* later bragged that "the new stable of Capt. Flavel's looks more stylish outside than any ordinary dwelling house." The historical society plans on converting this structure into an orientation center for the house.

Exterior

When Polly McKean Bell first saw the house, her initial impressions were "it stood stately and ornate, with tall bay windows, porches, handsome doors, and a tall and beautiful tower on the northeast corner." The tower was ornate as well as practical. At the top of a winding staircase is a small area surrounded by windows where George Flavel could look through a telescope and see ships crossing the bar.

The house displays a Queen Anne style shape with the tower and north and south gables extending from the main hip roof. A gabled dormer on the front façade has a balcony that is accessed through the attic. Another characteristic of the Queen Anne style is the porch that extends across the front façade, wraps around the bay window formed by the tower, and extends onto the side of the house (the tour entrance is now through the former side doors).

From the 1896 to 1984, the Flavel house was painted white. As a widow, Mary Flavel thriftily had the house painted all one color rather than repeat the costly multicolor paint scheme. When it was white, the decorative features such the brackets under the eaves and the window hoods supported by small brackets appeared to be in the Italianate style. After the historical society returned it to Victorian colors, however, the contrasting colors on the corner boards and the vertical bands extending above the second floor windows to the brackets emphasize a vertical design. These features are characteristic of what Virginia and Lee McAlester identify in *A Field Guide to American Houses* as Western Coast Stick style. Unlike its eastern counterpart that includes diagonal stickwork, the western version emphasized a vertical design and was common in San Francisco, where Carl Leick, the architect, had spent some of his time.

Captain George Flavel kept a telescope at the top of the tower so he could watch ships cross the Columbia River bar.

Interior

The architect designed a house that would initially seem as overwhelming on the interior as it does on the exterior. The ceilings on the first floor are fourteen feet high, and the doors are nine feet high. The hall alone was large enough to hold three chairs, two sofas, two tables, and a hat stand, all of which were there when Mary Flavel died in 1928. The main entrance today was originally used by family, and the best place to start the tour is in front of the entry doors located down the hall to the right of the cashier's desk.

Captain Flavel's love of the sea is demonstrated in the leaded glass transom over the two doors, that features a sailing ship set in an oval. The design of the ship is attributed to Cleveland Rockwell, a government surveyor who, after he retired in 1892, became a full-time painter. George Flavel commissioned Rockwell to paint the two pictures of the Columbia Bar that hang in the hall.

The Portland firm of "Foster & Robertson, Jobbers of Hardware, Iron and Steel, Guns and Ammunition, Fishing Tackle" supplied the front doors as well as the shutters in the house, including those seen in the parlor on the right. The shutters were designed to recess into the window reveals when not needed.

Marjorie Halderman and Marjorie Dubois, who played as children in the house, recalled that the parlor was rarely used, and that the doors were usually closed and the furniture kept under sheets. The parlor was used for the 1916 Regatta reception, and the *Evening Budget* newspaper headline was "Flavel Mansion Thrown Open to Receive Queen and Admiral." While the Queen of the Regatta and an Admiral stood in the parlor greeting guests, Mary Flavel and her daughters stood in the music room and welcomed visitors, and "Japanese boys in their native costumes served punch and cakes to the visitors."

Halderman and Dubois described the house as being without color and that "everything was dark: the wood, the furniture, the drapes the walls—everything." Part of this impression must have been created by the Eastlake style woodwork around the doors and windows. Charles Eastlake, an English designer, wrote *Hints on Household Taste*, a seminal work first published in 1868 that was printed in several editions in America. Despite its widespread popularity, American furniture manufactures developed their own interpretation of Eastlake's style, which was characterized by straight lines, shallow geometric carving, and incised decoration. Eastlake was the rage in America during the 1880s and 1890s, and the moldings in the Flavel house in the Eastlake design were another indication of the family wealth.

Ironically, Eastlake was disturbed with American manufacturers' interpretation of his designs. In the Preface to the 1878 edition of *Hints on Household Taste*, published in London, he wrote, "I find American tradesmen continually advertising what they are pleased to call 'Eastlake' furniture, with the production of which I have had nothing whatever to do, and for the taste of which I should be very sorry to be considered responsible." Though Eastlake wrote that the practice of false graining was "an objectionable and pretentious deceit," the Flavel parlor door, like others in the house, is Douglas fir faux painted to look like burled rosewood.

The 1928 household property inventory listed the value of the parlor furnishings as $271, of which $100 was attributed to a marble bust and pedestal. The music room, located across the hall, had $300 worth of furniture. The Flavel daughters were trained in music in San Francisco, New York, and Europe, and Katie sang with a coloratura soprano voice, while Nellie was an accomplished pianist and church organist. On Sunday afternoons, the women would give recitals to a select group of friends and acquaintances, who considered it an honor to be invited. Bell remembered the music room of "truly noble proportions and handsomely furnished."

One of the instruments in the room was a grand piano, which George Flavel had given to Nellie. Bell related that Nellie Flavel was her father's favorite child, and that both of them had "rather luxurious tastes." While it is likely that George and Nellie Flavel favored spending the money to build the house, Mary probably was against it. Bell noted that "Mrs. Flavel complained the house was too big and too difficult to care for properly with a cook, and a maid and a handyman."

Mary Flavel, born of pioneer stock, was apparently frugal throughout her life. When her sister asked her to purchase some gloves from San Francisco, Mary Flavel wrote her that she had some gloves that were too small for herself that she would send. The 1928 household property inventory noted that some of the carpets (likely the original ones installed when the house was new) were forty-one years old in order to explain their low value. Another "well worn" carpet was in the dining room and upstairs hall. In addition, two "damaged" cloisonné vases stood in the hall, while four "damaged" vases stood in the music room.

Because they were affixed to the wall, the fireplace mantels and overmantels were not counted as personal property, but the one in the music room as well as the other two located downstairs are so decorative that they seem to be a part of the furnishings. This mahogany mantel exhibits French tiles, and the iron firebox also displays a design. In addition,

Flavel daughters gave Sunday recitals in the
music room. A portrait is of George Flavel is
in the center of the photograph.

both the mantel and overmantel have space for the bric-a-brac popular
during Victorian times.

Halderman and Dubois remembered an unusual chair "that would
play music when you sat on it." In the library across the hall, the two
remember that there was a large Eastlake style chair on which they would
play "King of the Mountain." The two noted that the wood on the crest
rail would zigzag up and down at sharp angles, an apt description of the
style. By then, Eastlake furniture must have gone out of fashion, as the
two related that the chair was "unattractive as all of the furniture was."

Although the architect designated the room as a "library" on the plans,
the room was used as the principal family room. The family used the side
door now used as the main entry door as their primary entrance, and the
library was conveniently located right off this section of the hall. One of
the few Flavel pieces the historical society owns is the library table. Bell
remembered a "long library table holding magazines, stereoscope and
photographs," as well as "walnut book cases full of treasures in the
background."

Embodying a Victorian notion of bringing nature indoors, a
conservatory was designed off the dining room. Even when the pocket
doors between the two rooms were closed, clear glass inserts allowed a

view of the plants in the conservatory. Today, a couch occupies the room and on it rests a harp guitar, a musical instrument that first appeared in the United States around the 1880s.

When the Flavels ate in the dining room, the help served them through the pantry, a place where the china was stored in custom Eastlake style cabinets. As children, Halderman and Dubois did not like the meals, recalling them as "awful. … Everything was creamed." Their feelings about the food might have affected how they felt about the cooks, because they also related that they were afraid of them.

Perhaps the cooks were fearsome because of their working conditions. Carolyn Shepherd, whose grandmother was a domestic for the family, told stories about George Flavel inspecting the potato peels to insure that the employees were not wasting food. The historical society also has a letter describing an incident when a day maid fished a coffeepot out of the Flavels' garbage and was then docked a day's wages to "pay" for the item.

While the four chairs in the kitchen were given to the museum and did not belong to the family, they do have an appropriate marine connection. The donor's father purchased the chairs from Captain Jackson Gregory Hustler, who made them as a pastime during long days at sea in 1868.

The rest of the downstairs service area was converted to a caretaker's apartment after the house became a museum. According to the plans, there was another entrance to a back porch (still there), a room set aside for washing, and an attached "wood house." The Flavel mansion had a central boiler that burned three-foot-long logs, so a wood house was a necessity.

The entrance to the basement was originally located in the kitchen, but the historical society moved the stairway to the front hall. While the basement contains items from various Astoria persons and businesses, it also contains some Flavel items, including a horse-drawn sleigh that the family used to travel through the town when the streets were muddy. Also in the basement is a Victorian pool table from the luxurious Flavel Hotel, a business endeavor of the Captain's only son. The hotel was located across Youngs Bay in the town of Flavel, but it was not a prosperous enterprise and nothing remains of the building or the town.

To go up to the second floor, walk back to the servants' stairway to experience their typical route. Once you are upstairs, the main bathroom is on the left, a luxury that must have astonished Astorians. A marble counter encircles a porcelain sink, while the cabinetry below follows the pattern of the wainscoting. Except for the horizontal board across the lid, the remainder of the water closet enclosure is original. The wood around the water storage tank is fittingly in the Eastlake style.

Historians believe that a small bedroom near the bathroom was a servant's room. Another bathroom and two other bedrooms for the servants, fashioned from rough boards, were located in the third-floor attic. The rest of the attic was left unfinished, and it is now closed to the public due to fire code.

The first bedroom in the main hall was reserved for guests. Beyond, double doors in the hall separate the family bedrooms from the rest of the upstairs, including the guestroom. The historical society believes that Mary Flavel installed these doors after George died, and they still have brackets at the bottom that would hold a bar for additional security. Since the guest room is not within the secured area, apparently she was not concerned about a visitor's safety.

Nellie Flavel occupied the first room on the right, and shared the sink located in an adjoining passageway with Katie, whose room was located in the front of the house. Across the hall was Mary's room. If the house was large enough, Victorian husbands and wives frequently did not share the same bedroom, as was the case with the Flavels. George Flavel's bedroom has one of the three fireplaces on the second floor. Facing the fireplace is an armchair with velvet upholstery, which the historical society believes was a Flavel item. The remaining tassels on the bottom suggest that the chair was Turkish styled, a design prompted by the Victorian interest in things then considered "exotic."

Above the fireplace mantel hangs an oil painting by Cleveland Rockwell of the captain's barkentine, the *Jane H. Falkenberg*. The ship was a favorite of George Flavel, and he reportedly set several records in it. Even a local newspaper noted that it was "one of the fleetest vessels afloat, if not really the fastest one on the seas carrying the stars and stripes." George Flavel loved the sea, and the house he built with his profits embodied his great love.

Lindgren Cabin

Built: 1928

Cullaby Lake County Park
Astoria
503-654-0448
(Gene Knapp, editor of the Finnish-American Historical Society of the West)

The cabin is a handmade building built by Erik Lindgren, a man in his sixties, with just one helper. The cabin, so well constructed that only a few nails were needed, is rich in Finnish tradition.

Directions: The cabin is actually located in an unincorporated area south of Astoria. Drive eight miles south of Astoria along Highway 101, and watch for the sign for Cullaby Lake County Park. Turn east on Cullaby Lake Road and follow the signs to the park. The house is on the right beyond the park admission trailer.

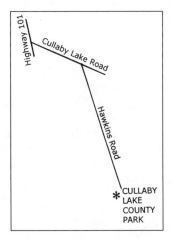

Open: Mid-June to mid-September, weekends and holidays
Hours: 10:00–5:00
Admission: Donation; park entry fee is $3.00 per car
Tour: Guided
Entry: At the front door
Additional Attractions: Cullaby Lake County Park has facilities for boating, swimming, hiking, and picnicking.

History

The Lindgrens were born in Finland: Johanna in 1857 and Erik in 1861. The couple had one child, Emil, in 1889 before Erik immigrated to the United States looking for work and a home for his family. His wife and child followed, and another child, Anna, was born in Massachusetts in 1902.

The Lindgrens migrated west to Astoria, a city with rich Scandinavian culture. Erik Lindgren worked at several jobs, including at a sawmill, but in 1907 he again left his family to establish a homestead in the Nehalem forest along Soapstone Creek. The Lindgrens lived primitively in a cabin with a dirt floor and one window and one door. The children attended a school in Hamlet, a small nearby community.

The Lindgrens lived on their farm, raising cattle and poultry, and planting cherry, apple, and pear trees. The family was without a horse, so every item they used was handmade or laboriously hauled up a narrow trail which wound along Soapstone Creek for about a mile and was the only way into the homestead.

The Lindgrens eventually erected a sauna, barn, guesthouse, and in 1928, finished the cabin now standing at Cullaby Lake. A friend with a two-horse team helped in moving the hand-hewed planks to the home site. The Lindgrens lived in the cabin for ten years before life in the wilds became too difficult. Erik Lindgren died in 1938 in Astoria, while Johanna died in 1943 in Deep River, Washington.

For many years, the cabin and the rest of the Lindgren buildings sat empty. Over time, hunters, anglers, and picnickers began stripping cedar from the structures to construct campfires. In the 1970s, concern for the fate of the cabin prompted its admirers to dismantle it, mark the pieces, and reassemble it on a site in Seaside. Members of the Finnish community were instrumental in moving and restoring the cabin at Cullaby Lake, and today, the Finnish-American Historical Society of the West operates the cabin.

Setting

The cabin and several of the Lindgren outbuildings stand within a cyclone-fenced area added for off-season protection. The largest outbuilding is the cedar-planked sauna/storage shed.

Exterior

Though many cabins were scattered throughout the Clatsop County wilderness, few were as well constructed as the Lindgren home. The horizontal cedar-plank walls are fitted so tightly that no chinking was needed. Dovetail notches and wooden dowels hold the planks together, and only a few nails were used. The width of the planks varies from about fifteen inches to an awe-inspiring forty-seven inches. Erik Lindgren hewed these planks by hand over several years with the help of a neighbor, William Merila. Merila had lost his hand while playing with blasting caps as a child, and Lindgren would say that "three able Finnish hands" made his house.

The placement of the inner walls is visible by the line of pegs that runs vertically up the sides of the house. The roof covering consists of planks running the full length from the ridge to the eaves. A long overhang protects the back of the house from rain, but the men carved a gutter from a long cedar log for the front of the cabin.

The front door is not original to the house. The Lindgrens' door now rests in the storage room adjacent to the sauna. Hunters built a fire in a sink and subsequently burned a large half circle into the door. The cabin also suffered after its move to Cullaby Lake, as the new glass windows lasted only a day before vandals smashed them. The shutters, a feature

Erik Lindgren and a helper constructed this well built cabin with cedar planks fit so tightly together that no chinking was needed.

that the Lindgrens did not have, now protect the windows during the off-season.

Interior

The interior is as rustic as the exterior, and just as functional. The main room, heated by the cooking stove, served multiple purposes: cooking, eating, and relaxing. Two small rooms off the main room, which were kept warm by the stove, served as the couple's bedroom and guest room, while a pantry and workroom were located on the other end of the main room. Above the workroom where the loom is located, a hole cut in the ceiling provided access to the attic, where the Lindgrens stored hay and put additional overnight guests.

Since every purchased item had to be hauled to the cabin, it would have been sparsely furnished. The Lindgrens likely would have built a table and bench similar to the one in the room today. They could not have constructed a wood-burning stove, so Erik Lindgren had to transport one the twenty miles from Seaside. He reportedly said that it was the heaviest load he ever carried.

Finnish handicrafts are displayed in the main room of the Lindgren Cabin.

Isolated from merchants, the Lindgrens depended on handcrafted items to furnish their home, and items from the Finnish tradition are displayed around the cabin today. Against the far wall hangs a *himmeli*, a Christmas ornament made by bending straw into various shapes. On the other side of the cabin above the glass display case hangs a *lippi*, a water dipper made by shaping a piece of bark into a funnel, held in place with a small forked branch. On the bottom shelf of the glass display case are *virsu*, handmade shoes made by weaving strips of birch bark. The human tendency to embellish appears even in the shoes, as one of the woman's *virsu* still exhibits a flowerlike applique made from the bark.

The rectangular rugs on the floor were created on the loom in the workroom, and are similar to ones Johanna Lindgren would have made. The loom itself is handcrafted, and can be broken down into pieces for storage. The Finnish docents at the cabin believe that Johanna Lindgren's loom would not have had a coat of paint, and therefore would not have been as "fancy" as this one.

Because of the distance from merchants, food preparation likely took a considerable amount of time, just as it did for early pioneers. The Lindgrens grew vegetables, planted fruit trees, and raised cattle. Deer and salmon provided additional protein. The Lindgrens preserved their meat by smoking it in the sauna and hanging it in the eleven-foot-high building located just north of the cabin. They preserved the salmon in a ceramic container like the one in the pantry, adding rock salt between the layers of fish. Their bounty from the homestead also provided them with something to trade for the provisions they could not grow, such as coffee, salt, and kerosene. However, life in the wilds had peril. Once when Erik Lindgren was carrying a slaughtered calf to Seaside to trade, he met a bear standing across a footbridge. The bear finally ambled off to the woods.

A knot in a plank in the guestroom is labeled "Finnish intercom system." On the wall is a tinted photograph of Hamlet, the nearest community to the Lindgren house. The scene shows a landscape including a road and fence, but no buildings. Like others in Hamlet, the Lindgrens eked out a living in the wilderness.

However, living primitively did not mean living without a sauna. The Lindgrens reportedly had the largest sauna in the neighborhood, and their neighbors would gather at their home on Saturday nights for the Finnish ritual. The sauna today has three benches, enough to hold a crowd. The Finnish believe that saunas promote good health. In the Lindgrens' sauna a wood fire would heat stones, and when water was poured on the stones they emitted a water vapor. A lit candle shining through a glass window provided the light in the sauna. The Finnish still take saunas in their homes today, although it is no longer the usual custom for gatherings of men and women to sauna together.

Yaquina Bay Lighthouse

National Register of Historic Places
Built: 1871

Yaquina Bay State Park, on the west side of Highway 101
Newport, OR
541-265-5679 (museum)
541-867-7451 (South Beach State Park)

The Yaquina Bay Lighthouse is the second oldest standing lighthouse station on the Oregon coast and the only lighthouse remaining in the state that was built as both a keeper's quarters and light tower. In service for only a short time (1871 to 1874), the lighthouse is known today for a legendary ghost.

Directions: From Highway 101, heading south just before crossing the Yaquina Bay Bridge, turn west into the state park. A parking lot and interpretive exhibit are located at the base of the lighthouse.

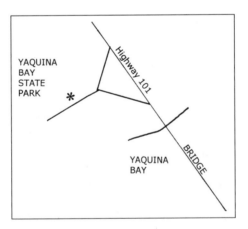

Open: Year around
Hours: Memorial Day through September, 11:00–5:00; October through Memorial Day, 12:00–4:00
Admission: Donation
Tour: Self-guided
Entry: Follow path from parking lot up to lighthouse
Additional Attractions: Yaquina Bay State Park has picnic facilities and trails.

Yaquina Head Lighthouse, located three miles north of Newport off Highway 101, has an interpretive center (call 541-574-3100 for information).

History

Construction finished on the Yaquina Bay lighthouse, designed to provide a light for the coastline, in late 1871. Lightkeeper Charles H. Peirce, his wife Sarah, and seven of their nine children lived together in the wood frame keeper's quarters and light tower. In 1873, however, construction began on the Yaquina Head lighthouse on its headland four miles north, replacing the one by Yaquina Bay because it was more easily seen from the ocean. The Yaquina Bay light was extinguished on October 1, 1874, and the Pierces moved to the Cape Blanco lighthouse.

The lighthouse stood empty for years, although the government periodically mended the roof and made repairs as needed. In 1888, U.S. Army Corps of Engineers workers occupied the lighthouse while they constructed the north jetty in the bay. From 1906 to 1933, the U.S. Life Saving Service (later called the U.S. Coast Guard) used the lighthouse as living quarters and a lookout station until their new compound was constructed near the water front.

The lighthouse is the only combination lightkeeper's quarters and lighthouse still standing on the Oregon coast.

In 1934, the Oregon State Highway Commission acquired the property around the lighthouse for a park, and in 1946, the state proposed demolishing the lighthouse since it was considered a safety hazard. The Lincoln County Historical Society was formed in 1948 to save the structure, and although the state delayed the demolition, the historical society was unable to raise the money to restore the building. In 1951, with the cause considered hopeless, a farewell party was held when the wrecking crew was reported to be on the way. However, the state relented again.

In 1955, the state decided that the lighthouse had scenic and historic interest, and the historical society began to use the building as a museum. Restoration of the lighthouse was completed in 1975. Today, a non-profit group, Yaquina Lights Inc., works with the Oregon State Parks Department to operate the lighthouse.

Setting

The combination lighthouse and keeper's quarters is located high up on a bluff. A stairway and path lead up to the building, which has sweeping views of the ocean and Yaquina Bay.

Exterior

The lighthouse has a classic box shape with a side-gabled roof. Its Folk Victorian style is based on a basic house shape with limited decoration, generally on the porch or cornice. In this case, the porch has the greatest amount of decoration, with jigsaw-cut brackets on the posts and jigsaw-cut ornaments on the porch roof. However, necessity was chosen over architectural considerations when the lighthouse was built, as a downspout ran across the western side of the front facade in order to connect to the cistern on the side.

A long woodshed extends out from the back of the house. The woodshed was important since the house had five fireplaces and one wood-burning stove for warmth and cooking. According to the plans, a water closet was to be installed at the end of the woodshed, so that in stormy weather the covered walkway could protect those who needed to visit it.

Interior

The sign on the entry door asks visitors to close the door due to the strong winds blowing off the ocean. Once inside, the double stairway visible from the hall in this small house suggests its special use.

For those preferring an overview of the house before they see it, a video about the lighthouse is shown in the basement. The bricks in the basement floor reportedly served as a ship's ballast from San Francisco.

The organ in the parlor displays the sheet music of a song called "The Lighthouse." A sewing basket rests on the table near an armchair, and a white handkerchief stained with drops of blood is among the basket items, representing the legend of the lighthouse. In 1899, Lischen Miller wrote a story entitled "The Haunted Light at Newport by the Sea" for the magazine *Pacific Monthly*. Miller wrote about Muriel Trevenard who along with some friends was exploring the old building. Muriel dropped her handkerchief, and returned alone to the room on the third floor to retrieve it. Her friends outside the lighthouse heard a blood-curdling scream, and when they returned inside they found the bloody handkerchief and blood on the floor in the hall, on the stairs, and in the upper chamber. Her body was never located, and one of her friends carried the handkerchief "next to his heart till the hour of his own tragic death."

In Miller's story, the haunting is in the form of moaning, cries for help, and a light shining from the lighthouse. Stories of a ghost do persist at the lighthouse. A curator of the local historical society reported in the

The basket on the floor in the parlor contains a handkerchief with bloodstains, representing the story of Muriel Trevenard, who mysteriously disappearance in the building and now supposedly haunts it.

October 19, 1975, *Eugene Register-Guard* that members of the Coast Guard on duty at the tower adjacent to the lighthouse have seen unexplained lights. While alone in the lighthouse, the curator herself has heard footsteps overhead.

The dining room, also at the front of the house, has the best view of any room on the ground floor. A small table now stands in the middle of the room, although the Peirces' table would have been larger to seat their family. The current chairs hold the body stiff and straight when sitting. During Victorian times, dining was a formal affair, and good posture was encouraged.

A framed hair decoration hangs over the dining-room fireplace, although Victorian women would likely have placed such handiwork in the parlor, where art objects and handicraft items were displayed. Nevertheless, this is an excellent opportunity to view an intricate hair weaving. On the other wall, a Currier & Ives print shows Chicago burning during the great 1871 conflagration; the caption states that one hundred fifty thousand people became homeless and five hundred lives were lost. If this lithograph had actually been displayed in a house, perhaps it was for homeowners to feel relief that whatever their situation might be, it was not as bad as that of Chicago residents in 1871.

The original hand pump, still in place by the kitchen sink, provided water to wash dishes, but drinking water had to be hauled up to the house by horse. The Peirces were relatively lucky in the location of the lighthouse, for instead of being in a lonely place miles from stores, they could walk to the merchants lining Yaquina Bay (now Newport's Old Town).

Schoolbooks from the 1870s are displayed in the built-in cupboard in the room opposite the kitchen. One of them, the Brooks Elementary Arithmetic from 1873, announces it contains the "New Normal Menial Arithmetic," showing that "new math" is nothing new. A copy of the architect's original floor plans for the lighthouse hangs on another wall. While these plans show this room as the oil room, the built-in cupboard and chair railing like that in kitchen and dining room suggest that the builder changed the plans during construction and the room was perhaps used as a library or study.

The large Peirce family undoubtedly appreciated the four bedrooms upstairs, although historians believe that the small room right of the head of the stairs likely was occasionally used by the lighthouse supervisor. A small room on the third floor, reportedly the location of Muriel's disappearance, was the watch room and a place where Peirce could supervise the lantern, which needed to be monitored in case it went out. The children sometimes assisted their father, relieving him of the burden

This bedroom, outfitted as the parents' room, overlooks the ocean and has one of the best views in the house.

of being awake at night from dusk to dawn. An excerpt from "Instructions and Directions to Light-House and Light-Vessel Keepers" is posted on the wall near a now off-limits ladder leading to the light. It reads, "Every evening, half an hour before sunset, the keeper provided with a lighting lamp, will ascend to the lantern of the tower and commence lighting the lamps." Constancy was required to prevent accidents and save lives.

Butterfield Cottage

Built: 1893

at the Seaside Museum
570 Necanicum Drive
Seaside
503-738-7065 (museum)

Seaside was already a vacation destination when Horace Seely Butterfield built this cottage in 1893. Horace and his brother Albert had purchased two lots on Second Street (now N. Columbia Street) between Oceanway Street and Broadway the prior year. The two brothers built identical cottages, each with a kitchen, dining and living room, and two bedrooms on the second floor.

Directions: From the main intersection in town at S. Holladay Drive and Broadway Street, head north on S. Holladay Street. Turn left on Fourth Avenue and cross the river. Turn right on Necanicum Drive. The museum is on your left.

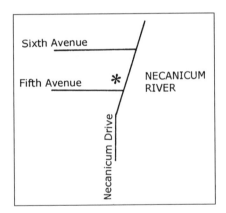

Open: Year around
Hours: Winter, 12:00–3:00; Summer, 10:00–4:00
Admission: $2.00 adults; $1.50 seniors; $1.00 students; children under twelve free
Tour: Guided
Entry: At the museum building

Additional Attractions: The admission price includes a visit to the adjoining Seaside Museum, which has exhibits depicting aspects of local history. Be sure to see the large black-and-white photograph of the Seasider Hotel on the wall and the diorama to get a sense of where the house was located in town.

History

The Butterfield brothers operated the first wholesale jewelry and optical goods company business in Portland. Horace Butterfield, who had been born in 1860, married Genevieve Newman in 1887, and they named their daughter Genevieve.

The brothers' cottages were built as summer residences, and were among the first houses built in Seaside (then called Grimes Grove). Most early visitors stayed in hotels or lived in "tent cities." About 1903, Albert Butterfield constructed five more identical cottages, three of which were along the Prom and faced the ocean. The Butterfield families then likely occupied the cabins with the better view when they vacationed.

Guy DeGolia, a carpenter living in Gearhart, became the caretaker of the cottages in 1907. He married Emelia Emma Bitterling about 1912, and for a time the couple lived in Albert Butterfield's first cottage before moving to Horace's vacation home. Altha, Emelia's daughter from a prior marriage, returned to Seaside about 1914 and helped with the caretaker duties for several years.

Horace Butterfield died in 1917, and Albert's first cottage burned that same year. Through several ownerships and two more marriages, Emelia Bitterling was an intermittent caretaker in the cottage. In 1960, George and Marion Roberts, who had moved to Seaside from Klamath Falls, used the cottage as the "House of Roberts," a millinery shop, and subsequent businesses included an antique shop and art gallery. In 1984, the cottage was donated to the Seaside Historical Society and moved from its original site that was being redeveloped for a commercial building to the property owned by the historical society.

The rehabilitation of the cottage was controversial, as the historical society needed to raise funds, and was unsure whether the effort to save the cottage was warranted. Local residents complained about the appearance of the disheveled building as it rested on blocks, and the historical society ran advertisements in the *Daily Astorian* for offers to move or salvage the cottage. With no takers, they contemplated turning it over to the Seaside Volunteer Fire Department, which planned to burn it for fire-fighting practice. Finally, in September 1985, society members voted to restore the structure.

Setting

The cottage looks east towards the Necanicum River. A garden around the building now makes it look homelike in its site near the Seaside Museum.

Exterior

The Butterfield cottage appears unbalanced as the two twentieth-century additions visible from the front were constructed for space rather than aesthetics. The initial design was symmetrical, a tall and narrow two-story house with a front gable. The original shape of the house can still be imagined if you mentally eliminate the one-story extension on the south side and the dormer and everything under the elongated gable on the north side.

The Butterfields had their cottage designed in the Stick architectural style, an appropriate choice for a beach house. The style was considered appropriate for a resort, since Richard Morris Hunt designed several exuberant examples built in Newport, Rhode Island. The style features horizontal and vertical bands on exterior walls that vaguely mimic the exposed structural members of medieval half-timbered houses. The bands,

This modest beach cottage is tied to Seaside's early history.

less apparent on the Butterfield cottage, are concentrated around the first floor windows. The cottage's gable roof has a decorative truss at the apex, another characteristic of Stick style houses.

Interior

The door now serving as the front entry leads to a hall that is part of the later addition. A black-and-white photograph on the far wall in the parlor shows the tall and narrow house as it was originally built. Draped between the front porch posts is a string of wooden fishing floats that adds a nautical flavor.

The photograph shows a tall chimney. A fireplace in the living room and the stove in the kitchen provided the heat for the house, with driftwood from the beach as the fuel. When the house was moved to its present site, the parlor wall with the fireplace caved in. Although the historical society president carefully set aside the bricks for a subsequent rebuilding, the next day she discovered that a workman had placed them in a burn pile, making them scorched and unusable. Today, a metal fireplace rests against the wall, waiting the time when the historical society has the resources to rebuild the fireplace.

The historical society decided to use the house to interpret beachside living in 1912, about the time the house was wired for electricity. The descendants of Flora Elizabeth Sohns, who had decorated a Seaside house in 1912, provided some of the furniture, including the wicker settee and the round oak dining room table and chairs. Sohns had been both smart and lucky. A divorcée with two children, she planned to marry a wealthy Portland man, although his parents objected to the match because of her marital status and poverty. In return for her signing away any claim to his inheritance, Sohns demanded $2,000 up front, with which she purchased a lot in Seaside, built a house, and furnished it. After they were married, her husband and his parents died without eliminating her from their wills and she subsequently inherited all of the estate.

Sohns's wicker settee followed the tastes of the time. Wicker had grown steadily in popularity since the late nineteenth century, when Victorian tastes focussed on nature and plants. In the early years of the twentieth century, wicker furniture became associated with resorts and country homes with brand names of the day such as Bar Harbor, Cape Cod, Newport, and Southampton, and it is appropriate that Sohns decorated her Seaside house with wicker.

The Victrola in the living room is the same vintage as the furniture, as evidenced by the August, 1913, *Ladies Home Journal* advertisement propped up nearby. The copy advises that you "take a Victrola with you when you go away this summer." The illustrations suggest places where it could be enjoyed: during an impromptu dance, on a porch, on the water, and while camping (doubtless provoking the first "Turn that darn thing down!"). For those unable to afford a trip after purchasing the machine, the advertisement helpfully suggests that it will "give you a delightful 'vacation' right at home."

A fold-down bed once in the kitchen served as the summer sleeping quarters for Emelia Bitterling's daughter, Altha, who lived in the cottage until 1922 while her mother was the caretaker. Summer accommodations were difficult to find in the beach town, and the two took in boarders during the season. Another alternative for visitors was the tent city that stood behind the Butterfield house. The tents were lined up in rows on the lot, each furnished with two double beds and a woodstove. The amenities included outdoor privies, running water, and stacks of wood.

For most of the year, Emelia Bitterling slept in the downstairs bedroom, although her thriftiness caused her to rent out her room in the summer and she then slept in the woodshed. The bedroom set from Sohns's 1912 house now stands in Bitterling's former room. The entrepreneurial spirits of both these women intersect in this room today.

A tall replica of a six-story tower covered in shells stands in the short hall by the kitchen. Originally, the staircase began here and doglegged up to the second floor. The historical society altered it to its present design to accommodate visitors. The daughter's upstairs bedroom, in the original part of the house, is now used as a storage space.

The Phillips family, another long-time Seaside family, sponsored the room across the hall from the storage space in memory of Edna Phillips, whose countenance is angelically illustrated in the portrait above the bed. A black-and-white photograph of Edna Phillips and her brother John with their nanny hangs just to the right. Including the nanny in the formal portrait suggests that the family held her in esteem, although her face suggests what might have been chronic glumness.

A window over the hall stairs provides a glimpse of the Necanicum River. While the Butterfield cottage was originally constructed facing the ocean, the demand for high value commercial lots near the beach has relegated the cottage to a secondary site facing the river.

Columbia Gorge

Surgeon's Quarters &
Anderson Farmhouse

National Register of Historic Places
Built: 1856 (Surgeon's Quarters), 1895 (Anderson Farmhouse)
Fort Dalles Museum
Fifteenth and Garrison streets
The Dalles, OR
541-296-4547 (museum)

The main building at the Fort Dalles Museum is the Surgeon's Quarters, the largest structure left from the 1850s army outpost constructed to protect settlers on the Oregon Trail from the Indians. The museum collection includes artifacts from the fort as well as items pertaining to local history.

Also on the museum property is the Anderson Farmhouse, barn, and granary, which was moved from a farm south of The Dalles.

Directions: Heading eastbound on Interstate 84, take Exit 84; heading westbound, take Exit 85. Follow signs to the city center. Once downtown, turn south on Union Street, away from the river, and go up the hill to the intersection of Thirteenth Street. Turn right and travel four blocks and turn left on Garrison Street. Go two blocks; the museum is on your right.

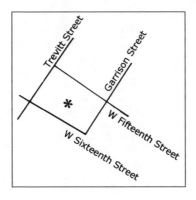

Open: Memorial Day through Labor Day, daily. Call for winter schedule
Hours: 10:00–5:00
Admission: $3.00 person; under eighteen free
Tour: Self-guided, except the Anderson Farmhouse
Entry: At the kitchen door of the Surgeon's Quarters
Additional Attractions: About four blocks away is the Rorick house, which was a noncommissioned officer's house. This quirky museum reflects the more contemporary life of Eck and May Rorick (see page 192).

Surgeon's Quarters (1856)

History

In 1848, a volunteer militia, responding to the Northwest Indian attack on the Whitman mission, occupied the Methodist mission buildings in The Dalles. The first U.S. Army troops in the Northwest stopped there in 1849, with some returning early in 1850 to construct a small post. With the help of local settlers, they erected a log barracks and several buildings, but the structures were of primitive construction with dirt floors.

In 1853, in response to a donation law amendment that allowed forts to reserve 640 acres, Commanding Officer Brevet Major Benjamin Alvord changed the name from "Camp Drum" to "Fort Drum" (even though the facility was never stockaded) and shortly afterwards the name was changed to "Fort Dalles." Colonel George Wright arrived in 1856, and the fort became busy. Treaties from the Yakima Indian War had to be enforced, and Fort Dalles became the headquarters for the regiment and the supply post for Forts Simcoe and Walla Walla, located to the north and east in present-day Washington State.

Assistant Quartermaster Captain Thomas Jordan, with the help of his civilian clerk, Louis Scholl, directed the construction of new fort buildings. Louis Scholl, a German immigrant, had studied engineering, drafting, art, and music, and he used an 1850 house plan book by Andrew Jackson Downing for the fort buildings that were situated around a grassy parade ground. Timber was cut nearby and sawn at the fort's mill, and sandstone was quarried at a nearby bluff. The doors, windows, and mantelpieces were hand-planed by personnel.

The Surgeon's Quarters, the smallest of the houses, cost less than $5,000 to construct in 1856. Scholl called Colonel Wright's house "the finest in all of Oregon." It cost $22,000, but astonished settlers labeled it the "$100,000 house."

The cost also astonished the federal government inspectors, who immediately forbade any further expenditure. Both Jordan and Wright were criticized for the ornate design and the anticipated cost of upkeep. However, the two men tried to refute the charges by noting that all construction on the frontier was costly due to the scarcity of material and labor. In addition, some of the expense attributed to Fort Dalles had funded other posts. Their protests went unheard.

By 1867, three of the officers' houses had burned down due to faulty mortar and the fort was no longer active. A caretaker lived in the Surgeon's Quarters until the mid-1880s, when the remaining buildings were left to squatters. After the turn of the twentieth century, local women banded together to save the Surgeon's Quarters, enlisting the help of the Oregon Historical Society. It opened as a museum in 1905, and is one of the oldest in the state.

Setting

The Surgeon's Quarters sits on the upper slopes of The Dalles on the former site of the fort. On the grounds are two iron fences that were originally part of the guardhouse. Two stands of ponderosa pine on the grounds are located where the commanding office's house and the major and captain's duplex stood. The only other surviving fort building on the grounds is the gardener's cottage, which with its small size illustrates the difference in quarters allotted to enlisted men and officers.

Historic cars, wagons, and stagecoaches from the Wasco County area are located in the barn and shed.

Exterior

Although the visitors' entrance is at the back of the house, the best view is of the front façade. Julia Gilliss, whose husband was stationed at the fort, described in an 1866 letter to her family that the Surgeon's Quarters and the quartermaster's house (which would burn down in 1867) were "very pretty Gothic villas." Ninety years later, Marion D. Ross, a University of Oregon professor, wrote that the Surgeon's Quarters was "one of the loveliest little buildings in the state."

In 1850, six years before the Surgeon's Quarters was built, Andrew Jackson Downing wrote a revolutionary book entitled *The Architecture of Country Houses,* which extolled the virtues of single-family homes and presented designs and floor plans. Downing divided houses into three categories, and the Surgeon's Quarters is modeled fairly closely after a design for a "Symmetrical Bracketed Cottage."

Because the design is an east coast idea imported directly to the West, the architecture is sophisticated in comparison to other Oregon structures of the time. Downing called the style "Picturesque," but today the style of the Surgeon's Quarters is more commonly called Gothic Revival due to its steep gable roof, center gable, and triangular arch windows. Embellishing Downing's plan, the architect designed triangular arches for the door opening and sidelights that mimic the above windows. The structure has board and batten siding. Downing wrote that he preferred a cottage of brick or stone, though if it had to be of wood it should be of vertical boards because that would provide "strength and truthfulness."

Interior

On the wall by the entrance door, a photograph shows Ezra Meeker and his oxen with President Theodore Roosevelt in front of the War and Army Building in Washington, D.C. Meeker, an advocate for marking and remembering the Oregon Trail, traveled it by wagon in 1852 and traveled the reverse of the route with oxen in 1906 and 1910, by car in 1915, and by plane in 1924. On the opposite wall, a map of the "Military Reservation at Fort Dalles" shows roughly how the fort was designed. Necessities

The Surgeon's Quarters, the largest structure left from Fort Dalles, has been called "one of the loveliest little buildings in the state."

such as a cemetery (indicated by small crosses) and stables are depicted. The map, however, was probably drawn in Washington, D.C., by someone who never had visited the fort, as it shows buildings that were never constructed and structures with the wrong shape.

The visitor first should venture to the front hall to get the best sense of the house and the front door from the inside. The location of the built-in cabinet in the foyer is unusual. One theory is that medicine was stored there, and the surgeon saw patients in the hall. Scholl likely designed this cabinet, as he designed other items at the fort such as the captain's desk, officers' bedsteads, and even an oil can.

The architect designed the built-in cabinet, as well as furniture for the fort.

Gillis wrote to her family in 1866 that her parlor furniture in the quartermaster's house included "relics of the furniture grandeur that formerly reigned here [and] several wooden armchairs belonging to the Post." Today, the parlor in the Surgeon's Quarters also includes donated furniture. A black leather settee, rocker, and chair display carved leopard faces in the armrests and paws for feet. Also in the room stands a combination bookcase and desk that were once owned by Dr. William Shackelford, who came to The Dalles in the 1850s. After the army left the fort, he remained in the area and developed a private practice. Perhaps because she understood the importance of a doctor's contribution, his wife Roxa was instrumental in saving the Surgeon's Quarters.

A framed wreath of human hair hangs on one wall in the parlor, while a cross and another wreath, also of human hair, hang in the former dining room. The dining room now displays the museum's arrowheads, photographs, and items related to the steamboat era.

The Gothic style windows visible in the second-floor hall are an indication of the attention paid to detail. In the bedroom on the left, a detailed wooden mystery object, about six feet high, shows another kind of devotion. A dedicated parishioner gave the Sisters of the Holy Name this item, but its intended use is unknown.

The spool bed came from England in 1864, but it was not always held in such high regard; it was once used as a roosting place for chickens before it was rescued. Nearby, a table designed by Scholl is further evidence of the extent of his design work. The bonnet under glass on top of the table was, according to a family lore, worn at Ford's Theater the night that Abraham Lincoln was assassinated.

The second bedroom displays guns and saddles. Over the fireplace, a framed advertisement of Winchester Repeating Arms Co. exhibits the company's assorted inventory of bullets and shells, clustered to form a large "W."

Anderson Farmhouse (1895)

History

Lewis Anderson was born in Sweden in 1859. At age fourteen, he went to sea as a cabin boy and traveled around the world several times. Anderson paid a sailor a penny a lesson to teach him English, and when he was twenty came back to Sweden to find that his sister Anna had joined a group planning to immigrate to America. Because of his knowledge of the language, he was persuaded to join them. (He once related that his sister's group shanghaied him and he awoke on ship to find a lump on his head.) He accompanied the immigrants to New York and then to a logging camp near Lake Michigan.

Lewis Anderson was dining in a railroad cafe in Milwaukee, Wisconsin, when he met the red-haired Carrie Jackobson, a Norwegian waitress. They married in 1878, and after the birth of two children, began planning to move to the Pacific Northwest. They chose Goldendale, Washington, because the name seemed promising. Goldendale, however, was sparsely settled and in the midst of an Indian uprising, so the Andersons decided to go to the "first place with trees," which was The Dalles.

While being employed at the Oregon Railway & Navigation Company, Lewis Anderson met two men who interested him in an available homestead on Pleasant Ridge, south of The Dalles. For the first summer, the Andersons camped by the creek and began planting a garden and building a cabin. By this time, they had four children. Although they farmed, Lewis Anderson continued to work at the railroad. He walked fourteen miles to town every week and walked home on weekends because it was too expensive to stable horses in town.

The Andersons erected the barn, the first main structure, in 1890. The house was constructed five years later. The granary had been a homestead cabin during the 1880s, but Lewis dismantled it, moved it to the farm, and reconstructed it in 1898. Because of its solid walls, it was ideally suited to be a granary.

Lewis and Carrie Anderson eventually divided the farm between their four children and retired to The Dalles. Carrie Anderson died in 1922, and Lewis eleven years later. The house was occupied until the 1950s before gradually falling into disrepair. A grandson donated the house, barn, granary, and outhouse to Wasco County in 1972, and these buildings were transferred to the site of the fort.

Setting

Today, the house sits a few feet behind a cyclone fence, although it was originally built on acreage and had a number of outbuildings, including the granary and the two-level barn. The Andersons' Swedish neighbors helped with the barn raising, and according to the couple's daughter-in-law, "The barn was constructed very rapidly because with a Swede on every corner, it didn't take very long."

Lewis Anderson was not a much of a farmer; he once admitted to engaging a neighbor in conversation just so that he could figure out how the neighbor's team of horses were directed to stay together and go in the same direction. However, inside the barn he was innovative; holes through the floor made it easy to drop hay from the loft into the feeding bins in the daylight basement. He also designed the log thresher shaped into a cone that lies on the floor, although apparently this was not successful.

Exterior

Although lumber was widely available in 1895, perhaps Lewis Anderson wanted a house that reminded him of his native land. The house and the nearby barn are exceptional examples of Scandinavian-American construction, following the tradition of log cabin building techniques that Swedish immigrants brought to the United States in the seventeenth century. Swedish descendants Ab Pearson and his son were the builders of the Anderson house, although Anderson is believed to have been the designer. He also cut and hewed the yellow pine logs himself while camping four miles from his homestead. The logs are joined so tightly that, unlike in most log houses, chinking was not necessary.

Despite lumber being widely available, the Andersons built a
two-story hewn log house in 1895.

The house has two and a half stories, which is unusual for a log building. Lewis Anderson reportedly stated before construction started he would probably be like that man who planned a big house when he cut the first log, then decrease the size of the house in half while he cut the second log, and decided after the third log that the old house would do. This proved not to be the case; when the Pearsons reached the gables, a dispute ensued over the height of the house and Lewis Anderson had to pay an extra $10.00 to raise the walls another two feet. The Anderson house was not all hand-made, since the windows and doors were of commercial manufacture.

Interior

The front door opens immediately into the living room. While the interior now appears rustic, when the Andersons lived there the ceiling was whitewashed and wallpaper graced the walls. A woodstove kept the room warm, and a chaise lounge and platform rocker helped to furnish the room.

The Andersons slept in a small room off the living room. A second bedroom, only large enough for a bed and table, once occupied the back of the house, although the wall placement has been altered. Nearby, Carrie Anderson loomed and sewed in what was a small enclosed room under the stairs.

Despite the availability of modern conveniences, the Andersons chose to live simply.

The original woodstove included a tank for heating water. Water was a problem in the original location in Pleasant Valley, and a cistern holding rainwater located in a small room off the back entrance supplied the water for the household. The kitchen now contains a sink with a pump, a later addition. Even though the house was last occupied in the 1950s, an inside toilet was never one of its luxuries. From the kitchen window, you can see the outhouse, now ramshackle and ivy-covered, which was also moved to this site.

A stairway off the kitchen leads up to a long hall, which accesses two large bedrooms. Although no longer open, an attic above provided more room. Its walls were once papered with the Salvation Army's *War Cry* newspaper and others from 1898, and for years the house's inhabitants could read about the effects of the Sino-Japanese war and other turn-of-the-twentieth-century events.

Rorick House

National Register of Historic Places
Built: circa 1850 (original section)
300 W. Thirteenth Street
The Dalles
541-296-1867 (museum)

While the nucleus of the Rorick house was the home of a noncommissioned officer stationed at what would become Fort Dalles, the museum really offers a view of an ordinary couple's life and the things that they would have had around them in the middle of the twentieth century. It is a bit like snooping through someone's personal things, but since Eck Rorick bequeathed the house and all its contents to the Wasco County Historical Society, he must have wanted it that way.

Directions: Heading east on Interstate 84, take Exit 84; heading west, take Exit 85. Follow signs to the city center. Once downtown, turn south on Union Street, away from the river, and go up the hill to the intersection of Thirteenth Street. Turn right and travel two blocks; the house is on your left at the corner of Thirteenth and Lincoln streets.

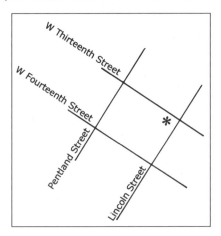

Open: Memorial Day through Labor Day, Friday–Sunday
Hours: 10:00–4:00
Admission: Donation

Tour: Guided
Entry: At the front door
Additional Attractions: The Surgeon's Quarters and Anderson farmhouse are located at the Fort Dalles Museum (see page 183).

History

The Rorick house consists of various additions constructed over about a hundred years. Historians believe that the central section was constructed about 1850 by a noncommissioned officer stationed at the U.S. Army post later called Fort Dalles. After the fort was disbanded and the federal government offered the buildings for sale, Malcolm Moody purchased the house in 1884. Between 1900 and 1915, he constructed a fireplace using the stone blocks from the fort's bakery, and added a bathroom wing on the east side.

Malcolm Moody died in 1925 and willed the house to Annie and Elizabeth Lang, sisters for both of whom he had felt unrequited love. The sisters never lived in the house, but sold it four years later to newlyweds Estell (Eck) and May Rorick. When the couple added a bedroom in

The core of the house was a noncommissioned Fort Dalles officer's quarters, but the dwelling has been expanded over the years.

1933, they found *New York Times* newspapers dating from the 1850s used as wall insulation.

The Roricks enlarged the kitchen and added a family room to the back of the house in the early 1950s. They spent most of their married life in the house. May Rorick died in 1986, and Eck then moved to a nursing home. He died in 1991, and bequeathed the house to the Wasco County Historical Society, which still runs the house.

Setting

May Rorick was a devout gardener, and the Wasco County Master Gardeners are restoring the grounds in the style of a 1940s cottage garden. Behind the house, a brick path meanders among the trees.

Exterior

The house began with cabin-like proportions, and over the years rambled to the east, west, and south as the owners saw fit to expand. Today, the different additions are discernible by the varying roofs. The entire exterior displays board and batten siding, which contributes to a sense that the house is one unit.

Since the construction date of the house is not precisely known, the historical society has placed a sign along the fence which reads "Built (about) 1850." This is one clue that the Rorick house is a quirky museum; another is the sign hanging from the tree that announces, "The Rorick's." Even the vinyl floor mat at the front door still declares their name.

Interior

On the inside, one would expect the house to be outfitted like a cabin, but the furnishings are quite different. Rather than reflecting its status as one of the oldest houses in The Dalles, the building portrays a home from the 1950s and 1960s. After Eck Rorick moved to a nursing home, the house was closed, and there was no family member to receive the possessions. Today, the house looks much as it did when the Roricks lived there. It is as if they went to the store and will return shortly.

Four casual chairs, one displaying a head of a horse stitched on its back and yokes for arm rests, echo the tan tones that predominate through the house. Light-colored wood was popular during the 1950s and 1960s, and the Roricks obviously liked it very much.

The house rests on slabs of basalt, and the steps up to the various spaces like that near the fireplace reflect the increase in the grade of the

The museum still displays the Rorick possessions that were in the house when Eck bequeathed it to the historical society.

rock. The Roricks added bookshelves and seating in front of the fireplace mantel to create an intimate space. Playing cards laying on the coffee table suggest that the Roricks must have spent many cozy evenings entertaining in this area. Although the basalt blocks forming the fireplace came from the Fort Dalles bakery (see Surgeon's Quarters at Fort Dalles, page 183), it is not known whether the stone came from the fireplace or the floor. One commemorative plate propped up in the windowsill displays a picture of the fort bakery.

Eck Rorick financed most of his education to Oregon State College (now Oregon State University) by playing in an orchestra that he started. While he lived in this house in the early 1930s, he and an orchestra played in towns from Goldendale to Bend. His baby grand piano, painted tan color to match the rest of the woodwork, stands in what normally would have been the dining room. The piano was not fully utilized, however, as Eck reportedly only played the black keys.

In the album on top of the piano, the personalized Christmas cards over the years suggest that the couple had a loving relationship. Their first meeting, however, was not friendly. While at college, Eck Rorick joined a fraternity, located a vacant lot away from the sorority to which

May Rorick even painted Eck's piano to match the rest of the woodwork in the house

May belonged. The sorority kept its supply of firewood on the vacant lot, and one day, the engineers at the fraternity determined by surveying and detailed measurements that the woodpile encroached on their property by four inches. Eck Rorick was sent over to inform the sorority that they had to move their firewood. May, as manager of the sorority, heard the request, and according to Eck later in *The Dalles Weekly Reminder*, "she promptly told me what I could do with the wood pile." Based on the success of his mission, his fraternity brothers then treated Eck Rorick to a tub of ice water.

May Rorick decorated the inside of the piano key cover and the cupboards throughout the house with tole painting. Originally, tole painting meant painting on thin metal, but its definition has evolved into decorative painting on many surfaces. At one point, while she was in the hospital, Eck Rorick would bring her one cupboard door at a time, and she would paint it in her hospital bed.

The bathroom is not usually open to the public, but it is worth a peek. The historical society has left much of the room the way it was when the Roricks lived there, and for those who enjoy snooping through other people's bathrooms, this is one place where it is permissible. The towels still display the "R" initial. May Rorick must have used "Smooth and Sleek Toni" for curling her hair, since a box stands on a nearby shelf. Their preferred air freshener is "April in Paris." The color of the "Klean-M-Klean" suede shoe dressing is bright red, suggesting that May Rorick had flamboyant-hued footwear.

May Rorick was the home economics teacher at The Dalles High School, and also served as the women's editor on *The Chronicle* newspaper. Fittingly, part of the wall in the family room, built on to the house in 1950, is filled with cookbooks. The usual classics are there: *White House Cookbook*, *The Joy of Cooking*, and *Beard on Food*. May Rorick, however, must have had a sense of humor, as her shelves also included a volume of Peg Bracken's 1960 irreverent classic, *The I Hate to Cook Book*. (One memorable line from a recipe is "Let it cook for five minutes while you light a cigarette and stare sullenly at the sink.") May Rorick's collection also includes *Caldron Cookery, An Authentic Guide for Coven Connoisseurs*. Recipes include a "Love Potion," "To Make Men Appear Headless," and "To Become Invisible."

The black-and-white photograph showing May Rorick roasting meat in the fireplace gives further evidence that few things have been disturbed in the house. The carriage lamps are still affixed to the brick, and by the fireplace rest the bellows.

The Roricks slept in a small, unpretentious bedroom off the living room. The biplane stands on the shelves above the bed, just as Eck Rorick, a former World War I pilot, would have enjoyed seeing it. On the dresser stands a white statue of the Virgin Mary, another piece of evidence that the things in the Rorick house once made it a home.

Eastern Oregon

Adler House

Built: 1889

2305 Main Street
Baker City
541-523-9308 (Oregon Trail Regional Museum)

Of Oregon's historic museum houses, the Adler house stands out for its fine display of reproduction wallpaper. The house also has an extensive collection of Victorian furniture that actually belonged to the Adler family. Both the furniture and the wallpaper afford a glimpse of middle-class Victorian interiors.

Directions: From Interstate 84, take Exit 304 and follow the signs to city center, which will place you on Campbell Street. After you have turned left onto Main Street, the house is located two blocks south on the right.

Open: June to October, Thursday–Sunday
Hours: Thursday–Saturday, 1:00–4:00; Sunday, 11:00–2:00
Admission: $5.00 per person; $15.00 families
Tour: Guided
Entry: At the front door
Additional Attractions: The Oregon Trail Regional Museum, which has exhibits on local history, is located a short distance away at 2480 Grove Street (call 541-523-9308 for admission and hours).

History

The Adler house is a mirror image to the privately owned Baer house, which stands on the same block at 2333 Main Street. J. E. Baisley constructed the Baer dwelling in 1882, and used the same floor plan seven years later for the Adler house. The Baers were related to the Adlers. Sam Baer had married Laura Adler's sister, and the Adlers had moved from Astoria to Baker City so that the two sisters could live in the same town. When his wife died, Sam Baer married the third sister.

Leo Adler was born in 1895 in Baker City, the youngest of three children. His parents, Carl and Laura Adler, owned the Crystal Palace, a jewelry and glassware shop which also at one time sold everything from bicycles to musical instruments. At the age of nine, Leo Adler peddled the *Saturday Evening Post* and the *Ladies Home Journal*. After graduating from Baker High School, he followed his father's advice to "stay at home and get a head start while the others are in college." In this case, it was sage advice. By the age of twenty, he was operating a magazine distribution business that eventually employed a staff of thirty. When Leo Adler retired at the age of seventy-seven, his business covered seven states with two thousand outlets selling more than three million magazines annually.

Despite his fortune, he was frugal in some aspects of his living. He continued to live in the family home, eventually using only four rooms on the ground floor. He never wired the upstairs for electricity. In other ways, he lived well. He dined out every night, and frequently bought a round of drinks. A lover of baseball, he attended twenty consecutive World Series. A Baker City acquaintance reported that Leo Adler once "called from Palm Springs, tipsy, partying with Roy Rodgers and Dale Evans."

Though he never married, for many years he had a woman friend named Zella Smurthwaite, who worked for his company and died in 1990. When Leo Adler died in 1993, he had accumulated a fortune of twenty million dollars that was bequeathed to a foundation designed to help Baker County residents. The foundation provides college scholarships to those who graduate from local high schools, and grants to other community groups, such as the Little League and the Baker City library.

Baker County currently owns the museum.

Setting

Once surrounded by an orchard, garden, barn, and stable, the house now stands on the edge of downtown on what appears to be a typical residential lot.

Exterior

The Adler and the Baer houses exhibit an Italianate style with a hipped roof and tall windows with window hoods supported by brackets. Finely detailed brackets are also under the eaves. Like the Baer house, the Adler home has two-story bay windows that flank the entrance and emphasize the structure's vertical appearance.

The Adler House has a foundation of tuff blocks, a material which is initially soft when quarried and hardens over time. Tuff has contributed to Baker City's distinctiveness. After the turn of the twentieth century, local builders began using it on the exterior of significant structures such as the city hall and courthouse. From the Adler front yard, a visitor looking southwest can see a portion of the 1905 St. Francis Cathedral and 1907 rectory, both constructed of tuff.

Although Leo Adler had $22 million when he died, he lived most of his life in this house.

Interior

The Adler house, like other Italianate houses, has double front doors under a transom that open to a small vestibule. A second pair of doors then leads to a central hall. Generally, the doors to the parlor on the right and to the family sitting room on the left would both have been closed off, leaving the hall somewhat dark in the daytime. (The electric lights along the south wall of the hall were added as a safety measure.)

Guests who were merely acquaintances would be ushered into the parlor, where they would have seen elaborately designed Victorian wallpapers that are similar to the reproductions hanging on the walls today. The Baker County Museum Commission spent about $20,000 on wallpaper for the first floor alone in an attempt to replicate the earlier Adler wallpapers covered during more recent remodeling. A member of the commission was delighted to discover that the Victorian reproduction wallpaper matched the Adler Victorian furniture.

The Eastlake parlor set in the Adler house once belonged to the Baers, Leo Adler's aunt on his mother's side. This set includes a settee, a ladies' chair, a gentlemen's chair, and, placed in the sitting room, a platform rocker with different upholstery. Augmenting the Adler collection is "Anglo-Japanese" furniture, so called because of the influence of the Japanese design. One example is the platform rocker in the parlor that has ebonized wood with incised gold. In the later years that Leo Adler lived in the house, most of this furniture, as well as the rest standing throughout the house, were crammed into the parlor and the adjacent dining room.

The two prints above the settee were hanging in those exact places when the museum commission took over the house. In the late 1880s and 1890s, art in a house expressed the refinement of its occupants, and Victorian homeowners would typically decorate with many art objects, creating an effect that would seem overwhelming to most homeowners today. On the opposite wall is a copy of an engraving of Johann Schiller enacting a part in his play *Don Carlos*, and, in the dining room, Shakespeare is reading his play *Macbeth*. Such prints were intended to suggest a level of culture and familiarity with those works.

Pocket doors separating the parlor from the dining room allowed the Adlers to expand their room for entertaining. A grander table than the one now standing in the dining room would have been located here. However, such a table was not among the furniture in the house when Leo Adler died, and it is possible that his brother Sanford took the table when he married.

Displayed in the dining room are examples of the Adler silver collection. In the process of cleaning the house after Leo Adler died, a volunteer found a heavy suitcase in the back of a closet. Inside were the individually wrapped pieces of the family's silver. Since the museum board members were unsure how to protect it, they took it to the county courthouse for safekeeping. Unfortunately, the county safe was full, so the treasure had to be locked in an old jail cell in the basement.

A less formal family dining room is located beyond the dining room. This room, as well as the kitchen, bathroom, and what is now decorated as Leo Adler's office were the four rooms in which he lived at the end of his life. He is said to have kept track of his millions in investments on a large table placed in the family dining room.

The bathroom off the kitchen was likely installed around 1915. When the museum commission took over the house, so much dry rot had developed under the tub that according to a president of the commission, "It's a wonder that it had not fallen into the basement." Maintenance must not have been a high priority to Leo Adler in his later years, as several doors still display claw marks from his German Shepherd.

Leo Adler maintained an office in a downtown building for several years, but commission members furnished one room of the house, originally a guestroom, as his office. One of the items displayed there is a *Saturday Evening Post* bag. Leo Adler peddled this magazine and the

The reproduction wallpaper and the family furniture
distinguish the museum.

The Adlers never wired the upstairs sitting area, nor the rest of the second floor, for electricity.

Ladies Home Journal when he was a boy, and according to the Adler foundation brochure, "his first business associate was his dog, Prince, who knew Leo's customers and routes as well as, if not better than, Leo."

About the time Carl Adler died, the family moved downstairs, perhaps as a cost-saving measure. This was practical, since the upstairs was not wired for electricity (the bedrooms still are not) and the only bathroom was located off the kitchen. Leo Adler's mother, Laura, occupied what was originally the guestroom, while his sister Theresa used the adjacent room. The iron and brass bed in this room is part of the Adler furniture collection. After the danger of germs was discovered by the experiments of Louis Pasteur and Robert Koch, furniture buyers, fearing that microbes lurked in thick upholstery and carved wooden frames, began purchasing iron and brass beds in the 1890s. The 1895 Montgomery Ward catalog reminded customers that iron and brass beds were "clean, no chance for vermin."

Theresa Adler, like Leo, never married, but her "Chap Record" on the desk by her bed suggests that she had plenty of opportunity. In the designated spaces, the girl is to record the name, date, and place of meetings with boys, and her opinion. Several pages are filled, not only about boys from Baker City, but from Eugene, San Francisco, and New York. One page, entitled "The Twelve Most Notable Chaps," provides blank spaces for the "handsomest," "youngest," "best name," "homeliest," "most hopeless," and, at the end, "the one." Theresa Adler never filled in this page, but she did write on the inside cover, "Beware to him who reads!"

A photograph of the family stands on the piano in the family sitting room. The family business, the Crystal Palace, also sold musical instruments, and the Ludwig & Co. piano, which Theresa played, likely came from their store. A piano in the house added status, suggesting not only that the family could afford a piano but that they could afford the lessons as well.

The upstairs walls still display the wallpaper that was hung before the Adlers moved downstairs about 1918. In the nursery, an iron hook stuck in the ceiling once held a kerosene lamp. The hook is not placed in the center of the ceiling, but rather on the joist. The ceiling paper shows another hole, as though someone had tried to find a joist and missed. Although the ceilings are now clean, volunteers worked for months to remove the soot deposited there by the smoking lamps, coal stoves, and the house's two coal fireplaces.

Theresa Adler's two theatrical costumes displayed in the nursery date from a time when movies and television did not exist and entertainment had to be self-created. Also in the nursery is a child's bed. The hole in the mesh in the center of the bed rusted out over the years, likely due to a number of "accidents."

The parents' room is a suite, encompassing two rooms in the front of the house on the second floor. Victorian women occasionally entertained in a sitting room off their bedroom, although this does seem a rather intimate practice in the context of the established formality of the parlors downstairs.

The Adler furniture collection included the overstuffed davenport and matching armchair, which are representative of the trend from "parlor" furniture to "living room" furniture after the turn of the twentieth century. The family also owned the armoire against the wall, which has a back that conveniently contains a folding bed. Despite his family's furniture collection in his possession, Leo Adler had little use for it, or even for more modern furniture later in his life. Though he could have well afforded to live in considerable comfort, it did not suit him.

Kam Wah Chung Museum

National Register of Historic Places

Built: circa 1867

Off N.W. Canton Street

John Day

541-575-0028 (John Day City Hall)

The Kam Wah Chung museum has one of the finest collections of original artifacts commemorating the nineteenth-century influx of Chinese immigrants into the West. Doc Hay vacated the building in 1948 and the structure stood untouched for twenty years. Today, the front door is a portal to another time.

Directions: From Highway 26 in John Day city limits, turn north on N.W. Canton Street and follow signs to the city park.

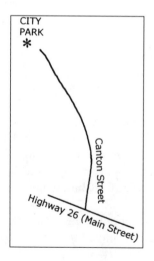

Open: May through October

Hours: Monday–Friday, 9:00–12:00 and 1:00–5:00; Saturday–Sunday 1:00–5:00

Admission: $3.00 per person

Tour: Guided

Entry: At the front door

Additional Attractions: The building stands adjacent to the John Day City Park, which has picnic tables and a children's play area.

History

Born in 1862, Ing Hay, or Doc Hay as he was later called, emigrated from southern China to North America with his father in 1883. Political unrest and a poor economic climate earlier had forced Doc Hay's five uncles, like many other Chinese males, to travel to the United States looking for prosperity. In 1887, his father returned to China, but Doc Hay moved to John Day, which along with the neighboring Canyon City, was once a major trading center for miners in the Eastern Oregon gold strikes.

Gold had been discovered in 1862 along Canyon Creek, which runs through Canyon City. By the early 1880s, the easily found gold was removed, but the methodical and patient Chinese miners panned for gold in the gravel banks left from the hydraulic and dredge mining. Shortly after moving to John Day, Doc Hay met Lung On, another Chinese immigrant from southern China who became his lifelong business partner and friend. Together with another Chinese partner (who may have soon sold out his share of the partnership), Doc Hay and Lung On purchased the Kam Wah Chung, which had been originally constructed as a trading post on The Dalles Military Road in 1866-67.

Kam Wah Chung, translated as "The Golden Flower of Prosperity," became the center of the Chinese community in Eastern Oregon. Initially, it sold both bulk lots to miners who came to John Day to stock up on provisions and individual items of daily use to the white community who found the location of the store convenient. The partners also were an important source of Chinese goods, such as food, books, and clothing. The Kam Wah Chung also had other roles, acting as a hiring hall for Chinese labor, a post office for Chinese immigrants, and a headquarters for religious needs.

In 1880, the Chinese population in John Day was nine hundred five; twenty years later it had dwindled to one hundred fourteen people, and by 1940, it was a mere twenty-one people. Although many Chinese had returned to their homeland, the two partners had remained. Lung On, who was extremely intelligent, had business interests in various places in the Pacific Northwest, while Doc Hay, a herbalist, had begun treating members of the white community as his reputation grew. Lung On died in 1940, but Doc Hay, almost totally blind, continued to live at the Kam Wah Chung until 1948, when he fell in the building and broke his hip. He then moved to a Portland nursing home, where he died in 1952.

His will bequeathed the Kam Wah Chung to Bob Wah, a relative and herbal doctor who had moved to John Day to be with him after Lung On died. Bob Wah deeded the property to the City of John Day in 1955 with the provision that the building be made into a museum to commemorate the Chinese contribution to the development of Eastern Oregon. The building stood dark and forgotten until the late 1960s when city workers began surveying the land around the structure for a park. In 1977, the museum opened.

Setting

Although the building once stood in the middle of the John Day Chinese district, this is the only building remaining from that time.

Exterior

Function was more important than the appearance of the Kam Wah Chung. The ground floor walls consist of volcanic rock, called rattlesnake tuff, cut into huge blocks. (One on the south wall is thirty-eight inches long.) The building has few windows, and the stone blocks create a fortress-like appearance that was helpful on Saturday nights when drunken ranch hands would have their fun by coming into town and shooting off their guns. A bullet hole in the iron plate that covered the front door likely remains from one of those incidents. In addition to protecting the inhabitants,

The exterior of the Kam Wah Chung is utilitarian and practical. The stone blocks helped preserve the artifacts which were untouched for twenty years.

the rock also moderated the temperatures inside the building, which helped to preserve the items inside over the years.

Around 1900, Lung On and Doc Hay built the addition on the north side, which is distinguished by its own gable roof. After 1900, they added a second story, which appears like a little house above the main section. According to one theory, the two were expecting that a new railroad line would be built through John Day, bringing more Chinese immigrants who would need a place to sleep. The railroad never came, and the space had only limited use for storage due to its narrow outside stairway.

Interior

The tour begins in the display room in the addition, the one place in the building that has been refurbished with a new floor, ceiling, and electric lights in order to illustrate aspects of the Chinese experience in John Day. The gradual acceptance of the Chinese who remained in John Day after long years of friction can be seen from the items in the glass cases around the room.

The Chinese in John Day celebrated the lunar New Year with fireworks like those hanging in one case and, by the 1920s, the local school closed so that the children could watch the celebration. In another exhibit case are Chinese gifts such as slippers and cups and saucers, which Doc Hay and Lung On gave to John Day residents, who in turn have gradually donated the items to the museum. A notebook above another glass case displays the $23,000 in uncashed checks that were found under Doc Hay's bed in the late 1960s. Perhaps he believed that the checks were "as good as money" and he hid them there because it was safe.

In the next room, the ceiling is still blackened from the opium smoke from the Chinese smoker reclining in one of the two bunk beds. The British introduced opium to the Chinese in the seventeenth century, and according to the *1911 Encyclopedia Britannica*, by 1906 over one in four Chinese males smoked opium. Perhaps at the Kam Wah Chung, a smoker could blissfully dream that he was home with the smells and sounds of a Chinese household in the background. In 1909, Congress banned the import of opium except for use in medicine, and it is likely that its use in the building stopped as well.

Besides the store, Lung On had numerous investments, including racehorses, stocks and bonds, and real estate in Washington and British Columbia. His sense of adventure had led him to the United States, and his intelligence helped him to prosper. On the wall opposite the beds is a photograph of the First National Bank building in Portland, with printed words calling him "a staunch friend and loyal supporter." Only a wealthy customer would have received such a plaque under the guise of "friendship."

As in many Chinese homes, Doc Hay and Lung On kept a shrine to the kitchen god Tsao Chun by their stove. This god not only watches over domestic affairs, but also enforced moral behavior, as he ascends to heaven every year during the Chinese New Year to present a report to the Jade Emperor. Customarily, the shrine includes a picture of the god, and believers smear his mouth with sugar or honey so that he may present a sweetened version of their actions. His ascent to heaven is accomplished by burning his image, and the rising smoke represents his journey to the Jade Emperor. While the Kam Wah Chung shrine is without a picture, an offering to the god—an orange and a pomegranate—has rested there in a shriveled state since the late 1940s.

From reports of local people, Doc Hay was skilled in the art and science of pulse diagnosis, or "pulsology," a fundamental part of Chinese traditional medicine. In the main room, a patient would enter the Kam Wah Chung, and place his arm on a pillow on the red table. Former patients have related that Doc Hay often told them what was wrong with them even before they related their symptoms. With fewer and fewer Chinese in the area, his practice grew to include white clients, and their trust in his methods over western medicine testifies to his abilities. His skill reportedly

The interior of the Kam Wah Chung reflects another time and place.

Doc Hay and Lung On used this primitive
kitchen for about sixty years.

even included diagnosing whether a woman was pregnant and the sex of
the child.

With such a gift, Doc Hay had to be careful with his hands. He never
handled anything rough, including coarse paper, which could rub the
delicate skin from his fingertips. To keep his fingers sensitive, he had to
rely on Lung On to drive him around in the buggy, and later, automobile.
Lung On also handled the work involved in the selection and mixture of
the herbal prescriptions under the scrutiny of Doc Hay.

In addition to diagnosing ailments, Doc Hay was also an excellent
herbalist. One of his significant entrées into white society occurred when
a prominent local ranch owner desperately sent for him to help his son,
who had blood poisoning. A doctor trained in western medicine had treated
the boy, but his condition had worsened. Hay drew out the infection
using an ointment applied with a feather, and treated him with an herb
preparation. The doctor stayed at the ranch for six days watching over the
patient, and after the boy recovered, Doc Hay had established his
reputation.

When the Kam Wah Chung was opened again in 1967, a city
representative found over five hundred herb preparations in cigar boxes
and homemade metal boxes. These boxes are still located behind the barred
area in the main room, and the contents of only two hundred twenty

boxes have been identified. They include Wild Asparagus (prescribed as a cough remedy, to expel gas, as a vermifuge, and an insecticide) and Chicken Gizzards (used for dyspepsia, dysmenorrhea, nausea, and vomiting). However, Doc Hay would not recommend just one type of herb; many times he would mix them to create the specific cure. One 1906 prescription made for a patient with swollen feet contained eighty-five herbs.

The herbs were stored in a barred area, which once served gold and opium transactions. A barred area also protected Lung On's grocery store section in the main room. The original rope is still tied to the bars that Lung On pulled back during business hours. The various sizes and inventory of Prince Albert, Hi-Plane, Beech-Nut, and Old Rover tobacco containers suggest the popularity of this product.

Behind the bars on the counter is an empty Joel B. Frazier whiskey bottle, one of the ninety-five pre-Prohibition liquor bottles that city workers, who were inspecting the building, discovered secreted underneath the floorboards. The cache was moved to a public building and the city leaders had a tasting party.

On the back walls of the grocery area is a shrine. Doc Hay was a religious man, and placed offerings of "Three Precious Things": wine, fruit, and incense. The altar also served as a center for religious life in the local Chinese community when the joss house, their religious building, was discontinued. Consistent with their religious practices, the Chinese community used the altar as a place of divination and fortune telling, and participated in the annual refurbishment of the shrine, services for which they paid the partners a small fee. However, the reason for the altar was not just economic, as Doc Hay continued to offer the "Three Precious Things" long after most of the Chinese had returned home or had died.

Doc Hay's bedroom is decorated with wallpaper with a border, probably from a Sears catalog. The other furnishings—the iron bed, makeshift tables, and pegs on the wall—are like most of furnishings in the Kam Wah Chung, merely practical. Though Doc Hay lived there until 1948, the building retained the characteristics of a crude cabin. While the lifestyle of Doc Hay and his partner was simple, their reputations were legendary.

Frazier Farmstead Museum

National Register of Historic Properties
Built: 1892

1403 Chestnut Street
Milton-Freewater
541-938-4636 (museum)

The farmstead was constructed as William Frazier's retirement home, the reward for a long life of farming. He lived in it only four years, but the house continued to be held by his descendants for almost ninety years. Although the house was constructed before the turn of the twentieth century, the last significant remodeling in 1913 transformed the house to the latest style.

Direction: From Highway 11, turn east on S.E. Fourteenth Street (located at the southern edge of town). Travel two blocks, turn right on Chestnut Street. The museum is on your right.

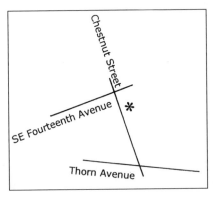

Open: April through December, Thursday–Saturday
Hours: 11:00–4:00
Admission: Donation
Tour: Guided
Entry: At the front door
Additional Attractions: The exterior of the 1918 Frazier barn and other farm outbuildings are also available for viewing.

History

William and Rachel Frazier and their seven children left Texas in 1867 in search of a better life. They settled in the Walla Walla Valley, purchasing a homestead claim of 320 acres and living in a cabin for the next twenty-four years. In 1872, William Frazier laid out the town of Milton (half of the present Milton-Freewater, which was a merger of two towns). Rather than calling the town Frazier, he named it after a favored English poet, John Milton.

Frazier built the present house in 1892, ten years after Rachel had died, and he lived there only for four years before his death. His youngest son, William Frazier, and his wife, Frances, inherited the house, which they remodeled by adding two bay windows that flanked the front door. When Chestnut Street was expanded, the Fraziers moved the house back about one hundred feet, and again remodeled the house.

William and Frances Frazier both died in the 1950s, but two of their three children, Earl and Lela, continued to live in the house. Earl Frazier died in 1978, Lela five years later. Lela Frazier bequeathed the estate to the Milton-Freewater Area Foundation, and the house, now operated by the Milton-Freewater Area Historical Society, opened as a house museum in 1984.

Setting

At one time, the Frazier property was as large as 350 acres, although today the parcel encompasses just six acres. Many of the outbuildings remain, including a 1918 two-story barn with an unusual central circular staircase. Smaller buildings still on the site include the former woodshed, garage, carriage house, and, near the Walla Walla River, a horse barn. In later years, the historical society moved an 1856 cabin, reportedly the oldest structure still standing in Umatilla County, to the back part of the site.

While the outlying acreage is left to grow wild, a caretaker maintains the grounds around the house, creating a contrast between the farm and house. South of the house is a shagbark hickory tree which was planted by the Fraziers from a nut they carried from Texas.

William Frazier built this house after living in a cabin for twenty-four years.

Exterior

The Frazier farmhouse today is considerably different from the house when it was initially constructed. An early photograph shows the structure with Italianate features such as its square shape and brackets supporting the eaves. Similar to many Italianate farmhouses throughout Oregon, the house was more functional than flamboyant. A photograph taken after the second remodeling shows twin bay windows with cresting on their roofs flanking the central front door, another Italianate feature.

The third remodeling occurred in 1913 when the house was moved out of the Chestnut Street right-of-way. The Fraziers dug a basement to the house, moved the front entry off the center, and added a porch across the front of the house. The porch, hipped roof, and square shape of the house suggest a Classic Box house, a subcategory of the Colonial Revival style, which was also popular at the time. These features communicated in a glance the house's fashionableness to those on the street.

Interior

One of the most astonishing features in the hall is the wallpaper, with its medley of colors and seemingly unmatched borders. In fact, many local people told the museum director that the Fraziers were "plain people," and therefore would not have had such a riot of colors and patterns. No known photographs of the Fraziers' interiors were available, but other photographs of the time do show that such "extravagances" were part of the decoration favored by the middle class.

The twenty-seven-inch-wide iris and cattail border in the hall, made by Bradbury and Bradbury Art Wallpapers, is based on an original design by Walter Crane, a cofounder, along with William Morris, of the English Arts and Crafts movement. The movement, based on the philosophy of simple but artistic living, began in England, and gained popularity in America after items in this style were displayed at the 1893 Colombian Exposition in Chicago. The style was first popular in wealthy homes, but middle-class homeowners also later embraced it.

The Fraziers added elements of the Arts and Crafts style in the 1913 remodeling. The original staircase consisted of a single flight of stairs in the center of the house, but the Fraziers relocated the staircase against

Remodeled in 1913, the fashionable interior has both Colonial Revival and Arts and Crafts features.

the south wall of the house, and added a landing. Built-in furniture such as the window seat on the stairway landing and the settle near the foot of the stairs was also an Arts and Crafts feature.

The Arts and Crafts style, however, was not the only style fashionable at the time for the interior. Colonial Revival was also popular, and the Frazier house has columns separating the hall from the living room. The theme is repeated in the 1913 living room light fixture that displays a Greek fret design on the glass. However, the beamed ceiling in dark wood is in the Arts and Crafts style.

Despite the simplicity advocated by the Arts and Crafts style, perhaps the Fraziers followed advice given by a 1901 pamphlet entitled "Nooks and Corners" in decorating a settle by the fireplace. The pamphlet advised for a "charming retreat," one should drape rich tapestries in colors of rich olive, red, yellow, and blue over the seat, and add "antique war implements, tabourets, arghiles, lamps and cushions of odd embroidered stuffs" to create a Turkish corner.

If the Fraziers did have a Turkish corner, the Maxfield Parrish print hanging on the wall, entitled "The Garden of Allah," would have fit in with the décor. The print, though faded, displays the artist's signature in cobalt blue, which has since become known as "Parrish Blue."

Pocket doors divide the dining room from the living room. In the dining room, the classical motif continues in the posts above the built-in sideboard and in the dentils under the plate railing. Dentils are a particularly apt decoration for the dining room, as they represented "teeth" in Greek symbolism. The rabbit and deer pattern in the border is another food reference in this setting.

The Fraziers reportedly brought the desk with them from Texas in 1867. The dining-room table is also part of the Frazier family collection, although only by luck did it remain in the house. Lela, the last Frazier heir to live in the house, was a meticulous housekeeper, and at one point she told a workman to take the table to the dump because it had a scratch on it. He assured her that he could buff it out, and she decided to keep it.

When Lela Frazier became too frail to climb the stairs, she used the room now outfitted as a gift shop as her bedroom. The adjoining bathroom was installed in 1913 in the location of a former porch. Hanging over the claw-foot tub is what would have been four risqué turn-of-the-twentieth-century scenes of a woman in various stages of undress getting ready to take a bath. She smiles coyly, while a mirror in the print conveniently displays her backside, but the most skin she shows is located below the knee and above the shoulder. Nevertheless, it is likely that these "forbidden" glimpses were intended to stimulate the male imagination.

The toilet is located in a small room adjacent to the bathroom. The room has an exterior door, which perhaps allowed farm laborers to use the facilities without venturing farther into the house.

The kitchen is compact, especially with the table perpendicular to the cabinets, which is as Lela Frazier had left it. She had a modern stove and refrigerator in the kitchen, but the woodstove and icebox now standing here were found in the basement. The name of the icebox is "The Automatic," and like other iceboxes, the food was put in one side, and in the top compartment on the left, a block of ice. The left door at the bottom allowed the receptacle for the melted ice to be removed. Modern refrigerators are taller than the typical three-door icebox, and the cupboards later had to be sawn to make room for the larger appliance.

The Fraziers took the family desk with them when they moved from Texas to Oregon.

A "labor-saving" device in the kitchen is the Dairy Swing Churn for butter-making, although the only difference is that one must rock the device back and forth rather than up and down as one would with a regular butter churn. A built-in Frazier laborsaving device is the dumb waiter that runs between the kitchen and the basement below. The Fraziers used the basement to store their canned goods, and had a summer kitchen there.

Family photos line the stairway and upper hall, just as one would expect to find in any home. While most of the family lived a long life, Claude Frazier, seen in a photograph hanging on the wall at the head of the stairway with his sister Zelma, had a tragic end. While he was pushing his rocking horse, the four-year-old slipped and fell into the fireplace. The museum director found a handmade headless rocking horse in the garage; perhaps the family stashed it in an outbuilding to help forget the tragedy.

In a display case in the northeast bedroom are sugar flowers which were found with a note by Lela Frazier that stated, "From Mama's wedding cake." Lela Frazier's mementos also included an 1884 wedding invitation addressed to the Fraziers from Walter Pierce, who later became governor of Oregon (1923-1927) and U.S. senator. The director was curious about the connection of this eminent man to the family until she located a newspaper clipping of Pierce's obituary, on which Lela Frazier had written, "used to chop wood for grandpa."

The bedroom across the hall displays photos of the Fraziers who fought on the Union side in the Civil War. Lela Frazier's collection included letters from her great uncles George, Lewis, and Jesse. The framed copy of the letter from Lewis is dated "August 18th, 1862," and states "Old Stonewall Jackson is out with his hordes of Miscreants, composed of Murders & Cutthroats, thives & robbers & that follower of the Arch Traiter Jeff –Davis." This was the only letter in the collection from Lewis, who was killed a short time after writing it. Jesse, who was wounded, was somewhat more fortunate. A transcript of a letter in the notebook on the table dated August 18th, 1864, states, "The reson that he [Jesse] done so bad was that he got Gang Green in his wound and it et a place as large as both of Eva's hands and one inch deep."

The bedroom also exhibits items donated by Milton-Freewater residents, as does the bedroom on the northwest corner of the house. An unusual child's swing stands near one corner. A similar contraption, which rocked the baby back and forth, was advertised in the July 1897 *Ladies Home Journal* as a "Combined Baby Jumper and Rocking Chair." The advertisement noted that "doctors will tell you that the side motion of the cradle is bad for baby's mental development," suggesting that the bulk of the population, who were rocked in a traditional cradle, were mentally impaired.

The last bedroom is outfitted with Lela Frazier's bedroom set, which she received in 1903 and used the rest of her life. Frazier family sheets and pillow shams cover the bed, reflecting the importance of linen handed down from mother to daughter. Because she treasured her family's furnishings and history, she left a legacy for others.

Southern Oregon

Hughes House

National Register of Historic Places
Built: 1898
Cape Blanco State Park
Sixes
541-332-0248 (museum)
541-332-6774 (Humbug Mountain ranger station)

With the Sixes River to the north and the Pacific Ocean visible to the west, the site of the Hughes House is tied to water. In this spectacular landscape, Patrick and Jane Hughes constructed one of the most elaborately decorated houses in Curry County.

Directions: Cape Blanco State Park is located about four miles north of Port Orford and twenty-three miles south of Bandon. From Highway 101, turn at the sign to Cape Blanco State Park and travel west on Cape Blanco Highway approximately four miles. At the sign for the Hughes house, turn right onto a short road that leads to the house.

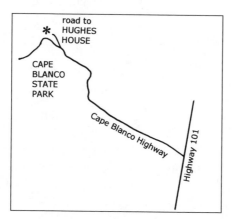

Open: April through October; Christmas season
Hours: 10:00–3:30
Admission: Donation

Additional Attractions: The state park also includes a small cemetery which once lay behind the now-demolished Catholic Church built by the Hugheses, as well as a campground, hiking trails, access to the beach, and horse camp with riding trails. The park also features Cape Blanco Lighthouse, one of the few working lighthouses in the nation with its lens room open to visitors (check hours by calling 541-332-6774). A trip to the lighthouse also gives a sense of the extent of the Hughes ranch holdings.

History

Born in 1830, Patrick Hughes left Ireland for America, and while in Boston, he met and married Jane O'Neil, who had also emigrated from the same area in Ireland, in 1855. Patrick Hughes traveled west in 1856, looking for gold and a way to improve the couple's fortune, and his wife followed later. Patrick Hughes began working on the A. H. Thrift ranch, located near Langlois, eventually accepting eighty acres in exchange for his labor. The couple still wanted gold, and so they purchased "Sullivan's Mine," a black sand gold mine on the south side of Cape Blanco that they operated until the early 1940s.

Over the years, the Hughes family expanded their operation to nearly two thousand acres and employed as many as fourteen ranch hands. They were shrewd businesspeople, selling butter locally as well as in the distant city of San Francisco. In addition, the ranch produced smoked and cured meats, milk, and fish.

The couple had nine children. Thirty-eight years after settling along the Sixes River, they built their grand home, though it was also a practical ranch house. Patrick Hughes died in 1901, only three years after the house was completed. A descendant of the family occupied the ranch until 1971. Today, 1,800 acres of the ranch is preserved as Cape Blanco State Park.

Setting

Patrick and Jane Hughes chose a spectacular site for their house with the Sixes River flowing on the north and emptying into the Pacific Ocean to the west. Green hills and fields dotted with livestock can be seen in the distance. The natural conditions affected the siting of the house, which was constructed near a cliff to avoid the brunt of southwest-flowing winter storms.

Exterior

One distinctive feature of the Hughes house is the unusual shingle pattern covering much of the exterior. Diamond shingles are located in the front facing gable and below in the brown bands above the foundation and between the first- and second-floor windows. The principal shingle design, however, is of circles crafted from alternating rows of fish scale and arched shingles.

The house, designed and built by Port Orford contractor P. J. Lindberg, is in the vernacular style, though the brackets under the eaves and on the porch posts are in the Eastlake style. Eastlake porches generally have spindle work, but this porch, with the exception of the brackets, is relatively plain. The Hughes home, designed as a ranch house, lacks a grand entry, which suggests that impressing guests was not a high priority. Instead, the front door is somewhat concealed under the L-shaped porch.

The paint color scheme of ochre and umber is based on analysis of samples of old paint taken from the house. According to local tradition, the paint base was seal oil from a Port Orford rendering plant. A rookery, once heavily populated with seals, was located southwest of Cape Blanco on the Orford Reef.

The Hughes house has an exterior with unusual shingles designed to look like circles.

Interior

Like the porch, the hall is designed as a functional space to connect the rooms in the house rather than to impress visitors. Members of the Friends of Cape Blanco, an organization working to restore the house, do not know how the Hughes family decorated the hall or the parlor off to the right, as very little remains of the Hughes' possessions. Today, the house is decorated with Victorian furnishings. While the house does not portray the clutter popular in decorating at the end of the period, the parlor furniture individually suggests elements of the Victorian era.

Grouped around the fireplace are a sofa and two armchairs, and although the sofa is covered in different upholstery, the similar woodwork on the three pieces indicates that they were part of a set. Sets, or suites as they were called, first gained popularity in the 1850s when mechanization allowed furniture to be mass produced and purchased in matching groups by those rising into the middle class. Prior to this, many families were unable to purchase even a sofa. By the 1870s, a typical suite included four small chairs that were referred to as wall chairs or parlor chairs.

While parlor suites came down from the upper class to the middle class, the folding rocker in the parlor exemplifies a furniture form that made its way up from the lower class to the middle class. Early rockers were simply chairs with rockers added to the legs, and initially they were used by the aged and infirm. Their popularity had spread by the 1880s and 1890s so that they were included in parlor suites, although generally those in the middle and lower price levels.

This parlor also includes the common Victorian fixture, the organ. The 1886 music book on the organ stand tells of the increased value of music in Victorian lives by noting in the preface,

> *Music in this county has until within the past few years, been considered an expensive luxury; enjoyed only by the favored few. But the introduction of the Parlor Organ, with its many improvements and reduced prices, has happily changed this luxury into what is almost a household necessity. The Organ has now found its way even into the humblest home, to cheer the lonely hours, and to give variety to the monotony of every day life.*

Other than the mahogany newel and balustrade in the hall, the cherry fireplace mantel in the parlor is the only wood not indigenous to the local area. Wooden mantels were common, but not everyone agreed with their use. In 1897, author Edith Wharton and architect-decorator Ogden Codman, Jr. in *The Decoration of Houses*, argued for marble mantels, as "there is indeed something of unfitness in the use of an inflammable material surrounding a fireplace. Everything about the hearth should not only be, but look, fire-proof."

Another wooden mantel stands in the "gentleman's parlor" at the end of the hall. Here, a local workman probably constructed the mantel and likely left behind the pencil markings on the wood. On the side of the fireplace, a cutout in the wall allows a view of the rough-sawn two- by eight-inch Port Orford cedars used as structural members. Port Orford cedar grows only along the coasts of southern Oregon and northern California. Left untreated, the wood's rot-resistant qualities make it ideal for high stress applications such as acid battery separators. The cedar emits a spicy but fragrant odor. Cape Blanco rangers report that during the summertime when the house is warmed by the sun, the smell of the cedar still permeates the rooms, even after a hundred years.

The parlor is also where family members gathered to discuss business and operate the ranch. On the rolltop desk is a ledger book with ranch receipts from San Francisco, evidence that the Hughes family traded more with merchants of that city than of Portland. Difficulty in transportation at the turn of the twentieth century, whether with local merchants or those several hundred miles away, dictated ordering in quantity. One bill for cigars lists "160 Shonish Puff, 100 Del Norte Puff, and 100 Spanish Puff."

The Hughes family purchased the parlor fireplace piece, one of the few places in the house where local materials were not used.

A vintage photograph of the Hughes house is above the
fireplace mantel. During hot summer months, park
rangers report that they smell the Port Orford cedar, the
house's structural members.

The Hughes family owned the Brunswick phonograph standing in the
corner of the room. A booklet included with the machine gives insight
into the Hughes family's tastes in music. Their collection includes records
relating to their Irish heritage, such as "Dear Little Shamrock Mine," and
their Catholic faith, such as "The Rosary." Despite the religious music,
on the same page is listed "Questa o quella," an aria from the opera
Rigoletto, in which a lecherous prince sings, "I laugh at the fury of
cuckolded husbands."

All the ranch hands ate at an oval table in the dining room, so perhaps
it was not as elegantly wallpapered as it is today. The reproduction
wallpaper, border, and ceiling papers are in the tradition of an English
Victorian designer, Christopher Dresser (1834-1904). Dresser, in his book
Principles of Victorian Decorative Design, noted that "Sharp or angular
forms, where combined in ornament, act upon the sense much as racy

and pointed sayings do. Thus … works in which there is a prevalence of angles and points so act upon the mind as to stimulate it." Although he died just after the turn of the twentieth century, many design motifs in his work, such as that in the border paper, foreshadow the Art Deco style which would become popular in the mid-1920s and 1930s.

Before continuing with the other rooms on the ground floor, the tour usually travels upstairs. One son, John, was the second native-born Oregonian to be ordained a Catholic priest. When he stayed in the house, he celebrated Mass in the room at the head of the stairs outfitted with an altar. This room, and the one bathroom in the house, located on the ground floor, are the only two rooms that still have a painted ceiling. While elaborately painted and stenciled ceilings were still in vogue during the last decade of the nineteenth century, very few are visible in Oregon's house museums because homeowners painted them over as the trend shifted to plainer ceilings.

The upstairs floor contains five bedrooms, but what we today call the "master" bedroom is located on the first floor, an arrangement not uncommon in Victorian houses. Patrick and Jane Hughes occupied this bedroom, which was conveniently located next to the house's only bathroom. Behind one door in this bedroom is the evidence of two layers of older wallpaper, and the burlap which separated the first sheet of wallpaper from the fir walls. Observant visitors will notice that the walls throughout the house are smoother than one would expect for a structure over a hundred years old. To comply with fire marshal regulations, Oregon State Park employees added a layer of drywall to the walls, and then newer wallpaper has been hung on top.

The original stove stands near the middle of the kitchen, a forerunner of the "island" stoves that are popular today. With a width of about four and a half feet, this French Range No. 2 must have been deluxe, but a large stove was undoubtedly needed as the Hughes family fed their ranch workers.

Before eating, ranch employees washed their hands in the porcelain sink by the rear entry. Black-and-white photographs hanging on the wall to the left of the sink commemorate the Hughes family's community contributions. The family constructed a Catholic Church, called "Mary, Star of the Sea," on their land, and organized the local school that for some reason was called Cape Blanco University. Another photograph shows the house constructed by their second son, James, which is still a working ranch. The house in the photo is visible through the window in the porch door, suggesting an intersection between the past and the present.

Drain House

National Register of Historic Places
Built: 1893

500 S. Main
Drain
541-836-2223 (North Douglas School District)

The North Douglas School District occupies the Drain house, and although much of the dwelling has been turned into an office, the school district allows visitors to see the interior. The exterior of the house, locally known as the Drain Castle due to its extravagant Queen Anne style, is well restored.

Directions: Southbound travelers on Interstate 5, take Exit 162; northbound travelers, take Exit 150. Follow the signs to Drain, about eight miles west. Once in town, turn east at N. Cedar Street and W. B Street, and after crossing the railroad tracks and the creek, turn south on Main Street. The house is at the end of the street.

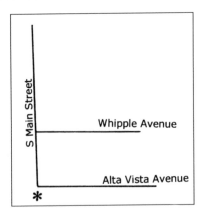

Open: Year around except holidays, Monday–Friday
Hours: 9:00–4:00
Admission: Free
Tour: Self-guided
Entry: At the front door

Additional Attractions: Behind the Drain civic center and library on W. A Street between N. Second and Third streets is the 1925 Pass Creek covered bridge, one of the few within a city limits. The bridge was moved about a block to this location in the late 1980s and is closed to vehicular traffic.

History

Charles Drain Jr. and his wife, Anna Kent, built the Drain house, but his parents made the family fortune. Charles Drain Sr. was born in Pennsylvania in 1816, and with his wife, Nancy Ensley Drain, and their children, traveled to Oregon with a wagon train. The family took a donation land claim near Shedd, and Charles Drain became active in Oregon's territorial and state legislatures. In 1860, he resigned as president of the state senate and a year later purchased 320 acres from Jesse Applegate in Douglas County. The family eventually acquired an additional 1,700 acres.

The heavily embellished Drain Castle was an appropriate dwelling for the town's leading family.

Charles Drain Jr. was born in Douglas County in 1861. Ten years later, the Drains traded sixty acres to the Oregon & California Railroad Company for a railroad station, and the family then planned the town of Drain. The new townsite was a promising shipping point and grew to a population of three hundred in the mid-1880s. Besides selling land, the family operated a mercantile. John Drain, the oldest son, was the first mayor of the town, but Charles Jr. acquired the family store and fortune after John and Charles Sr. died in 1891, followed shortly by Nancy in 1893.

The July 24, 1890, *Plain Dealer*, a Roseburg newspaper, reported that "Charles D. Drain is preparing to erect a fine residence in East Drain ... finest and most costly ever built in Douglas County." It was to have seventeen rooms of "elegant design and elaborate finish." Charles Drain lived in the house for seventeen years until he died in 1910, and Anna Drain remained in the house until her death in 1959. Drain descendants sold the property in 1963, and the North Douglas School District purchased the house in 1966 in order to avoid a lawsuit, as excavation for the nearby high school football field had caused the house to settle.

Setting

East Main Street leads right to the house sitting on a terrace overlooking the town. Originally, the Drains planted palm trees in the yard, an exotic yet fashionable landscape material of the period. The trees lived until the 1970s, a living reference to the status of the family.

Exterior

For their dream house, the Drains chose a design by George F. Barber & Co., an architectural firm that sold house plans through the mail. In 1892, Barber issued a catalogue containing over two hundred original designs and plans of "artistic dwellings." However, he also urged readers to write to his company if they desired alterations or wanted personalized plans. The catalogue included a form that asked such questions as "Is your house to be 1, $1^1/2$, or 2 stories high?", "Do you want transoms over Second Story Doors," and "Do you want Water Closet in Bath Room?" Client satisfaction was an important part of the service, as the catalogue stated: "Write to us concerning any changes wanted in plans and keep writing till you get just what you want. Don't be afraid of writing too often. We are not easily offended."

No correspondence remains that ties the Drains to the company, but Design No. 37 in a Barber catalog appears exactly like the Drain house, and one of the renditions of the plan states "residence of C.D. Drain, Drain Oregon." The company advocated that "a perfect house should look as if it had grown where nature intended it should." Barber must have believed that the Queen Anne architectural style was a natural design, as the Drain house and many of his other designs displayed this style.

Queen Anne style buildings have asymmetrical plans and the Drain house includes a tower, bay window on the north side, and front and side balconies. The company's catalogue noted that "towers, verandas and bay windows are all large parts of the design, and should be in exact proportion with the rest of the building, that it would seem impossible to dispense with either one of them without injuring the effect of the entire structure."

PERSPECTIVE VIEW.   *Residence of C. D. DRAIN, Drain, Oregon.*

DESIGN No. 37.

Cost to build, as per description, $4,535.

Profuse ornamentation is another aspect of the Queen Anne style, and the Drain house wholeheartedly embodies this principle. Barber had strong beliefs about ornamentation as well. "Each ornament must in itself be a proportional gem, and they [must be] equally and artistically distributed over the entire structure, not crowded or jammed into clusters to be unsightly or unmeaning in their positions."

The flamboyant paint schemes of the Victorian houses was one way of proclaiming status, since more colors required more work and therefore was more costly. In the mid-1990s, University of Oregon students from the Historic Preservation department spent hours trying to discover what the original colors had been, as the Drain house had been painted simply white at least as far back as the 1930s. Town residents were surprised to learn that the current colors—lima bean green, slate gray, burgundy brown, and light and dark chocolate browns—were the original paint scheme. The contrasting colors made the ornamentation more visible, so that after it was repainted several townspeople asked the school board about the new trim that had been added.

Interior

Unlike many other Victorian houses, the dark interior wood trim of this house was never painted, and the doors still show false graining, a form of decoration in which the natural wood grain was imitated. Graining was done with tools such as metal or leather combs, shade and pencil brushes, and badger softeners, brush-like implements that softened the hard line or stripe. The *Textbook on Architecture and Building Construction*, published in 1899, advised its students how to imitate wood types from bird's eye maple to rosewood, but noted that graining required "a degree of taste, observation, and dexterity of hand, placing this art far in rank above that of plain painting."

The Drain House still has the original unpainted woodwork.

The plans in Barber's book label the present secretary's office as the parlor, and the adjoining room as the living room. This room, however, had a broader function than the living rooms we have today, doubling as a dining room, a typical use in "smaller" Victorian homes. Under design No. 37, Barber related that "in this design the main living and dining room has been given prominence, being large and provided with a nice bay window, thus affording a good view to the front." Charles Drain reportedly sat in a chair in the bay window, dressed immaculately in a three-piece suit, watching his wife tend to their orchard visible through their windows.

On the far wall hangs the Drains' marriage certificate. While it includes a drawing of a couple idyllically sailing together from the church towards the house, the individual photos of Charles and Anna Drain, arranged so that they face away from each other, suggest another reality. Perhaps the certificate hints at another aspect of Victorian marriages in the border of chains and heart-shaped locks.

The school district displays treasures on the fireplace mantel that were found in the house or on the grounds. Someone, perhaps a Drain, owned the mended overstuffed catcher's mitt, the broken glass cup, or the twisted and dented clarinet. One definite Drain family possession is the trunk in the second-floor hall by the balustrade.

Barber relates that for Design No. 37, "The tower is round above the first story and is a very attractive feature." Stories persist about Charles Drain's ghost inhabiting the tower. Windows throughout the house rattle and floorboards creak with no obvious explanation. However, Charles died while hunting in the hills surrounding Drain, not in the house. When he failed to return, the police and townspeople searched for him. If anyone found him, he or she was to ring the church bell, but it was silent that night. Charles Drain's body was found the next morning, apparently killed when he slipped and his gun accidentally fired. In the conference room hangs a portrait of Anna Drain, who lived another forty-nine years in the house.

The fireplace mantle displays items found in the house and on the property.

Schmidt House

Built: 1901

508 S.W. Fifth Street
Grants Pass
541-479-7827 (Josephine County Historical Society)

The Schmidt house embodies a philosophy of financial caution. Built by immigrants Claus and Hannchen Schmidt, the house was initially a one-story four-room structure. As the family's fortunes improved, they slowly added onto the house.

Directions: From the center of Grants Pass at S.E. Sixth and G streets, drive south three blocks and turn right at S.W. J Street. Travel one block; the house is at the southwest corner of S.W. Fifth and J streets.

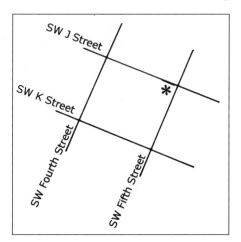

Open: Year around, except major holidays, Tuesday–Saturday (other times by appointment)
Hours: 10:00–4:00
Admission: $3.00 adults; $1.00 children; children under six free
Tour: Guided
Entry: If no one is at the house, go to the research library next door at 512 S.W. Fifth Street.
Additional Attractions: A research library on local history is next door in a remodeled house.

History

Claus and Hannchen Schmidt were immigrants from a Danish province that was later ceded to Germany. They met, however, in a German-speaking club in San Francisco, and came to Josephine County in 1887. The couple homesteaded about two and a half miles from Grants Pass, but after several years, Claus Schmidt decided that he disliked farming, and joined the gold rush in Alaska in the mid-1890s. Learning that gold mining was a matter of luck, he became a cook for the miners. While many miners returned home with nothing to show for their efforts, Schmidt came back to his family with enough money to start a grocery store in Grants Pass.

The family continued to live on the farm while Claus Schmidt walked to the store each day. After several years, the Schmidts began planning a house in Grants Pass, and bought two lots at the corner of J and Fifth streets. They constructed a modest four-room house of locally made bricks on the corner lot, and built a barn on the second lot.

As their four children grew, the Schmidts expanded their house by constructing a bedroom, bathroom, and a new kitchen. They eventually added a second floor that included three bedrooms and a storage room. A third lot behind the house was purchased for the barn, still standing, which was used for storing hay and grain and the horse that pulled the grocery store's delivery wagon.

Hannchen Schmidt died in 1924, and Claus died three years later. The Schmidts' two girls, Flora and Anna, never married and spent most of their life in the house. For many years, Flora Schmidt worked for a bank while Anna was the bookkeeper in the family grocery. After their father died, Anna and her brother Herman ran the store until he died in 1949. Six years later, Anna Schmidt sold the contents of the store and the building. After moving to a nursing home, the women in 1978 bequeathed the house to the Josephine County Historical Society, which still operates the house. Flora Schmidt died in 1981; Anna in 1987.

Setting

In the rear of the house stands the former barn, now available as a meeting space.

Exterior

Although the house was expanded several times, the quality of workmanship is so good that it is difficult to tell what was original and what was a later addition. Both the older and newer sections shared architectural elements so that the structure appears to have been constructed at one time. For example, the new porch and bay window have exposed rafter tails and triangular knee braces just like the roof.

Both the exposed rafter tails and knee braces are elements of the Craftsman style, which was popular after the turn of the twentieth century and espoused values such as beauty and honesty in traditional handcraftsmanship and natural materials. Brick Craftsman houses, however, are less common than those of wood, but then most of them, unlike the Schmidt house, did not begin as simply.

Interior

The large hall is atypical for a Craftsman home of this size. The Schmidts likely did not intentionally create this floor plan. The hall was one of the four original rooms and the Schmidts probably decided it was easier to keep its original size.

The historical society believes that the room off to the right, added at a later date, was initially used as a bedroom. Today, it displays mementos bequeathed to the historical society from local resident Colonel Leroy Heston, a U.S. Air Force pilot who spent most of his life in Asia. A desk standing against one wall is the handiwork of Claus Schmidt, who had trained as a furniture maker in his native land. When he came to America, he found that furniture making was largely a mechanized process, so he chose another profession.

From the sidewalk, it is difficult to tell that the house started as a modest four room structure and was enlarged over the years.

The Schmidt sisters lived in the house for most of their lives, and owned the 1920s sofa in the parlor.

In the living room are two tables that Heston acquired while in Asia. Only a limited amount of Schmidt furniture remained in the house when Anna and Flora Schmidt bequeathed the house to the historical society. One piece found upstairs is the fine 1920s overstuffed couch. The amount of upholstery on the couch represents a trend in home design after the turn of the twentieth century from stiff, formal parlors for guests to relaxing living rooms for family use.

Drapery holders protrude from the wall between living room and dining room, suggesting that at one time the Schmidts closed off these two rooms with portieres in the Victorian manner. The small rooms, typical in pre-1900 floor plans, were in part due to the requirements of gas lighting. Small rooms helped to prevent drafts from open windows, which would have extinguished the gas. Electricity, which the Schmidts installed about 1910-1911, did not have such a requirement, and allowed open floor plans typical of the Craftsman style houses. The sole heating unit, a woodstove, is located in the dining room. Perhaps the Schmidts continued to close off the parlor in order to keep the rest of the house warm during the winter.

The family initially used the small pantry beyond the dining room as the kitchen before they expanded the back of the house. An example of needlepoint work by one of the sisters hangs on the wall in the pantry and proclaims in German, "My kitchen is my pride"; another hangs in the kitchen and reads, "Clean and whole, the kitchen shines." Needlepoint was considered to be a virtuous occupation for Victorian women, who were seen as the guardians of basic values and creators of a "haven of morality" in the home. Needlepoint mottoes abounded during Victorian times, ranging from "In God we trust" to "Labor has sure reward." The two examples of Schmidt needlework reflect pride in their heritage as well as their lack of servants in the kitchen. Both women worked in jobs outside the home for the majority of their lives, yet they still were well versed in "womanly virtues."

The Electrical Appliance Mfg. Company manufactured the wood-burning stove in the kitchen; perhaps the company was moving forward to the new technology of electricity and changed their name to appear progressive. Initially, homeowners were slow to purchase major electrical appliances such as stoves, and only bought with small appliances such as irons or vacuum cleaners. To increase acceptance of electric irons, an advertisement by General Electric about 1912 depicts a man standing by a mountain of two thousand flat irons in the manner of a big game hunter.

Visible through the window in the back kitchen door is a water pump on the porch. For as long as they lived in the house, the sisters obtained their drinking water from this source. Friends still brought them water from the pump after they moved to the nursing home.

The house still is equipped with the original light fixtures installed when the Schmidts wired the house for electricity. Typical of the times, a large central fixture was installed in the primary rooms such as the living and dining rooms. The lighting fixtures in the kitchen, pantry, bathroom, and upstairs bedrooms, however, are utilitarian single light bulbs hanging from a cord. Illumination without a shade was not as harsh as it appears with today's light bulbs as early bulbs produced a softer, warmer light.

Upstairs, the bedroom facing Fifth Street has two large closets that flank the main room. While the tables in the parlor actually came from Asia, the bedroom set with its faux bamboo design is an American interpretation of Asian furniture.

The Schmidt children's toys are displayed in a second bedroom. Flora's framed paper dolls exhibit turn-of-the-twentieth-century dress. The boys' metal and tin toys also reflect life in the miniature. The two toy fire engines not only speak of the excitement of fire but also of a time of wooden buildings and great conflagrations. The toy wagon, pulled by two horses, likely reflected their father's livelihood, although the name on the wagon, "Good Boy & Co.," perhaps reflected their parents' expectations.

A third bedroom is outfitted as Claus and Hannchen Schmidt's room, while a fourth room is filled with items that the family sold at the grocery store.

Beekman House

Built: circa 1873

406 E. California Street
Jacksonville
541-773-6536 (Southern Oregon Historical Society)

The Beekman house provides a living history tour, in which "family members" are stationed in various rooms of the house and talk about aspects of the room from their points of view. Cornelius Beekman even walks home from the bank at 3:00, and the family has tea every afternoon. The house is interpreted as of 1911, so don't ask the family members about anything pertaining to a later time period; they will feign confusion.

Directions: From the center of Jacksonville at S. Third and California streets, travel four blocks east. The house is on the right at the intersection of E. California and Laurelwood streets.

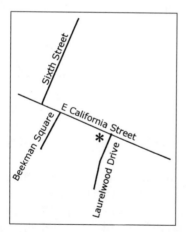

Open: Memorial Day through Labor Day, Wednesday–Sunday
Hours: 1:00–5:00
Admission: $3.00 adults; $2.00 seniors and children under twelve
Tour: Living History (house is interpreted as of 1911)
Entry: Pay at the former wood shed; visitors watch a video about the Beekmans before seeing the house

Additional Attractions: The house is near the trail system of the Jacksonville woodlands, which offers miles of hiking trails through the town's southern and eastern forested areas.

The Beekman bank is located at California and Third streets, and the interior is visible from viewing porches that are open the same hours as the house.

History

Cornelius Beekman was born in New York City in 1828. At the age of twenty-two, he traveled along the isthmus through Panama, hoping to make a fortune in the California gold mines. He worked as a miner, but then began carrying "express"—gold dust, parcels, and letters—between Jacksonville and Yreka and Crescent City, California. When the express company went out of business in 1856, he bought its stables in Jacksonville and began his own company along the same route.

Beekman's express company grew into banking as he began storing gold for miners for a rate of one percent per month or purchasing it outright. His business occupied part of a one-story wood-frame building in Jacksonville on "Express Corner," so named because it was the arrival and departure point of stagecoaches and pack trains. By 1863, Beekman had constructed an express and banking office on its current site at California and Third streets. That same year, he became a Wells Fargo Express agent, a position that he retained for forty-two years.

Cornelius Beekman had married the twenty-two-year-old Julia Hoffman in 1861. Hoffman's father had unsuccessfully tried farming, but had moved his family to Jacksonville, where he held several public service positions and then became a businessman. The couple had three children: Ben in 1863, Caroline (Carrie) in 1865, and Lydia, who died when she was six, in 1867.

The Beekmans constructed their house sometime between 1870 and 1876. Cornelius Beekman died in 1915, and Julia and Carrie Beekman continued to live in the house until Julia's death in 1931. Carrie Beekman then moved to Portland to be near her brother, although caretakers kept the house ready for her visits to Jacksonville.

Ben Beekman died in 1945, and after Carrie's death in 1959, the house and its contents were bequeathed to the University of Oregon. The house was leased to Jackson County for a brief period before the university decided to auction off the house and its contents in 1961. Only the last-minute intervention by a local pioneer association saved the house, and Jackson County subsequently purchased it in 1966. The Southern Oregon Historical Society (SOHS) currently manages the property.

Setting

The house is situated on a residential lot a few blocks from the center of town. Unlike many of Oregon's house museums, the Beekman property still retains some of the original outbuildings: a two-hole outhouse, a cool house, and a wood shed, which has since been converted to an interpretive room.

Exterior

The Beekman house is in the Gothic Revival style. Sir Horace Walpole, a wealthy English dilettante, was influential in starting the style when he remodeled his country home in 1749. Landscape architect Andrew Jackson Downing furthered the style's popularity when he advocated it in *Cottage Residences* (1842) and in *The Architecture of County Houses* (1850). Downing and others suggested the style was appropriate for rural settings, which is why few Gothic Revival houses were constructed on narrow, urban lots. The style's high, multiple gables and wide porches demanded more space.

Although this was a banker's house, the Beekmans dried their laundry over the railing above the porch.

The Beekman house exemplifies a later evolution of the style called Western Farmhouse (this term suggests the style's rural nature.) The Beekman house has the steeply pitched roof and asymmetrical floor plan with cross gables that are characteristics of the style.

The side porch off the parlor and guest bedroom faces California Street, the main thoroughfare. The architect of the house is unknown, and so is the reason why the front door, usually a focal point of a house, faced what was then a field. Passersby on California Street could not see the front façade, nor could they see the Beekman laundry which dried above the front door on the second-floor railing.

Interior

While the architect of the Beekman house is unknown, the Southern Oregon Historical Society (SOHS) believes he (the architect would almost certainly have been a man at this time) lived in the community. Because so little is known about this person, we must examine his work without fully understanding the reasoning that created the unusual aspects of the Beekman floor plan. The hall is small and compact, not grand, as one would expect to find in the house of a leading member of the town. On the left, the wall runs at an angle, although the reason for this extra carpentry effort is not apparent.

Turn-of-the-twentieth-century chores such as baking and laundry are illustrated on the living history tour.

The formal parlor is on the right. This room has an entrance to the side porch, as does the guest bedroom, making the porch a quasi-public space. A photograph in possession of SOHS shows Julia Beekman's father in an open coffin on this porch; apparently it was a functional place for viewing the body.

The photograph on one wall in the parlor shows the family in a formal studio portrait. Who sits or stands determined rank in Victorian photographs, and the parents are appropriately sitting while the now grown children stand behind them. Perhaps by design, Carrie Beekman stands closer to her father, with whom she felt the greater affinity, and Ben stands near his mother, to whom he was more attached. Julia Beekman would write letters to Ben informing him of details that she dared not tell her husband. Another portrait of Julia Beekman in the parlor subtly shows the family's economic standing, as she wears a gold necklace, brooch, and earrings.

A copy of the Lord's Prayer, complete with pictures of some very stern apostles, hangs on another wall. The bottom of the print boasts that it was the "resulting of six years close labor." Julia Beekman was religious, and attended the Presbyterian Church diagonally across California Street faithfully every Sunday; the pink steeple is visible from the parlor window. From Julia Beekman's letters to Ben, we learn that her husband was a less regular attendee, but as the family paid for the salary of the minister, it is unlikely that the latter badgered him to attend.

Carrie Beekman played organ in the church and taught piano lessons to children in the community. Cornelius Beekman bequeathed everything to his wife except the piano standing in the parlor, which was specifically given to Carrie. Another source of music in the house was the Victrola phonograph. The Beekmans purchased this phonograph sometime between 1909 and 1910. At a time when the 1909 Sears, Roebuck and Co. catalog was selling table model phonographs ranging from $7.50 to $45.00, a source shows that the Beekmans paid at least $200 for their phonograph. Unlike the table models, in which the sound came out of a horn, the Beekmans' Victrola produces sound from the two upper doors in the stand, and the volume can be adjusted by opening and closing the doors.

The other doorway in the hall leads to the sitting room, the symbolic center of the house. Four other rooms can be accessed off the sitting room: the guest bedroom, the dining room, the kitchen, and, after 1915, the newly added bathroom. While the location of the sitting room allowed the family to monitor the comings and goings of each other and the help, it undoubtedly led to some awkwardness. An overnight guest exiting the bedroom was immediately in the presence of the family, and day visitors invited to formal dinners had to cross the private family space to dine. Since the bathroom was not otherwise accessible, anyone going to use the facilities, including the maid, was in full view of the family in the sitting room.

Bessie Smith Johnston, who did light housekeeping for the family in 1916, remembers that Julia Beekman spent a great deal of time in the sitting room doing needlework and reading by the window. Her husband had died the previous year, and Johnston recalled that the Julia and Carrie were "very quiet, very sedate. They didn't seem to have that bond that [most] feel with our daughters ... nowadays." Johnston remembered that both women wore "dark dresses and high-laced collars held up with whalebone insets ... very formal ... all old-style dresses ... out of style even then."

SOHS has chosen 1911 as the year to represent the environment of the house, a time that encompasses many of the changes to the house and when Cornelius Beekman was still living. Almost all of the furniture in the house belonged to the Beekmans. Historic houses with the owners' furniture are somewhat rare in Oregon, and the pioneer association was fortunate to be able to acquire it. A flier for the furniture auction scheduled for Sunday, June 25, 1961, had already been circulated when the local pioneer association intervened. The auction was slated to be held at the house, the flier informed interested buyers, adding that "all items extremely old," and promised that luncheon would be served on the grounds.

The Beekmans were avid readers, and books were at one time in almost every room. Julia and Carrie Beekman were members of a reading group, and even on her European vacation, Carrie spent time reading in her hotel room. Ben Beekman was also a fervent reader. However, based on the assumption that he would have stayed in the guest room while he was home visiting, a weight set and Indian clubs now rest in that room. Too much reading apparently was considered part of the problem when the Beekmans took ten-year old Ben to a phrenologist, someone who practices the lost skill of reading skulls to determine personal traits. Ben Beekman's report related that he needed to develop his physical side, as "anything for exercise will all make him brave for cowardice is one of his chief faults." The report also related he "must marry a cousin of the Amazons who will do her own fighting and help him do his."

Like his father, Ben Beekman was short of temper, and during his visits, the help did not eat at the dining-room table when he was present. SOHS believes that it was Ben Beekman who crafted the motto "God Bless Our Home" out of pipe cleaners that hangs on the wall. Short inspirational mottoes made by hand had been part of Victorian culture, and typically represented Protestant sentiments. Generally, they were located high on the wall, symbolically inspiring the connection with God above.

In 1915, the year Cornelius died, Julia Beekman installed the bathroom, replacing the need for the two-hole outhouse in the backyard. (The tour interprets the house as of 1911, but because of the difficulty in pretending that this room, which occupies part of the original summer kitchen space, does not exist, the tour includes this room.) The stove in the kitchen heated the water, which was then piped to a cylindrical holding tank standing next to the claw-footed tub. The medicine on the shelf above belonged to the family; one bottle for "internal treatment" was to be taken in doses of ten drops with a little water three times a day. The medicine may have been for Cornelius Beekman. The February 23, 1915, *Medford Mail Tribune* reported that he had died of "hemorrhage of the bowels." Perhaps because of this, Ben Beekman's personal motto was "Trust in God and keep your bowels open."

Along with other turn-of-the-twentieth-century chores, the SOHS demonstrates cooking on the wood-burning stove. While recipes today suggest turning on the oven before mixing the ingredients, a wood- or coal-burning stove, requiring even more advanced preparation, took at least forty-five minutes to heat. One of the cooks in the Beekman house before the turn of the last century was a Chinese immigrant named Yan (also spelled Yang). Affection seems to have existed between the family and the servant as noted in the letters that the family wrote. However, one letter to Ben Beekman written by Julia in 1887 still suggests consciousness of the difference in their positions, as she relates, "Yan, faithful boy, took good care ..." Yan was thirty-eight years old at the time.

The dark cupboard against one wall in the kitchen is a pie safe in the bottom section, complete with metal doors that have false graining to imitate wood. Pie safes (also called food safes and pie chests) were made obsolete by the use of refrigerators such as the model standing against another wall. However, ice blocks kept the food cold in these early appliances, and a sign for Medford Ice & Storage Co. would be placed in the front parlor window during the late spring, summer, and early fall months, notifying the iceman how many pounds were needed. The refrigerator itself includes instructions not to "place in a cellar or other damp place as [it is] made of thoroughly kiln-dried lumber and is liable to swell." Doubtless homeowners needed that instruction, as they were accustomed to putting their food in cool places.

During hot months, servants would cook in the summer kitchen to keep heat out of the house. One of the Beekman servants, Louise Ensele, worked at the house for at least seven years, likely starting when she was twenty years old. Her son later related that she was unable to finish high school because she had to support her family. Her personal space, located off the kitchen, is without a closet.

Upstairs, Carrie Beekman's room has the luxury of two closets, although possibly the Beekmans originally intended Carrie to share the room with Lydia, the daughter who died in 1873. The total of six closets in the house is an unusual feature, as houses of that time period were usually built without any. For the lower class, clothes hung on a hook on the wall; for the upper class, an armoire, or wardrobe, served.

Standing in Carrie Beekman's room is a tall mirrored etagere, an elaborate form of the Victorian whatnot shelf. This piece would usually be displayed in the parlor, but perhaps like many families, the Beekmans retired the older furniture to the bedroom when they purchased newer pieces. This could have been the reason for the chaise lounge, which dates from the 1880s, to be located in the parent's bedroom. With its burnt-orange color and fringe, the iron-frame chair has an exotic appearance. Perhaps Cornelius Beekman relaxed in it after working long hours at the bank.

Naucke House

National Register of Historic Places
Built: circa 1883
at the Kerbyville Museum
24195 Redwood Highway
Kerby
541-592-5252 (museum)
541-592-6414 (Sandy Hare, President of the Kerbyville Museum Board)

The Naucke house is only a part of the 3.9-acre Kerbyville museum complex. The house is outfitted to look like a comfortable farmhouse.

Directions: The house is located approximately three miles north of Cave Junction in the unincorporated community of Kerby. The museum is on the east side of Highway 199, north of Kerby Street.

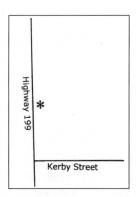

Open: March through December
Hours: Sunday, 12:00–4:00; Monday–Saturday, 10:00–5:00
Admission: $3.00 adults; $.50 children under sixteen; children under six free
Tour: Guided
Entry: At the museum building
Additional Attractions: The main portion of the museum is located in an adjacent building that includes a display of Indian artifacts, a re-creation of an old country store, and musical instruments. The grounds include a collection of farming, logging, and mining implements, and a miner's cabin and Grimmette School.

History

William and Nannie Naucke, both Prussian emigrants, constructed the house sometime around 1883. William Naucke operated a prominent dry goods and general mercantile in Kerby, and had served as the Josephine County Treasurer for fourteen years. After he died in 1894, Nannie Naucke remained in the house with their sons Alfred and Theodore and daughter Delia, her husband Frank Stith, and their three children.

Frank Stith was a carpenter by trade, and a persistent family story is that he met Delia when he was working on remodeling the house. He became a partner in the reorganized "Stith and Naucke" store with his brother-in-law Theodore, and served as Kerby's postmaster when the post office was located in the mercantile. After Frank Stith died, the family sold the home in 1923. The house was sold several times over the next twenty-five years until the Illinois Valley Federated Women's Club purchased the house and formally opened it as the Kerbyville Museum in August 1959.

Setting

The Naucke house stands on its original site; the rest of the museum was constructed around it. On the pathway between the house and the blacksmith shop is a "drilling rock" from a miners' contest held during the 1908 July 4th celebration in Takilma in Josephine County. The miners had to drill through the rock to win, and although there are ten drill holes, apparently only three contestants were able to perform the feat.

Exterior

The Naucke house is a variation of a common folk form called the I-house, which is distinguished by its floor plan of two rooms wide and one room deep. I-houses typically extended toward the rear as the family grew or acquired greater affluence. The date of the addition on the back of the Naucke house is unknown (and it also could be original), but it changes the floor plan to a T-shape.

The house exhibits Classic Revival style pedimented windows on the front ground floor and some windows on the side. The front door, believed to be original, is also pedimented, and exhibits a transom and sidelights.

Interior

The front door opens into the sitting room, now comfortably outfitted with cushions on the chairs and afghans across the back of the sofa and rocking chair. The furniture is of different styles and ages, suggesting the practice of a homeowner who acquired a piece here and there over the years. The carpet and wallpaper date from after the women's club acquired the house. Despite being a museum, the informal sitting room seems as if someone still lives here.

Black-and-white photographs, placed in a hodge-podge manner, fill the walls. Historical photographs of Victorian house interiors show that it was fashionable to have large amounts of clutter on the walls, and a profusion of pictures was important to the decoration. One of the photographs in the Naucke house is of Josephine Rollins, for whom the county is named. Rollins, the first white woman in the area, was the daughter of a miner who was seeking gold in the Illinois Valley. For a short time, the community of Kerby was named after the French emperor, reportedly because "Josephine (County) should have her Napoleon."

In addition to photographs, Victorians also decorated their walls with pictures and "art" prints. An ad in the June 1900 *Ladies Home Journal*

The Naucke house stands on its original site, and the museum developed around it.

The parlor is outfitted as a
comfortable room.

featured an advertisement for "Famous Pictures" at a cost of one cent
each or one hundred twenty for $1.00. The company offered "one hundred
fifty on Life of Christ" and "one hundred Madonnas." For those who
could not afford prints, businesses provided images suitable for hanging
as part of their advertising. By the hat rack hangs a picture in glass of a
secluded shack in the woods with the words "Nels Swanson Fuel and
Transfer." On the opposite wall, in the guise of a calendar, the *Christian
Herald* provided the nymphs wearing butterfly wings or checking bird
nests for eggs.

The extensive decoration on the central light fixture's pressed metal
exemplifies the extent of Victorian embellishment. The lamp, now
converted to electricity, was originally fueled with kerosene. Kerosene
lamps required daily maintenance; the chimneys had to be washed, the
wick trimmed, and the fuel container refilled. This lamp has a smoke bell
above the chimney to protect the ceiling from carbon deposits.

An organ stands in the sitting room while a piano is located in the
parlor. Generally, families would have one or the other, and those with
limited income would have an organ (which is one reason why they are so
prolific in historic homes). In the December 1892 *The Delineator*, two
companies offered pianos starting at "$175 and up." Organ prices,

however, started at $35, illustrating why they were called "the poor man's piano."

The pump by the kitchen sink still works, indicating that it was the house's source of water as late as the 1950s. Unlike faucets, pumps have to be primed if not used regularly. One had to pour water down the pump at least once in the morning to get rid of any air in the pipe and then crank until the water appeared.

Historians are not certain when the side porch and the shed behind it were constructed, but if they were not original, they were very early additions. The side porch and connection to the shed were likely working areas instead of places of leisure. Here, one could chop wood and pluck chickens sheltered from the weather.

In the upstairs landing, more pictures adorn the wall. One depicts Abraham Lincoln, James Garfield, and William McKinley, under the title "Our Martyrs." According to the display, before his death James Garfield managed to say, "It is God's will, so be it," while McKinley said a similarly noble sentiment: "Goodbye all, goodbye. If it is God's way, his will be done, not ours." Sinclair Lewis in *Main Street* (1920) gave insight to the meaning of displaying the assassinated presidents. Schoolteacher Vida Sherman, speaking about a bust of McKinley, noted, "Isn't it an inspiration to have the brave, honest, martyr president to think about!"

The house has four bedrooms on the second floor, one of which is furnished as a sewing room and dedicated to an Illinois Valley resident who owned the extensive button collection displayed there. While saving buttons suggests frugality, the doll collection in the next bedroom would be largely for the pleasure of the collector. Some of the dolls in the room wear costumes of different countries, which is appropriate since dolls are found in many cultures including those of antiquity. The word "doll" was not a common word in the Middle Ages; one term used was "children's babies."

In the last room stands a bed, commode, and dresser that was purchased in 1887 in Kansas. Apparently it was a significant investment, as it went to Texas before it came to the Illinois Valley. Clyde Hayes, who donated the set, was born in the bed. With most babies being born in hospitals today, beds lose one of their assigned functions.

Floed-Lane House

National Register of Historic Places
Built: circa 1866 and 1876

544 S.E. Douglas Street
Roseburg
541-459-1393 (Secretary of the Douglas County Historical Society)

The Floed-Lane house is only tacitly connected to Joseph Lane, Oregon's first Territorial governor. His daughter and her husband actually lived in the house, but reportedly Joseph spend some of his time there. His own home, which he built after he retired, was on the same street. The Floed-Lane house has some of the furniture that belonged to the Lane family, but the collection includes a significant amount of pieces from another Roseburg family.

Directions: From Interstate 5, take Exit 124 and travel east, following the signs to city center. After crossing the river, get in the left lane and turn left on S.E. Spruce Street. Go two blocks and turn right on S.E. Douglas Street; the house is on the left.

Open: Saturdays and Sundays
Hours: 1:00–4:00
Admission: Donation
Tour: Guided
Entry: At the front door
Additional Attractions: The house is located within one block of Riverside Park, a linear park that overlooks the South Umpqua River.

History

Emily Lane Floed, the daughter of Joseph Lane, and her husband, John, moved to Roseburg and purchased the one-story portion of this house in 1866. In 1876, they added the two-story section that fronts Douglas Street.

Joseph Lane, born in 1801, had already served as Oregon's first Territorial governor, Territorial delegate to Congress and United States senator by the time he settled in Roseburg in 1870. A widower, he constructed his house on Douglas Street to be near his daughter Emily and son Lafayette. The railroad tracks run immediately east of Emily Floed's house, and according to the lore, while sitting at the bay window he routinely watched for sparks from the wood-burning steam trains that might start a fire.

Emily Floed eventually sold the house to her brother Simon Lane. After his death in 1925, it was willed to his daughter, Eva Lane Waite, and then bequeathed to her daughter, Katherine Waite Bain. She in turn gave it to the Douglas County Historical Society in 1961.

The two-story part of the Floed-Lane house was constructed in 1876 and was connected to the rear section, which was built ten years earlier.

Setting

The neighborhood was once residential; however, several nearby homes were razed after being damaged in a 1959 dynamite blast that detonated in the downtown. Today, the immediate area has some industrial buildings.

Exterior

The two-story portion appears to have been two rooms wide and one room deep, following the shape of an I-house, a folk form that has its roots in seventeenth-century England. This section displays elements of the Classical Revival style with its symmetrical front façade with sidelights and a five-light transom around the entry door. On the porch are squared columns with simplified bases and capitals. Each porch story has a frieze and a small row of dentils.

However, this two-story section is properly an "addition," as historians believe that the one-story section in the back of the house was constructed on the site about ten years earlier. The gabled roofline of this section has been altered at least twice, indicating several remodelings.

Interior

Over the years, the interior floor plan has undergone changes. The front door originally opened into a hall, which divided a parlor to the right from a room used as a bedroom to the left. Today, the front door opens up into a sitting room, which displays a collection of furniture largely from the Lanes and the Moores, another Roseburg family. The Moore melodeon, reportedly the first musical instrument in Roseburg, was carried on the back of a mule from Scottsburg, over fifty miles away. After the road was improved, the Moores purchased the piano that is standing against the opposite wall from the east coast.

The Lane family owned the card table by the window. Today's "card tables" are lightweight and manufactured with folding legs in order to be easily stored, but eighteenth- and nineteenth-century card tables were substantial, with a back leg that swung out to support a hinged, folded top. When not in use, these tables could be placed against the wall out of the way.

Other pieces from the two families are located in the back of the house, and the museum also includes artifacts that are tied into other parts of Roseburg history. On the shelf by the pantry stand two buckets from the local butcher, who gave away lard to his best customers at Christmas.

In the exhibit room left of the front door hangs a portrait of Aaron Rose, the founder of Roseburg and a shrewd landowner. Before the election to determine the county seat, he invited the citizens of the rival town of Lookingglass to come for a large dinner, and according to the *Roseburg News-Review*, "he was such a perfect host" that the Lookinglass citizens showed their appreciation by casting their ballots for Roseburg.

Underneath the display case, the twisted axle from a truck carrying two tons of dynamite and four and a half tons of ammonium nitrate carbonitrate represents the disaster that struck the town on August 7th, 1959. A trash can fire ignited the truck, and the resulting fireball created a crater fifteen feet deep and forty-five feet wide. The tremor was heard as far away as fourteen miles. Whole city blocks were flattened, while fourteen people eventually died and one hundred twenty-five were seriously wounded. According to the August 7, 1960, *Oregonian*, town promoters, however, soon set up signs along the major roads into Roseburg, stating, "Thirty-four city blocks BLASTED ... Tour the Area, See a City Rebuild."

The display case contains a "hair book," a collection of human hair used to create decorations. The owner of the book wrote names such as "Rob," "Elizabeth," and "John" below the groups of hair. Victorians also created other items from hair such as bracelets and watch chains, one of which is also in the display case.

Tours of the second floor, which contains more items from the Moore and Lane families, are sometimes available.

Southeastern Oregon

Fort Rock Valley Homestead Village Museum

Built: between 1910 and 1918

Fort Rock, OR
541-576-2251 (museum)
541-576-2282 (Jean Flegel, museum executor)

Fort Rock was quickly settled after 1909, and seemingly just as quickly deserted, as homesteaders found that they could not make a living farming. The conditions were harsh, ranging from dust storms to jackrabbits that consumed the crops. The Fort Rock Valley Historical Museum has preserved a collection of cabins and other buildings, assembling in one place a sense of that homestead era.

Directions: From Highway 31, follow the signs to Fort Rock. The museum is near the center of the community on the south side of the road.

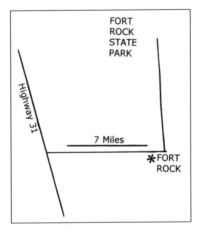

Open: Memorial Day weekend to mid-September, Friday–Sunday and holidays

Hours: 10:00–4:00
Admission: Donation $2.00 per person
Tour: Self guided (guided tours available on request)
Entry: At the small building off the parking lot
Additional Attractions: The museum also includes Dr. Thom's Office (1907), Sunset School (1912), and the former Widmer Cabin (1912), now converted to a post office/patent office.

Fort Rock, a remnant of a volcano, rises abruptly in the high desert, is about a mile and a half northwest from the town, and is a state park.

History

Government land laws were the impetus for the settlement in Lake County beginning in the 1840s, but the Enlarged Homestead Act of 1909 and the Stock Raising Homestead Act of 1916 were what caused the population to increase in the Fort Rock Valley. The 1909 act allowed a person to make a claim of 320 acres of non-irrigable, non-mineral, and non-timbered land, and settlers came in droves, hoping to stay and prove up their claim for the required five years, when the land would become theirs. From 1908 to 1915, eight post offices sprang up in the Fort Rock Valley.

Most of the Fort Rock homesteaders abandoned their claims within five years. Dry farming, or farming without irrigation, proved difficult, if not impossible, because of the low annual rainfall, the short growing season, and the hordes of jackrabbits that ate whatever the settlers planted. The population of Fort Rock Valley, which had been at twelve hundred in 1910, plummeted to three hundred by 1920. Irrigation, powered by electricity, came in the 1950s, years too late for most settlers. Today, alfalfa and stock raising are economic mainstays of the valley.

The Fort Rock Valley Historical Society was formed in 1984, when residents became concerned about the deterioration of and vandalism to the early homesteader cabins. Four years later, the society purchased twenty acres in the town of Fort Rock and moved the Webster cabin, Dr. Thom's office, and St. Bridget's Catholic Church onto the property. Because the homesteaders were more concerned with just surviving than with preserving their history, the historical society, which runs the museum today, has been unable to determine precise dates and information about the cabins.

Setting

The paths running between the sagebrush that surrounds the structures add a sense of realism. Although modern structures are visible from the museum, you can still get a sense of how a homesteader's cabin looked as it stood in the desert.

Menkenmaier Cabin (c. 1910)

Exterior

Settlers in Oregon generally put up rough log cabins as their first homes. George Menkenmaier, who had moved to the desert with his father around 1909, reportedly built this log structure in 1910. Menkenmaier constructed the entrance to the cabin under the side of the gable, the traditional location. The doors of commercial structures built of logs, such as the nearby office of Dr. Thom, were typically placed under the gable.

Chinking, a mixture of soil, straw, water, and other materials, was used to fill the spaces between the logs in an attempt to make the cabin weatherproof, of particular importance since the desert has tremendous dust storms. Chinking is difficult to maintain between rounded logs as

The Menkenmaier cabin symbolizes the basic shelter of many Fort Rock Valley settlers around 1910.

the material rests on curved surfaces, and so strips of wood were placed in an attempt to hold the chinking. The denim and burlap stuffed between the logs on the inside demonstrates that the wood strips were not effective.

Interior

The interior consists of one room commonly called a "pen." An attic loft, accessed by a ladder through the square hole in the ceiling, provided additional space, and was traditionally a sleeping area for children.

As in the other houses at the museum, few items remain in the cabin from the original occupants. An iron bedstead, light enough to transport in a wagon, occupies one half of the cabin, while a cook stove and table stand at the other end. Tables in pioneer cabins served not only for eating, but for food preparation, reading, and writing. Even in the bright desert sun, the light inside the cabin is dim with the door closed. Nails stuck in the joists held lanterns which brightened the otherwise dark evening hours.

Nails in the wall provided places to hang pans and pots that otherwise would have occupied the limited storage space. The built-in shelf by the bed provides another space for personal items. The settlers would have used local materials to make cupboards, such as the one standing by the foot of the bed, since transportation of such furnishings would have been cumbersome, or beyond the settlers' finances. Although the carpentry of this cupboard is rough, its maker embellished the top with a cornice.

The Menkenmaier Cabin is sparsely furnished with pioneer pieces, illustrating the few domestic comforts in the family's life.

Money was scarce for most of the settlers, and necessities were handmade whenever possible. By the front door hangs a broom made of bundled twigs, while nearby stands a lightweight rake, which was used for lifting bundles of rye hay, which fed the cattle in the winter. Except for the crosspieces, the rake is made of a single wood piece, and still exhibits the skill of its maker in separating and bending the four prongs.

Boedigheimer House (c. 1911)

Exterior

The Boedigheimer House is different from the museum's other dwellings; the front entry is under the gable and siding is board and batten. Simon Boedigheimer (one source lists his name as Bodenheimer) was a carpenter, so perhaps he was familiar with a variety of building methods.

Like other settlers, Boedigheimer thriftily used available materials to build his house, which still has the flattened five-gallon kerosene cans he used to shingle his roof. He also used the cans for roof and window flashing.

Boedigheimer built a house with a gable front and used flattened kerosene cans to shingle his roof.

Interior

The Boedigheimer House has a number of "amenities." The structure is equipped with windowsills, two exterior doors, and storage that includes shelves built in the corner of the first room as well as a closet located under the stairs. The front room still displays remnants of wallpaper, although the blue floral print on the back bedroom walls is more intact.

On a wall in the front room is a framed certificate bearing the name "Fremont Wastena Threshing Company." Fremont and Wastena were both small towns in the high desert. The company, a cooperative effort by local residents, supplied a threshing machine to cut the rye to those who had purchased stock at $20.00 per share. It took twelve people to operate the machine, five of whom were hired by the company.

The dishes and silverware on the dining table are mismatched, representing the homesteader's make-do mentality. Tableware was difficult to make, but chairs could be crafted with some effort. The chair at the table, though homemade, displays three ornamental holes in the back. Two store-bought chairs rest in the back room. Like other rural homesteaders, the high desert settlers could purchase chairs and other items through the Sears and Roebuck catalogue, called "Sears and Sawbuck," or the Montgomery Ward catalogue, referred to as "Uncle Monty" or "Monkey Ward." The catalogues not only provided access to a greater variety of goods, but, as E. R. Jackman noted in *The Oregon Desert*, they also served as "means of entertainment, fashion guide, seat for the baby at the table, cutouts for the kids, and when replaced by the new issue next year, it was a standard toilet article."

Sewing machines were important for making and maintaining clothes. The sewing machine against the wall in the back room once belonged to local resident Vivian Stratton's mother. When the Strattons decided to improve their fortunes by trading their three hundred twenty homesteaded acres for forty acres in Columbia County, Vivian's mother was forced to sell her sewing machine to help finance the trip and she wept at the loss. Sixty-eight years later, after Vivian had moved back to the high desert, she discovered her mother's machine still in the possession of the second owner and repurchased it.

The Boedigheimer House's second floor, accessed by a staircase, was likely used as a sleeping area. Among the furnishings in this dimly lit room is a trunk, one of the settlers' versatile pieces of furniture, which was used not only to transport possessions, but later could become a table, seat, or cupboard. With limited funds, settlers had to press everything they could into multiple uses.

Webster Cabin (c. 1912)
Exterior

The Websters reportedly built this cabin as their first home when they arrived. After they constructed a more substantial house, their son Carl stayed, living here for most of his life. Its function as a permanent home likely explains the double-wall construction, a better grade than the typical cabin. Carl Webster was a recluse, and the small cabin, away from his parents' house, must have suited him.

Interior

A black-and-white photograph on the inside of the cabin near the front door shows Carl's parents, possibly on their wedding day. In the second photograph is the home they left in Illinois, a substantial dwelling that must have seemed palatial in comparison to the cabin. The Websters had not made a direct trip from Illinois to Lake County. Before moving to the desert, they lived in Pasadena, California, and Riddle, Oregon, each time doubtless looking for a better place to live and prosper.

Carl Webster supported himself by trapping. On the post outside the cabin hangs a coyote trap, while rabbit traps rest in the flower garden. The house also contains records of his trapping success. On the inside door of the built-in cupboard are the numbers of rabbits he trapped written in pencil. Calculations in pencil are also around the door to the bedroom.

Jackrabbits, which would eat crops and gardens, were a particular pest to the homesteaders, who would frequently organize drives to kill thousands. They would construct a large pen with sides that extended for up to a half a mile. A line of people would advance, beating cans and making noise, which would scare the rabbits to run into the enclosure. Once the rabbits were trapped, the homesteaders would club them to death. The November 11, 1915, *Fort Rock Times* reported on a successful rabbit drive the previous Saturday.

> *Though the drive was the largest in the history of the valley, thousands of rabbits escaped, especially when nearing the pens. At this one drive more rabbits were killed than in the entire seven drives held last fall and winter. After the big slaughter, which lasted about a half hour, the rabbits were counted and a total of 3,540 were found to have been killed.*

From Fleetwood, a town in the Fort Rock Valley, the paper noted, "Some of the ladies who thought they could never endure to see the poor

Carl Webster lived most of his live in this cabin. The Belletable House is on the right.

things killed became as excited in the chase as anyone and were even present at the final slaughter."

Carl Webster was a bachelor all his life, so the cabin's arrangement are entirely his. This cabin, with the kitchen cupboard, wall pocket to hold lids and a muffin tin, and a shelf over the bedroom doorway, likely has more built-in storage because he lived here for most of his life. Two closets in the adjoining room occupy scarce space, but they must have been a necessity to maintain tidiness. The historical society has added a piece of homesteader furniture in the corner of the main room: wooden boxes stacked on their sides that provided additional shelving.

One of the smaller rooms holds various implements, while the other room is outfitted as Carl Webster's bedroom, although the space between the walls is only big enough to hold a mattress and frame. Hanging on the bedroom wall is a thermometer from the Owl Service Station, which was located "on the Dalles–California Highway, North Entrance to Bend, Oregon." The instrument boasts the advantages of the station, doubtless listing in order of importance, "Dependable Service, Sanitary Restrooms, Beautiful Grounds, Parking Space." The service station, like the Webster cabin, was vibrant years ago.

Belletable House (c.1911-1918)

Exterior

The Belletable house, like the Boedigheimer and Webster dwellings, has walls of planed pine. The Embody sawmill, located at the edge of the ponderosa pine forest about twelve miles west of Fort Rock, provided lumber for the "construction boom" in the area. The pine boards are a favorite of the Yellowhammer, a member of the woodpecker family that drills large holes in walls for nests. Someone subsequently nailed tin can tops over several holes on the walls.

A feature of this house was a screened-in front porch, and the strip of wood still nailed to the wall indicates how high the porch stood. Below, you can still see traces of the ochre and burnt-orange exterior paint that the porch protected from the weather. Vivian Stratton recalls that the Belletables were among the richest folk in the area, and the paint and porch, in addition to the size of the house, were symbolic of their wealth.

Interior

A photograph of the sturdy-looking Belletables in front of their house is placed just inside the front door. In the kitchen rests a "wash machine," a contraption which a homesteader built after seeing a similar one in a catalogue. It was still being used when electricity came to the Silver Lake area in the 1950s. Posted on the wall is "Grandma's 'Receet' for Washing Clothes," a thirteen-step process which starts with "bild fire in back yard to heat barrel of rainwater," and concludes with "go put on clean dress, smooth hair with side combs, brew cup of tea, set and rest and rock a spell and count blessins."

Guests at the Belletable house were likely ushered from the front door through the kitchen into the adjoining parlor, which was made grand by a larger than average opening in the wall separating the two room. Unlike the kitchen, which is painted white, the parlor is outfitted in pink and mint-colored paint. The parlor also has two cupboards built into the corners, one of which is open to display dishes. It is possible that the Belletables also used the parlor as their dining area, a practice common in smaller homes before the turn of the twentieth century.

The stairway railing leading to the second floor displays the ochre and burnt-orange colors, likely left over from the exterior paint. With two large rooms and a third that could have been used as a closet, the second floor was as "luxurious" as the rest of the house. From the window in the second bedroom, you can see the rabbit brush, the ubiquitous land cover of the high desert, which likely was the same view the Belletables had in the original location of their upscale house.

Schminck Memorial Museum

Built: 1922

128 S. E Street
Lakeview, OR
541-947-3134 (museum)

The town of Lakeview is about a hundred miles from a town of any size, but the Schminck museum is worth the trip. Located in a bungalow, the museum is crammed full of artifacts.

Directions: From the Lake County courthouse in the center of Lakeview at Center and F streets, travel south two blocks, and then turn left onto S. First Street. Turn left on S. E Street and drive about one block; the house is on the left.

Open: Tuesday–Saturday except in December and January
Hours: Summer, 10:00–5:00; winter, 1:00–4:00
Admission: $2.00 adults; $1.00 children twelve or under
Tour: Guided
Entry: Ring front doorbell
Additional Attractions: For those wishing to learn more about local history, the Lake County museum is located next door (call 541-947-2220 for admission and hours).

History

Lula Foster was born in 1878, the youngest of fifteen children born to Elizabeth and James Foster. Her family house, which still stands along Highway 31, is located about sixty miles from Lakeview. Dalph Schminck, who was born in 1876, worked at his father's hardware store in Lakeview. On weekends, Dalph Schminck pedaled his bicycle the long distance to court Lula. He would stay the weekend at Summer Lake, and then pedal back home to be at work on Monday morning.

The couple were married in 1901 in the parlor at the Foster home, and began living together in Lakeview. Both received a number of antique items from their parents, which they stored away in their attic and basement. Friends and relatives would often ask to see a piece, which they would gladly unpack, tell its story, and then repack.

They began collecting other items, and it soon became their passion. In 1936, they decided to turn the basement of their house into a museum. Many Lake County residents began donating items to their museum, although some items came anonymously; the Schmincks would frequently find a box or bundle on their porch that someone had left during the night. The couple welcomed interested visitors to their home, some of whom in turn contributed items to their museum.

The Schminck museum looks like a small house, but it is crammed full of artifacts.

Dalph Schminck died in 1960, and Lula Schmink in 1962. Her will donated the house and its contents to the Oregon State Society of the Daughters of the American Revolution (O.S.S.D.A.R.). The O.S.S.D.A.R. remodeled parts of the house in the late 1970s and added some display cases. The organization still operates the museum, which has over five thousand items in its collection.

Setting

The house is sited on a residential lot near the center of town. Within walking distance are the Lake County courthouse and library, as well as Lakeview's shops and restaurants.

Exterior

Without the sign in front, the one-story house on a residential street would still look like someone's home. The flag, white aluminum siding, and plastic lawn carpeting on the porch are the choices of a homeowner. Few, however, have a 1917 machine gun poised on the porch.

The Schminck house is a bungalow, a type of house that became popular after the turn of the twentieth century when the style was touted in magazines such as *Ladies Home Journal, House Beautiful,* and *Good Housekeeping.* Bungalows are typically one to one and a half stories, and like the Schminck house have a wide gable roof, a porch which extends across the front of the house, and hefty, tapering porch posts.

The Lake County Museum occupies the house next door at 118 S. E Street. This bungalow, constructed in 1926, is similar in appearance. However, the exterior of this structure consists of concrete blocks made to look like stone.

Interior

Despite its twentieth-century exterior, the front room of the Schminck house recreates the exuberance of the Victorian era: chairs have pillows or afghans, tables are covered with a scarf, and photographs and mementos cover every surface. Unlike many house museums, the mementos in the Schminck house are arranged in a scattered yet artful manner, just as one would find in a Victorian interior near the turn of the last century.

The piano standing against one wall was purchased in 1871 by Lula Schminck's parents in Corvallis and hauled by wagon to Lake County. Schminck's eldest sister was to take lessons, which she did, and then to teach her sisters, which she did not. Although a piano or organ was once considered a necessary component of a well-furnished parlor, phonographs gradually replaced them as the source of music in the house. The museum has two Edison phonographs (a word derived from the Greek "sound" and "to write"), one from 1898, the other 1905. Both use a wax cylinder to produce the music, which has a scratchy sound. The cylinders in the collection are labeled on the edge, but Edison's pre-1904 cylinders were unmarked and the selection was "self-announcing." Edison continued making cylinders and disk records until he quit the business one day before the stock market crash in October 1929.

The dining room has six cases full of glassware and china. Sherrain Glen, the current curator at the time of writing, sets the dining-room table according to the season, utilizing the museum's vast inventory. For Valentine's Day, the table will display settings in red, black, and white, while during the summer green and purple dishes will accent the lilac plates. Glen admits that she doesn't set the table for what is "proper," rather basing it on color.

The museum has over one hundred sixty pressed-glass goblets, possibly the largest collection on the West Coast. The goblets represent a time span from 1830 to 1920, and include patterns with descriptive names like "Frosted Waffle," "Pleat & Panel," and "Owl & Possum." Bakewell, Pears & Company was awarded the patent for making pressed glass in 1825, a

Although the house is a modern bungalow, the interior is artistically arranged to portray a Victorian interior.

process which consisted of pouring molten glass into a mold, which allowed glasses to be made quickly and cheaply.

While pressed glass is a reasonable facsimile of blown glass, it nonetheless has identifying characteristics such as having rounded as opposed to sharp facets, and a line on the glass indicating where the molds joined. There is also a difference in sound. While fine glass has a melodic "ting," the pressed glass sounds like "thunk."

The collection started when Dalph Schminck was courting Lula Foster. He later recalled in the March 20, 1958 *Lake County Examiner*, "Did much of my courting by bicycle. It was a long, rough steep road up and down over the mountains. … Anyway, she knew I really loved her, riding one hundred twenty miles by bicycle to see her." Since flowers would fade by the time he pedaled to see his sweetheart, he gave her a series of pressed-glass goblets which came from his father's store where he worked. The number of goblets in the collection today might lead visitors to wonder how why it took her so long to make up her mind.

In the kitchen, on the floor by the sink is an early mousetrap with the product name "Catchemalive." The little wood box has a ramp which leads up to the mouse prison, and it advises one to "place a piece of smoked bacon, cheese or cake in the bait box" (a good last meal). To kill the mouse, the trap suggests turning them out in a pail of water. However, to avoid a mouse getting caught, dying, and smelling bad while the trap was for sale in the store, it advises that the box should be turned up side down when placed on the shelf.

In the pantry stand two early appliances: the Savage Washer and Dryer and the Golden Rod Vacuum Cleaner. The Savage is just one machine, suggesting perhaps that the boast of a dryer meant that it included an electric spin cycle, which would have eliminated the need for a wringer. The Golden Rod is hand operated by placing it on the floor, holding one grip, and pulling the handle. While it appears to be an excellent way to develop arm muscles, it might have been easier just to pick up the dirt by hand.

In the hall between the two bedrooms hangs a picture frame with a beaded bag that was owned by Lula's mother, Elizabeth Currier Foster. When Elizabeth Currier Foster was traveling with her family on the Oregon Trail as a young girl, another little girl in their group died along the way. Elizabeth Currier couldn't bear to leave her there with nothing, so she cut out one of the beaded roses from her purse, and left it on top of the grave.

Elizabeth Currier Foster was a fine quilter, and the museum has several pieces of her work. Quilts occasionally need to be refolded in different ways so that the fabric doesn't record the fold marks, and if the job needs

Photographs and mementos cover almost every surface in the Schminck parlor.

to be done, lucky and careful visitors will have a chance to touch and examine these 150 years old works of art.

If Elizabeth Currier Foster was a good seamstress, Lula was even better. In the yellow bedroom lies Lula Schminck's pansy quilt, which was hand sewn between 1931 and 1933. No two pansies are alike, and the story is that when she needed another pansy to design, Dalph would go to the garden and pick her one. Her husband also made the hand-woven rugs in the pansy design to complement her quilt.

Schminck items are particularly concentrated in this bedroom. The oak bedroom suite was a wedding present that they received in 1901. The wedding certificate displaying both their pictures hangs on the far wall. On the bureau and vanity are celluloid toiletry articles displaying their initial. Lula Schminck also made several other quilts displayed in the room.

The curator's office was the Schmincks' bathroom, and the shower stall was innovative with four handles and seven heads placed at various points. A toilet in the garage is unusual as lowering the oak seat activates the flushing action. The Schmincks likely had these plumbing innovations in their house because they owned part of the general store.

While the Schmincks lived in the house, the full basement was used as the museum; today, it is still filled with memorabilia. One item that ties the land-locked town of Lakeview to U.S. naval history is the desk from the ship Battleship Oregon standing at the foot of the stairs. It was one of three battleships commissioned for long-range cruising capacities in 1890. Isolationists in Congress, advocating only coastal defense, opposed the idea of sea-going ships that could be involved in world conflict. To appease them, the assistant secretary of the U.S. Navy, Theodore Roosevelt, called them "Sea-going coast-line Battleships", clearly an oxymoron. The Battleship Oregon's most famous entanglement was during the Spanish

American War when it raced 14,700 miles from the Pacific to the Atlantic to joint the American fleet. When the ship was gutted, the War Board gave the desk to Lake County in 1943 for their outstanding war bond purchase the prior year; the Oregon was finally scrapped in Japan in 1956.

The basement also contains other treasures, including a basket made of an armadillo that rests near the stairs. An advertisement in the 1907 Ladies Home Journal calls the armadillo basket the "oddest and most handsome basket shape ever known". (Likely happy news to the armadillo.) The 1890s work dress on the mannequin standing in the middle of the aisle on the south side also comes with an advertisement, although it is not so obvious. The mud ruffle is made from a flour sack, which still advertises the State Line Mill in the back

In one of the display cases featuring "men's things," tobacco ribbons are displayed. Tobacco manufacturers once included these ribbons, which displayed flags, sports figures and female movie stars, in their boxes. Quilters, however, found a useful place for them in their "crazy" quilts, a patchwork of different fabrics, which typically included clothing scraps. The crazy quilt on display with the bird's eye maple bedroom set includes a ribbon that still reads, "Eighth Annual meeting, Hotel Keepers Association."

In the toy area stands a dollhouse modeled after Lula Schminck's childhood home at Summer Lake. In the same case is a model of cattle baron Peter French's round barn, which he used for training horses in the winter in Harney County. A local resident, using tongue depressors and Popsicle sticks, had constructed the replica and offered it to the curator. The people of Lakeview, as well as many from around Oregon, have contributed their treasures to create the extraordinary museum it is today.

Glossary

arch—A curved, flat, or pointed structural member used to span an opening, such as a window or doorway.

Arts and Crafts—An interior design movement started in the late nineteenth century in England that advocated craftsmanship in response to the machine-made products of the Industrial Revolution.

balustrade—A series of pillars or uprights that form a railing, handrail, and bottom rail. Part of a balcony, porch, or staircase.

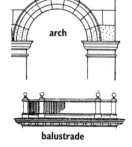

arch

balustrade

bargeboard

bargeboard—A board, usually decorative, that hangs from the incline of a gable roof.

bay window—An angular window that projects outward from the wall and extends the interior living space.

board and batten siding—Siding that consists of boards with small strips of vertical wood covering the joints.

brackets—Projecting members that support eaves, door and window hoods, and other overhangs. Can be plain or ornamental.

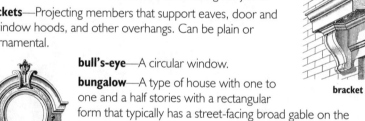

bracket

bull's-eye—A circular window.

bungalow—A type of house with one to one and a half stories with a rectangular form that typically has a street-facing broad gable on the house and porch. The porch usually is the full width of the front of the house and has square piers or posts with sloping sides.

bull's eye window

capital—The upper decorated part of a column.

capital

chinking—A mixture of mud, straw, and other materials that is used to fill cracks and openings between logs forming an exterior wall.

Classic Box—A type of architectural style characterized by its box shape, hipped roof, hipped dormer, and usually a full width porch. A subcategory of the Colonial Revival style.

Classical Revival—An architectural style characterized by a symmetrical façade, eave returns or pedimented gables, windows with six-over-six panes, and a transom and sidelights around the door.

Colonial Revival—A style of architecture characterized by a symmetrical façade with multiple-pane windows, and a front porch decorated with a pediment and pilasters.

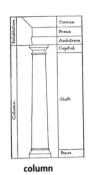

column

column—A cylindrical structure, usually a supporting member in a building.

corner boards—The vertical boards on the corner of a building which are used as trim.

cornice—A horizontal projection, usually ornamental, that crowns the top of a wall at the intersection of the roof, and the uppermost main division of an entablature (see definition below and illustration of the parts of a column).

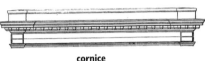

cornice

cornice return—A horizontal molding that partially extends across the gable to simulate a pediment.

corner board

Craftsman—An architectural style characterized by a rectangular form, roof with wide overhanging eaves, exposed rafters, and a porch with piers.

crest rail—The exposed upper horizontal rail on a chair or sofa.

cresting—Ornamental work, usually metal, which projects above a roofline.

cross gable—A gable which is parallel to the ridge of a roof.

cross gable

dentils—A band of small tooth-like blocks found in cornices, moldings, etc.

Doric—One of the Greek classical orders.

dormer—A window projecting from the slope of a roof.

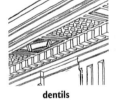

dentils

dormer

double-hung windows—A window with two sashes, each of which is moveable.

dovetail notch—A mortise and tenon shaped like a dove's tail.

eave—The portion of a roof projecting beyond the walls.

double-hung windows

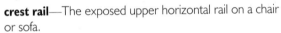

eave

entablature—The part of a building carried by columns, horizontally divided into a cornice, frieze, and architrave.

Federal—A style of architecture characterized by a symmetrical façade, cornice, double-hung windows with six-over-six panes, and a center door with sidelights.

finial—An ornament at the end of a spire or tower.

finial

fluting—Vertical concave grooves on columns and pilasters.

Folk Victorian—A house in a folk form which has been embellished with modest Victorian detailing, such as spindles on the porch.

French door—A door that has a frame enclosing multiple glass panes, usually half or full length.

fret—An ornamental design consisting of continuous lines arranged in rectangular forms.

frieze—A decorative band near the top of a wall immediately below the cornice, or the middle section of a classical entablature.

gable—The triangular end of a vertical exterior wall on a structure that has a pitched roof. (new illus)

gable-front-and-wing—A folk type of house with a gable facing the street and a side-gabled wing placed at a right angle to the front gable.

gable roof—An inverted V-shaped pitched roof.

Gothic Revival—An architectural style characterized by a steeply pitched roof usually with steep cross gables, and windows that form a point at the top, called gothic windows.

fluting

fret

gable

half-dovetail notch—A mortise and tenon which, instead of being shaped like a dove's tail, forms half of a dove's tail on the top while the bottom is shaped at a right angle.

hall-and-parlor—common house type, one or one and a half story, which contains essentially two rooms. The hall serves as the center of family activity and the parlor as the place for the best furniture. A central hall can separate the two rooms.

hew—To cut with an ax.

hipped roof—A roof with four sloped sides.

hood

hipped roof

hood—A decorative or sometimes protective cover found over windows and door frames.

I-house—A common two-story house type, containing essentially two rooms per floor. The hall serves as the center of family activity and the parlor as the place for the best furniture. The two rooms per floor can be separated by a central hall.

Italianate—An architectural style that displays low-pitched roofs with widely overhanging eaves having decorative brackets underneath, and tall, narrow windows.

Italian Villa—An architectural subcategory of the Italianate style characterized by eaves with brackets, an asymmetrical façade, and a square tower.

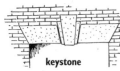
keystone

jigsaw—A narrow-bladed saw with a vertical blade used to cut sharp curves and intricate patterns.

keystone—A wedge-shaped member found in the center of an arch.

knee brace—A diagonal support placed between two members that are joined at a right angle.

lean-to—A one-story addition that has a single pitched roof.

molding—A continuous decorative band that serves as an ornamental device on either the exterior or interior of a structure.

overmantel

mortise and tenon—a joint comprising a mortise (a cavity) and a tenon (a projection).

newel—An ornamental post supporting the hand rail at the head or foot of a stairway.

overmantel—A mirror or panel, usually decorative, that is placed over the fireplace mantel.

pediment—A triangular section used ornamentally over doors and windows.

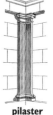
pilaster

pier—A rectangular vertical support structure.

pilaster—A rectangular column attached to a wall for ornamentation.

pediment

porte cochere—A covering over a driveway that protects passengers going in to and coming out of vehicles.

rafter

pyramidal roof—A hipped roof which has four sides of equal shape.

Queen Anne—An architectural style using an asymmetrical façade, irregular shape, patterned shingles, varying window styles and other devices to avoid a smooth-walled, balanced appearance.

rafter—An inclined structural member which runs from the ridge of the roof down to the eaves.

rafter tail—The end of the rafter, sometimes decorated, which extends beyond the wall.

sash—The framework of a window, usually moveable.

saltbox—A house with a short front roof and a longer back roof that extends to close to the ground.

segmental arch

segmental arch—An arch formed by a segment of a circle.

side-gabled roof—A roof where the gable faces the side of the house, not the front.

sidelights—Long narrow windows flanking a front door.

sidelights

Stick—An architectural style characterized by a steeply pitched roof, decorative trusses in the gable, and vertical and horizontal bands used as embellishment.

surround—An encircling decorative border.

transom—A small window or series of panes above a door or window.

trusses—Structural members that form a triangular shape to support the roof.

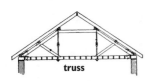
truss

Tuscan—One of the classical Roman orders characterized by simplicity, with no fluting on the columns, and unadorned capitals.

wainscot—A facing or paneling applied to the walls of a room, generally on the bottom half.

Western Farmhouse—A category of the Gothic Revival architectural style characterized by a steeply pitched roof, and a "T" or "L" shape.

Major Sources Consulted

General

American Technical Society. *Cyclopedia of Architecture, Carpentry and Building.* Chicago, IL: American Technical Society, 1907.

Ames, Kenneth L. *Death in the Dining Room and Other Tales of Victorian Culture.* Philadelphia, PA: Temple University Press, 1922.

Baker, John Milnes, A.I.A. *American House Styles: A Concise Guide.* New York: W.W. Norton & Company, Inc., 1994.

Blumenson, John J.-G. *Identifying American Architecture.* 2nd ed. New York: W.W. Norton & Company, Inc., 1979.

Bridgeman, Harriet, and Elizabeth Drury. *The Encyclopedia of Victoriana.* New York: Macmillan Publishing Co., Inc., 1975.

Butler, Joseph T. *Field Guide to American Antique Furniture.* New York: Henry Holt and Company, 1985.

Calloway, Stephen, and Elizabeth Cromley, eds. *The Element of Style.* New York: Simon & Schuster, 1996.

Canby, Henry Seidel. "God Bless Our Home." In *America Remembers*, edited by Samuel Rapport and Patricia Schartle. Garden City, NJ: Hanover House, 1956.

Carey, Charles. *General History of Oregon.* 3rd ed. Portland: Binfords & Mort, 1971.

Carley, Rachel. *The Visual Dictionary of American Domestic Architecture.* New York: Henry Holt and Company, 1994.

Clark, Clifford Edward Jr. *The American Family Home: 1800-1960.* Chapel Hill: The University of North Carolina Press, 1986.

Clark, Rosalind. *Architecture Oregon Style.* Portland: Professional Book Center Inc., 1983.

Corning, Howard McKinley, ed. *Dictionary of Oregon History.* Portland: Binford & Mort, 1989.

Cross, Mary Bywater. *Treasures in the Trunk.* Nashville, TN: Rutledge Hill Press, 1993.

Dole, Phillip. "Farmhouses and Barns of the Willamette Valley." In *Space, Style and Structure: Building in Northwest America*, edited by Thomas Vaughan and Virginia Guest Ferriday. Portland: Oregon Historical Society, 1974.

Downing, A.J. *The Architecture of Country Houses.* 1850. Reprint. New York: Dover, 1969.

Eastlake, Charles L. *Hints on Household Taste.* 1878. Reprint. New York: Dover, 1986.

Fitzgerald, Oscar P. *Four Centuries of American Furniture.* Radnor, PA: Wallace-Homestead Book Company, 1995.

Foy, Jessica H., and Karal Ann Marling, eds. *The Arts and the American Home, 1890-1930.* Knoxville: The University of Tennessee Press, 1994.

Gowans, Archie. *The Comfortable House: North American Suburban Architecture, 1890–1930.* Cambridge, MA: The MIT Press, 1986.

Grier, Katherine C. *Culture and Comfort: Parlor Making and Middle-Class Identity, 1850-1930.* Washington, DC: Smithsonian Institution Press, 1988.

Harris, Cyril. *American Architecture: An illustrated encyclopedia.* New York: W. W. Norton & Company, Inc., 1998.

Harris, Cyril M., ed. *Illustrated Dictionary of Historical Architecture.* New York: Dover, 1977.

Hawkins III, William J., and William F. Willingham. *Classic Houses of Portland, Oregon: 1850 –1950.* Portland: Timber Press, 1999.

International Correspondence Schools. *A Textbook on Architecture and Building Construction.* Scranton, PA: International Textbook Co., 1899.

Johnson, Laurence A. *Over the Counter and On The Shelf.* New York: Bonanza Books, 1961.

Kaye, Myrna. *There's a Bed in the Piano: The Inside Story of the American Home.* Boston, MA: Bulfinch Press, 1998.

McAlester, Virginia, and Lee McAlester. *A Field Guide to America's Historic Neighborhoods and Museum Houses.* New York: Alfred A. Knopf, Inc., 1998.

McAlester, Virginia, and Lee McAlester. *A Field Guide to American Houses.* New York: Alfred A. Knopf, Inc., 1984.

McMurry, Sally. *Families and Farmhouses in 19th Century America.* New York: Oxford University Press, 1988.

Miller, Judith, and Martin Miller. *Victorian Style.* 2nd ed. London: Reed Consumer Books Limited, 1998.

Moss, Roger. *Lighting for Historical Buildings.* Washington, DC: The Preservation Press, 1988.

Moss, Roger W., and Gail Caskey Winkler. *Victorian Interior Decoration.* New York: Henry Holt and Company, Inc., 1992.

Myers, Denys Peter. *Gaslighting in America.* Washington, DC: U.S. Department of the Interior, 1978.

Nye, David E. *Electrifying America: social meanings of a new technology.* Cambridge, MA: The MIT Press, 1991.

Ormsbee, Thomas H. *A Field Guide to American Victorian Furniture.* New York: Bonanza Books, 1952.

Phillips, Steven. *Old House Dictionary.* Washington, DC: The Preservation Press, 1992.

Ross, Marion D. "Architecture in Oregon, 1845-1895." *Oregon Historical Quarterly* (March 1956): 7-64.

Roth, Leland. *Building at the End of the Oregon Trail.* Eugene: School of Architecture and Allied Arts, University of Oregon, 1997.

Seale, William. *The Tasteful Interlude: American Interiors Through the Camera's Eye, 1860–1917.* 2nd ed. Walnut Creek, CA.: Altamira Press, 1995.

Sears, Roebuck and Co. *1902 Catalog.* Reprint. New York: Bounty Books, 1969.

Sears, Roebuck and Co. *1909 Catalog.* Reprint. New York: Ventura Books, Inc., 1979.

Upton, Dell, ed. *America's Architectural Roots.* New York: John Wiley & Sons, Inc., 1986.

Young, John H., comp. *Our Deportment, or the Manners, Conduct and Dress of the Most Refined Society.* Springfield, MA: W.C. King & Company, 1881.

Wharton, Edith, and Ogden Codman Jr. *The Decoration of Houses.* 1902. Reprint. New York: W.W. Norton & Company, Inc., 1978.

Whiffen, Marcus. *American Architecture since 1780.* Cambridge, MA: The MIT Press, 1981.

Wiederhold, Kathleen M. *Exploring Oregon's Historic Courthouses.* Corvallis: Oregon State University Press, 1998.

Adler House

Kelley, Tina, and Samantha Miller. "Land of Leo." *People* (August 10, 1998): 67-68.

"Leo Adler Foundation." Baker City: Leo Adler Foundation, 1997.

Van Duyn, James N. National Register of Historic Places Inventory–Nomination Form: Baker Historic District. State Historic Preservation Office, Salem, 1978.

Aurora Colony Museum

Communal Studies Association. "Guide to Historic Communal Sites in the United States." Amana, IA: Communal Studies Association, n.d.

Dole, Philip, and Judith Rees. Aurora Colony Historic Resources Inventory. State Historic Preservation Office, Salem, 1985.

Nordhoff, Charles. *The Communistic Societies of the United States.* 1875. Reprint. New York: Dover, 1966

Beekman House

Southern Oregon Historical Society. Docent information handbook. Southern Oregon Historical Society, Jacksonville. Photocopy.

Brunk House

Polk County Historical Society. Docent information package. Polk County Historical Society, Rickreall. Photocopy.

Bush House

Blau, Martha, Ellen Foster, Jennifer Hagloch, and Edith Schryver. *Vignettes of the Bush Family.* Salem: Bush House Auxiliary, 1983.

Hagloch, Jenifer. "The History and Development of Bush's Pasture Park." SAA newsletter (December 1998). Photocopy.

Hartwig, Paul. National Register of Historic Places Inventory–Nomination Form: Bush (Asahel) House. State Historic Preservation Office, Salem,1973.

Powell, Anna. Reminiscences. http//earthisland.com/AMPowell/index.html.

Snyder, Susan. "The Development of the Bush House." *Marion County Historical Society* (1954): 3-8.

Butterfield Cottage

Dennon, Jim. "Butterfield's 1893 Beach House." *Cumtux* (Spring, 1989): 32-36.

Bybee-Howell House

Cleaver, J.D. *Island Origins: Trappers, Traders and Settlers* (Sauvie Island Heritage series; v. 1). Portland: Oregon Historical Society, 1986.

Cleaver, J.D. *Island Immigrants: The Bybees and the Howells* (Sauvie Island Heritage series; v. 2). Portland: Oregon Historical Society, 1986.

Cleaver, J.D. *Island Life: Pioneer Homesteading* (Sauvie Island Heritage series; v. 3). Portland: Oregon Historical Society, 1986.

Hartwig, Paul. National Register of Historic Places Inventory–Nomination Form: Bybee-Howell House. State Historic Preservation Office, Salem, 1974.

Vaughan, Thomas. *Bybee-Howell House on Sauvie Island*. Portland: Oregon Historical Society, 1974.

Caples House

Becker, Pearl. "The Caples House of Columbia City." *Columbia County History* (1971): 14–16.

Deepwood Estate

Duniway, David. *Dr. Luke A. Port: Builder of Deepwood*. Salem: Marion County Historical Society and the Friends of Deepwood, 1989.

Hartwig, Paul. National Register of Historic Places Inventory–Nomination Form: Deepwood. State Historic Preservation Office, Salem, 1973.

Helphand, Kenneth, ASLA, and Nancy Rottle. "Cultivating Charm." *Garden Design* (Autumn, 1988): 27-34.

McMath Hawkins Dortignacq. Historic Deepwood Estate: Historic Structure Report. Deepwood House files, 1990.

Thompson, Polly Povey, A.I.A. "Povey Brothers." *Stained Glass* (Winter 1984-85): 331- 37.

Dibble House

Hartwig, Paul. National Register of Historic Places Inventory–Nomination Form: Dibble House. State Historic Preservation Office, Salem, 1974.

Drain House

Brown, Tracey, and Valerie Patton. *The Castle in Drain, Oregon*. Drain House, Drain.

Smith, R.A. National Register of Historic Places Inventory–Nomination Form: Drain House. State Historic Preservation Office, Salem, 1978.

Barber, George F. The Cottage Souvenir No. 2. Revised. Knoxville: S. B. Newman & Co, 1892.

Ermatinger House

Fowler, Daniel. National Register of Historic Places Inventor –Nomination Form: Ermatinger House. State Historic Preservation Office, Salem, 1987.

Flavel House

Anonymous. "Household Property." Clatsop County Historical Society vertical files, Astoria.

Anonymous. "The Historic Flavel House." *Cumtux* (Summer, 1991): 2-19.
Bell, Polly McKean. "Polly McKean Bell Remembers." *Cumtux* (Winter, 1986):
    28-35.
Dennon, Jim. "Captain George Flavel." *Cumtux* (Summer, 1991): 20-30.
Goodenberger, John. Notes on tour given by Marjorie Halderman & Marjorie
    Dubois. Clatsop County Historical Society vertical files, Astoria, 1984.
Staton, Julie A., comp. *Interpretive Material: The Captain George Flavel House
    and Family.* Clatsop County Historical Society, 1999.

Flippin House
Flippin, Thomas J. Jr. "The Castle." *Columbia County History* (1976): 3-7.

Floed-Lane House
Powers, D. W. III. National Register of Historic Places Inventory–Nomination
    Form: Gen. Joseph Lane House. State Historic Preservation Office, Salem,
    1974.

Fort Dalles Museum
Anderson, Dale L. *The History and Preservation of the Lewis Anderson
    Homestead.* Oxon Hill: Silesia Printing, 1974.
Knuth, Priscilla. *Picturesque Frontier.* rev. ed. Portland: Oregon Historical Society,
    1987.
Gillis, Julia. *So Far From Home.* Portland: Oregon Historical Society, 1993.
Seufert, Gladys. National Register of Historic Places Inventor –Nomination
    Form: Anderson (Lewis) House, Barn and Granary. State Historic Preservation
    Office, Salem, 1979.
Walton, Elisabeth. National Register of Historic Places Inventory–Nomination
    Form: Fort Dalles Surgeon's Quarters. State Historic Preservation Office,
    Salem, 1971.

Fort Rock Valley Homestead Village Museum
Buckles, James Slama. "The Historical Geography of the Fort Rock Valley, 1900-
    1941." Master's thesis, University of Oregon, 1959.
Chappel, Jill. "Homestead Ranches of the Fort Rock Valley: Vernacular Building
    in the Oregon High Desert." Master's thesis, University of Oregon. 1990.
Chappel, Jill. "An Investigation into the Construction Methods Used in the Fort
    Rock Valley of South-Central Oregon, 1909-1920." Thesis, University of
    Oregon, 1988.
Fort Rock Valley Historical Society. *Portraits: Fort Rock Valley Homestead Years.*
    Fort Rock, Fort Rock Valley Historical Society, 1989.
Jackman, E. R., and R.A. Long. *The Oregon Desert.* Caldwell, ID: The Caxton
    Printers, Ltd., 1964.

Foster Farm
Cody, Mary E. National Register of Historic Places Inventory–Nomination Form:
    Foster Farm (Philip) House. State Historic Preservation Office, Salem,1979.
Cody, Mary E. *Philip Foster: A History.* Eagle Creek: Jacknife-Zion-Horseheaven
    Historical Society, 1993.

Frazier Farmstead Museum

Biggs, Diane. National Register of Historic Places Inventory–Nomination Form: Frazier Farm. State Historic Preservation Office, Salem, 1985.

Harlow House

Troutdale Historical Society. Docent information package. Troutdale Historical Society, Troutdale. Photocopy.

Nesbit, Sharon. "The Families of the Harlow House" Troutdale Historical Society files, 1999.

Nesbit, Sharon. *Vintage Edgefield: A History of the Multnomah County Poor Farm and McMenamins Edgefield*. McMenamins Edgefield, 1995.

Nesbit, Sharon, and Curt Kaiser. National Register of Historic Places Inventory–Nomination Form: Harlow House. State Historic Preservation Office, Salem,1983.

Hoover-Minthorn House

Barker, Burt Brown. Autobiography of Burt Brown Barker. Hoover House files.

Barker, Burt Brown, comp. "Home of Dr. Henry John Minthorn." Herbert Hoover Foundation, n.d.

Olsen, Deborah. "Minthorn House: Boyhood Home of Herbert C. Hoover Thirty-First Present of the United States of America." Herbert Hoover Foundation, 1979.

Hughes House

Fryberger, Georgia. National Register of Historic Places Inventory–Nomination Form: Hughes House. State Historic Preservation Office, Salem,1980.

Kam Wah Chung Museum

Barlow, Jeffrey, and Christine Richardson. *China Doctor of John Day*. Portland: Binford & Mort, 1979.

"Chinese Folk Religions: The Kitchen God." http://www.csupomona.edu/folkreligion/kitchengod.

Hartwig, Paul. National Register of Historic Places Inventory–Nomination Form: Kam Wah Chung Company Building. State Historic Preservation Office, Salem, 1973.

Lindgren Cabin

Manttila, Walter. "The Forest Home and Its Hewers." *Finnish-American Historical Society of the West* (October, 1996) 2-27.

McLoughlin House

Barker, Burt Brown, comp. *The Dr. John McLoughlin House: A National Historic Site*. Oregon City: The McLoughlin Memorial Association, 1949.

Smelser, June. "A History of the McLoughlin House." *Clackamas County Historical* (1960): 27–55.

Mission Mill Museum

Hartwig, Paul B. National Register of Historic Places Inventory–Nomination Form: Parsonage of the Methodist Mission. State Historic Preservation Office, Salem, 1974.

Hickok, Neysa. "Living in the Jason Lee House in 1841: An Interpreter's Guide." Thesis, Oregon State University, 1989.

Judson, Lewis H. "The Jason Lee House." *Marion County Historical Society* (1962-64): 9-11.

Peterson del Mar, David. "Violence Against Wives by Prominent Men in Early Clatsop County." *Oregon Historical Quarterly* (Winter 1999): 434-50.

Potter, Elisabeth Walton. National Register of Historic Places Inventory–Nomination Form: Lee (Jason) House. State Historic Preservation Office, Salem, 1975.

Walton, Elisabeth. "Jason Lee's "Mill Place"—A New Mission House of the Willamette." *Marion County Historical Society* (1962-64): 5-8.

Walton, Elisabeth. National Register of Historic Places Inventory–Nomination Form: Boon (John D.) House. State Historic Preservation Office, Salem, 1973.

Walton, Elisabeth Brigham. "'Mill Place on the Willamette: A New Mission House for the Methodists in Oregon, 1841–1844." Master's thesis, University of Delaware, 1965.

Mission Mill Museum. Tour guide. Mission Mill Museum, Salem.

Monteith House

Asai, Barbara, Meredith Wiley, and Phillip Dole. National Register of Historic Places Inventory–Nomination Form: Monteith (Thomas & Walter) House. State Historic Preservation Office, Salem, 1975.

"Gilbert Stuart—Washington." http://americanrevolution.org/washstu.

Goddard, Kimberly, and Ellen E. Frances. "Restoration of the Dining Room and Kitchen of the Monteith House, Albany." Thesis, University of Oregon, 1980.

Smith, Ianthe. "Monteith Daughter Tells Stories of Old Albany and City's First Home." *Albany Democrat-Herald* (August 25, 1948): 3.

Morse House

Heald, Leslie, and Corri Jimenez. National Register of Historic Places Inventory Nomination Form: Wayne Morse Farm. State Historic Preservation Office, Salem, 1998.

Moyer House

Hartwig, Paul. National Register of Historic Places Inventory–Nomination Form: Moyer House. State Historic Preservation Office, Salem, 1973.

Donovan, Sally. "A Restoration and Preservation Plan of the J.M. Moyer House, Brownsville, Oregon." Master's thesis, University of Oregon, 1987.

Naucke House

Kramer, George. National Register of Historic Places Inventory–Nomination Form: William & Nannie Naucke House. State Historic Preservation Office, Salem, 1999.

Newell House

Dobbs, Caroline. *Men of Champoeg.* 1932. Reprint. Cottage Grove, Ore.: Emerald Valley Craftsmen, 1975.

Hussey, John A. *Champoeg: Place of Transition.* Portland: Oregon Historical Society, 1967.

Zorn, Henry. "Robert Newell and Newell House." *Marion County Historical Society* (1962-1964): 39-42.

Pittock Mansion

Kraus, Kevin. "A Social, Architectural and Technical Discussion of the Pittock Mansion." Thesis, University of Oregon, 1984.

Renfrow, Emily C. "Servants at the Pittock Mansion: Architecture, Society, and "The Servant Problem." Thesis, Portland States University, 1994.

Pittock Mansion Society. "Pittock Mansion Remembered." 1984.

Pittock Mansion Society. "Simply Splendid: Portland's Pittock Mansion." 1999.

Schuber, Stephen. "Frederick C. Baker: making art of light." *Architectural Lighting* (January, 1987): 46-50.

Staehli, Alfred. "The Pittock Mansion Portland, Oregon: Historic Structure Report." Pittock Mansion files, 1994.

Stewart, Kenneth. "The Four Careers of Henry Lewis Pittock." Pittock Mansion files, 1983.

Rorick House

Cramer, Fredrick K. "Eck Rorick The Dalles' Original Music Man." *The Dalles Weekly Reminder* (February 10, 1988): 3.

Deach, Carolyn. "Turning Back Time." *The Dalles Weekly Reminder* (September 1, 1995): 3.

Seufert, Gladys. National Register of Historic Places Inventory–Nomination Form: Moody, Malcolm A., House. State Historic Preservation Office, Salem, 1980.

Rose Farm

Hartwig, Paul B. National Register of Historic Places Inventory–Nomination Form: Rose Farm. State Historic Preservation Office, Salem, 1974.

Stafford, Roma. "The Historic House of Rose Farm." 1937. Reprint. Rose Farm files, 1987.

Settlemier House

Anonymous. "A Fine Residence." *Woodburn Independent* (January 2, 1892). Reprint. Settlemier house files.

Anonymous. "An Enterprising Nurseryman." *West Shore* (August 1889). Settlemier house files.

Monnier, Ron. "Jesse H. Settlemier: Oregon Pioneer, Nurseryman, and Founder of Woodburn, Oregon." Settlemier house files, 1993.

Schminck House

Anonymous. "Museum Holds History of a Fabulous County" *Lake County Examiner* (March 20, 1958) Lakeview library vertical file.

Anonymous. "Schminck Museum Displays Pioneer Past." *Lake County Examiner* (April 29, 1982). Lakeview library vertical file.

McSherry, Patrick. "USS Oregon." http://www.spanam.simplenet.com/oregon.

Schmidt House

Bradford, Margaret. "Sisters Share Home Nearly 9 Decades." *Daily Courier* (December 14, 1982): 6.

Josephine County Historical Society. "Remembering the Schmidt Family and Their Legacy to the Josephine County Historical Society." 1997.

Shelton-McMurphey-Johnson House

Anonymous. "Shelton-McMurphey-Johnson House: Self-Guided Tour" Eugene: Shelton-McMurphey-Johnson House, n.d.

Crow/Clay and Associates. "Shelton-McMurphey Master Development Plan." Eugene Public library, 1990.

Sussaman, Nancy, and Robert Warwick. National Register of Historic Places Inventory–Nomination Form: Shelton-McMurphey House. State Historic Preservation Office, Salem, 1983.

Whipple, Andy. "The House on the Hill." *Eugene Register-Guard* (February 17, 1975): page 1D.

Tigard House

Sharp, LaVerne B. National Register of Historic Places Inventory–Nomination Form: Tigard House. State Historic Preservation Office, Salem, 1979.

Yaquina Lighthouse

Howes, James M. "The Old Yaquina Bay Lighthouse." Lincoln County Historical Society (1968).

Miller, Lischen. "The Haunted Light at Newport by the Sea." *Pacific Monthly*, Vol II, 1899. Reprint. Lincoln County Historical Society files, n.d.

Walton, Elisabeth. National Register of Historic Places Inventory–Nomination Form: Old Yaquina Bay Lighthouse. State Historic Preservation Office, Salem, 1974.

Index